THE OUTWARD PATH

ALSO BY SEBASTIAN PURCELL

*Discourses of the Elders: The Aztec "Huehuetlatolli,"
a First English Translation*

THE OUTWARD PATH

The Wisdom of the Aztecs

SEBASTIAN PURCELL

Copyright © 2025 by L. Sebastian Purcell

All rights reserved
Printed in the United States of America
First Edition

For information about permission to reproduce selections from this book, write to Permissions, W. W. Norton & Company, Inc., 500 Fifth Avenue, New York, NY 10110

For information about special discounts for bulk purchases, please contact W. W. Norton Special Sales at specialsales@wwnorton.com or 800-233-4830

Manufacturing by Lakeside Book Company
Book design by Brooke Koven
Production manager: Julia Druskin

ISBN 978-1-324-02056-1

W. W. Norton & Company, Inc.
500 Fifth Avenue, New York, NY 10110
www.wwnorton.com

W. W. Norton & Company Ltd.
15 Carlisle Street, London W1D 3BS

10 9 8 7 6 5 4 3 2 1

For Lani

Contents

LESSON 1
You Don't Really Want to Be Happy,
You Just Think That You Do — 1

LESSON 2
What Makes Life Worth Living Also
Makes It Fragile — 13

LESSON 3
Success Is Uncertain, Slipping Is Not — 26

✢ SPIRITUAL EXERCISE I ✢
The Kinder Words Practice — 43

LESSON 4
All Are Born Unbalanced,
Some Stand for a Time — 49

✢ SPIRITUAL EXERCISE II ✢
The Truer Words Practice — 59

LESSON 5
A Good Life Is a Rooted Life — 62

LESSON 6
A Rooted Life Is Not a Product,
but a Performance — 77

LESSON 7
Great Courage Concerns Small Things — 87

✢ SPIRITUAL EXERCISE III ✢
The Social Vulnerability Practice — 105

LESSON 8
The Wise Don't Think for Themselves — 108

✦ **SPIRITUAL EXERCISE IV** ✦
The Personal Vulnerability Practice 131

LESSON 9
Willpower Is Three Things, Not One 134

✦ **SPIRITUAL EXERCISE V** ✦
The Consistency Practice 142

LESSON 10
Justice Is a Path; Fairness Is Accounting 144

✦ **SPIRITUAL EXERCISE VI** ✦
The Intensity Practice 154

LESSON 11
Love Is What You Do, Not What You Feel 157

✦ **SPIRITUAL EXERCISE VII** ✦
The Craving Practice 176

LESSON 12
You Cannot Prepare for Tragedy,
but You Can Learn to Live After It 179

Postface 187

Acknowledgments 204

APPENDIX I: *What's in a Name
(And How Do I Pronounce It)?* 207
APPENDIX II: *Are All the Virtues One?* 210
APPENDIX III: *Blood Sacrifice* 216
APPENDIX IV: *Guadalupe as Goddess, Demon,
Masterwork* 227

Abbreviations and Editions 237
Notes 239
Index 277

THE OUTWARD PATH

LESSON 1

You Don't Really Want to Be Happy, You Just Think That You Do

The "pursuit of happiness" figures into the United States of America's Declaration of Independence as an inalienable right. When Thomas Jefferson penned the line, he was recalling a standard and ancient view of the good life in the history of "Western" philosophy. The opening lines of Aristotle's *Nicomachean Ethics*, written some 2,100 years earlier, declare, "Every craft and every inquiry, and similarly every action and choice, seems to seek some good; that is why some people rightly described the good as what everything seeks." Aristotle goes on to dub this apex good; our main goal in life, "happiness." Of course, Aristotle later develops "happiness" in a technical way, rather distant from our colloquial English meaning. Jefferson gave Aristotle's idea a modern twist by framing the pursuit of happiness as both a legal and an existential right. Still, there is something of a tradition visible across the millennia. Today it appears that hardly anyone can conceive of an alternative goal for their lives. If not happiness, then what exactly is it that we should be otherwise pursuing? Misery?

But what if the "West's" conventional wisdom is wrong? What if we only think of happiness as a goal because we have lost sight of other alternatives? What if the heart of the problem is a lack of imagination? Aztec philosophers would urge us to reconsider our "Western" position. They would implore us to question the conventional wisdom of our culture. You are not really after "happiness," they would tell us, you just think that you are.

A scene from Homer's *Odyssey* underscores the Aztec point. It occurs after Odysseus has been shipwrecked on his homeward voyage and has been living on an island with the goddess Calypso for seven years. He has been crying and lamenting his fate, and the gods take pity on him. Hermes arrives and informs Calypso of Zeus's decision to have Odysseus leave. She agrees, provided that she may attempt one last time to convince him to stay. In the next scene, we witness Odysseus seated across from Calypso. She offers him what any human would apparently want: immortality, agelessness, and a leisured existence on an island paradise with the romantic company of a goddess. He turns her down, choosing instead to build a raft and then venture onto the open waters in search of his wife and child.

Unlike the biblical Adam and Eve who are forced from paradise, Odysseus *chooses* to leave. That choice might at first seem puzzling, but Aztec philosophers would be willing to bet that you would make the same choice. Aren't you willing to sacrifice your happiness for those who you love? Isn't that, to put it another way, exactly what it means to love someone?

Now a reasonable rejoinder is that Odysseus is given the prospect of infinite, or at least indefinite, happiness. Isn't that result something entirely different from our lives of mundane sacrifice, ones where you and I exchange definitive pleasures and pains? The Aztecs would wager that this indefinite prospect matters very little. To prove it, let's move from this hypothetical commitment to the real commitment many have already made—and if you haven't made it yet, to one that an overwhelming majority of you intend to make—namely the choice to have children.

Most spring semesters, I teach a class called Happiness. It's always packed with students because, like most people, they want to learn the secret to feeling fulfilled. "How many of you want to be happy in life?" I ask. Everyone raises a hand. "How many of you are planning to have children?" Almost everyone raises their hand again.

Then I lay out the evidence that having children diminishes most people's "happiness." Here is a taste of that evidence:

- A study found that parental levels of well-being drop off after the very first child, perhaps explaining why parents in more well-off countries, where childbirth is largely elective, tend to have only one or two children.

- According to four separate studies, marital satisfaction drops steadily until a couple's children age to between twelve and sixteen years; and couples only return to previous levels of satisfaction after the last child has left the house. Empty nest syndrome, it turns out, is largely a myth.

- Another study found that those with the most active lifestyles before having children are the most likely to experience a drop in feelings of well-being.

- Finally, while parenthood is likely to contribute to life satisfaction on its own, the positive effects are (for most) entirely negated by the costs of child-rearing (both in terms of time and money).

After presenting this material to my classroom, I give my students a second chance: "How many of you still want children?" I say. Maybe it's just obstinacy, but the same people who wanted to be happy at the beginning of class raise their hands.

Like Odysseus's choice to leave paradise to find his wife and child, my students choose to have children even though they know that having them is likely to diminish their "happiness." Since, generally, they are not yet parents, they do not object, as parents often do, that children are a great source of happiness. The students recognize what many often confuse, namely that some things in life are more important than elevated emotional states. And if we must make sacrifices to achieve these more important things, then so much the worse for "happiness."

Such would be the first Aztec lesson on the good life if they could speak to us today: You should stop searching for happiness, because that's not really what you want. When given the direct choice between a pleasurable, happy course of action and a meaningful one bound up with commitments to our closest few, we consistently choose something other than happiness.

In a genre unique to Aztec culture called the "discourses of the elders" (*huehuetlatolli* / way-weh-tla-TOL-lee), you can find speeches and dialogues that consider the nuances of happiness wherein elders, often fathers and mothers, speak to younger persons, often their sons and daughters, with the goal of educating them on how best to live. In an exchange with his daughter, recorded in volume 6 of the *Florentine Codex*, a father delivers the following speech.

> "O my daughter, my child, hear well: the earth [*tlalticpac*] is not a good place. It is not a place of happiness [*pacoaia*] or contentment. It can only be said that the earth [*tlalticpac*] is a place of happiness-fatigue, happiness-pain," so the elders often say. That we may not go on weeping forever, we are in debt to Our Lord, who gave us laughter and sleep, our food and strength, our life and love.

The father implores his daughter to recognize that human life on earth isn't simply a "happy" one. Though you and I might escape great tragedies, lesser ones are bound to dapple the smooth veneer of our lives. "Happiness" comes and goes in waves. The Nahuatl language has at least three terms for "happiness": *paqui* (PAH-kee), *ahuiya* (a-WEE-ya), and *huellamati* (wel-a-MAT-ee). The first means happiness as experiencing pleasure and enjoying yourself. The second means happiness as having what's necessary, or perhaps indulging a bit. The final term means happiness as contentment, but its related terms may suggest a connection with the pleasure of taste. At stake in this passage about the father and daughter is a form of *paqui*, the happiness of pleasure and enjoyment. We only ever experience these states in contrast with their opposites, joy then pain, or joy then fatigue. The pursuit of happiness, so understood, proves an impossible goal because it is not even a logically coherent candidate for a good life. With the pursuit of happiness comes the pursuit of its opposite.

My fellow philosophers might have more elaborate conceptions of "happiness" in mind, such as an "all things considered" view. For example, you might distinguish short-term happiness from long-term happiness, and then develop a principle for how to balance these competing goals. In general, such views distinguish forms of happiness and suggest a program for discerning what's the best overall view. Maybe one of those approaches is the right one. But the Aztecs would point out that these types of intellectual reconstructions often settle on conceptual shores far from our ordinary discourse about "happiness." Why not pursue a more forthright path and admit that the good life has nothing to do with "happiness" in the colloquial sense? Could we not then consider the Aztecs' positive proposal, that we are instead after a rooted life?

Though long excluded from academic consideration, undeniable evidence shows that the Aztecs were a philosophical people. Even more interesting, they advanced views about human life that both challenge dominant points of agreement in "Western" philosophy and might be right in their challenge. You've just learned of one such lesson, that you are not after happiness, though you may think you are, but a single thread in a tapestry of wisdom which answers a common human question: How shall we live?

· · ·

IF WE are to learn any of their other answers to this concern, then we must take the Aztecs seriously. The Aztecs, more accurately referred to as the Nahuas because they spoke Nahuatl, have, by turns, both fascinated and mortified "Westerners" since the Spanish officer Hernán Cortés first encountered them in the early 1500s. The nineteenth-century historian William H. Prescott, writing in what is today still among the most widely read books of the Spanish-Aztec war, crystallizes this ambivalence:

> In contemplating the religious system of the Aztecs, one is struck with its apparent incongruity, as if some portion of it had emanated from a comparatively refined people, open to gentle influences, while the rest breathes a spirit of unmitigated ferocity.

Much of that view, in my judgment, still rests comfortably in our broader cultural imagination.

Yet Prescott penned those lines in 1843, and his view is, to a significant degree, mistaken. In the nearly two centuries that have since intervened, a cohort of multidisciplinary specialists have shown us just what he was missing. Archaeologists and anthropologists have revealed that Prescott did not have available to him the entirety of the *Florentine Codex*, which is a principal source for our understanding of the Aztecs. Moreover, many of the major architectural and artistic artifacts of the Aztecs remained buried under the central square of Mexico City while he wrote. Linguistic studies nearly a century after Prescott identified, through the separate work of Richard Andrews and Michel Launey, that Nahuatl has an especially peculiar feature: It has no words. Instead, it has "nuclear clauses," so that individual terms may act as complete sentences on their own. The term *michin*, for example, is typically translated into English as the noun "fish." But were it to appear on its own, it would stiltedly read as "it is a fish," thus serving as its own sentence. Historians of the era have worked to correct myriad misconceptions about Montezuma, Cortés, and the global events that are often called the "conquest" of the Aztecs. Matthew Restall, for example, has worked indefatigably as a myth buster for dozens of misconceptions for roughly two decades now, and only recently did another historian, Camilla Townsend, stitch together the history of the Aztecs according to their own statements, as recorded in Nahuatl.

In the context of these intellectual efforts, philosophers have, like the owl of Minerva, arrived at dusk, that is to say, with most of the day's intellectual labor now complete. Nevertheless, I understand this book to constitute a contribution to the reevaluation of the Aztecs. I do wish to note, however, that the resulting view of the Aztecs will differ from what these other disciplines have represented—and for good reason. Philosophy responds to its own set of questions. In the Postface to this book, I explain what methodological assumptions guide my research, the tradition of analysis that I use, and why I think this approach is best given the centuries of cultural misrecognition the Aztecs have faced.

What you most need to understand is that the field is young and nearly everyone has a different view. My purpose in this book is to provide you with a contemporary reconstruction of Aztec philosophy—advancing an interpretive tradition favored in Mexico—that could be practiced today. Something similar transpires when philosophers address other ancient traditions in the world's canon. The philosopher Daniel Russell, for example, defends an "updated" form of Aristotle's virtue ethics in his *Practical Intelligence and the Virtues*. Author and philosopher Massimo Pigliucci defends an updated form of Stoicism in his *How to Be a Stoic*. I see no reason why we cannot treat the Aztecs similarly—learning from ancient sources to address our modern concerns. This reconstruction will inevitably differ from what contact-era (1519–1640) Aztecs would have said in no small part because it is updated according to our best (scientific) evidence today. But it should, for just these reasons, be of interest to the broader public.

• • •

THERE IS a formula intrinsic to the Aztecs' worldview that insists that we are after a meaningful and worthwhile life, a rooted one, rather than a happy one. The formula lays out for us the secret to enduring trials, how to enjoy the peaks of life, how to form lasting romantic partnerships, how to find your purpose, how to live with nature, and how to be well in both physical and emotional senses.

It is a formula that Nezahualcoyotl (Neza-wal-COY-ot / Hungry Coyote), the philosopher king of Tezcoco, followed while transforming his city into a flourishing arts and cultural center and toward a peaceful succession of power after his death in 1472. It is a view that finds a surprisingly clear articulation in Simón Bolívar's philosophical and political writings, as he led Venezuela, Colombia, Ecuador, Peru, Bolivia, and Panama to independence from European powers in the early 1800s. And, of course, it is a view that sustained Emiliano Zapata, in the early twentieth century, as he led the rural and Indigenous peoples of Mexico to revolutionary action.

You and I may not be kings, or liberators, or revolutionaries, but the world tests us all the same. If there is wisdom here that could sustain them through their trials, that could enable them to find meaning and joy in dark times, then perhaps we might find some solace ourselves.

For more than half a century, the United States has served as a laboratory for the modern popular exploration of ancient philosophies, from the reception of (especially Zen) Buddhism in the 1960s, to the recent resurgence of interest in ancient Greek and Roman Stoicism. The Aztecs offer a distinctive new voice in the chorus of recovered ancient wisdom. Without simplifying too much, what has been recovered of philosophical texts around the globe follows an inward path. The Stoic philosopher Epictetus begins *The Handbook* with the following claim:

Some things are up to us and some are not up to us. Our opinions are up to us, and our impulses, desires, aversion—in short whatever is our doing. Our bodies are not up to us, nor are our possessions, our reputations, or our public offices, or, that is whatever is not our doing.

The Stoic path to the good life, then, is one of detachment. One must learn to assent to the things under one's control and to let the rest go. It is the *inward* work on oneself, then, that leads toward a better life.

The form of Buddhism that has been imported to the "West" is primarily Zen Buddhism, and when approached from a Western perspective, the task is similarly inward-looking. Consider, for example, the purpose of the koan exercises. A novitiate might receive one of the following problems to work on:

> *What was the appearance of your face before your parents were born?*
> *We are all familiar with the sound of two hands clapping. What is the sound of one hand clapping?*

The pupil working at this initial (*hosshin*) stage is meant to undertake meditative practice (*zazen*) and work on a solution until their mind is exhausted. In the first case, the pupil might return to the master with a description of their face, or a leaf, or a rock—all of which would be dismissed as wrong. Then, after significant toil, and in a moment of exasperation, the student will have a flash of insight into some basic, ineffable truth. They will thus have taken their first real steps toward *satori*, enlightenment.

Zen Buddhism is unlike Stoic philosophy on the role of discursive, as opposed to intuitive, reasons. Zen Buddhism holds that the enlightenment that we each seek cannot be formulated into words, and instead must come from direct intuition; while

Stoicism made significant advances in formal logic and requires its followers to master that. In both cases, however, the path to a better life is still *inward* looking. It still proceeds through one's ordinary consciousness, whether in logical reflection, or in working on a koan, until your individual, rational mind is exhausted. The path toward enlightenment lies in understanding and working on your inward self.

Aztec rootedness, by contrast, follows an outward path. The aim is to look *outward*, in the right way, to stabilize oneself internally. In a long discourse, recorded as one of the preserved *Discourses of the Elders*, a father tells his son that there are two paths in life: the path of principles, of excellence, and the path of the rabbit and the deer. On the first path, the father tells his son, you will be able to stand on your feet, to be rooted, by living alongside human society. On the second path, the path of the rabbit and the deer, he warns, you will harm your character and lead a broken life. You will not even "emerge as a human."

Let me illustrate this outward path with a story. When Halloween last arrived, my wife and I were prepared to be greeted by scores of eager trick-or-treaters. Guided by the thought that too much candy was better than too little, we bought *entirely* too much, and, after the holiday, poured the excess onto a platter in our living room. The problem is: I have a sweet tooth. "I can't stop eating these!" I said to my wife, peevishly, a few days later. Nearly every time I passed the coffee table, I succumbed to my cravings for a sugar rush, and would immediately feel frustrated and irritated. When I returned from work that evening, I noticed the platter was empty. "Oh, I just took it to work and gave it away to the students," my wife said, when I asked. Just like that, my cycle of transgression and guilt was broken.

This anecdote illustrates two ways in which the Aztec path is distinct from "Western" philosophy, such as Aristotle's or the Stoics', as much as from "Eastern" paths to enlightenment, such as Zen Buddhism. The first is that I did not overcome my vice so much as manage it. The second is that I did not manage it on my own, but rather did so (almost entirely) with the help of another person.

The fact that my wife did most of the work illustrates what I mean by the outward path. The Aztecs believed that you learn to live well by living with others and by means of their help. The goal is to set up your circumstances and relationships in the right way. If those are set up well, they thought, then you will learn to manage your interior self. *That* is the path to a good life.

It's reasonable to think that these paths, the inward and the outward, may be complementary. But it remains important first to recognize how they are different. This book seeks to illustrate how the outward path to enlightenment has been missing in the "Western" reception of the world's philosophies. Its apex aim is merely to help you live a better life by recovering these Aztec ideas for modern times.

If these introductory points make sense, then you might reasonably have a follow-up question, "If we are not after happiness, then maybe we are after invulnerability?" Many who are attracted to Stoicism and Buddhism believe so, but the Aztecs would disagree.

Emiliano Zapata

LESSON 2

What Makes Life Worth Living Also Makes It Fragile

In the countryside of Morelos, Mexico, on November 12, 1911, Emiliano Zapata awaited news from an official messenger, sent by the new president, Francisco Madero. The message was to be that Zapata could put down his arms as a revolutionary, that the peasants he had fought for would finally receive their due, and that Zapata could go back to life as a private citizen. Madero, after all, had only succeeded in deposing Mexico's ruling autocrat, Porfirio Díaz, with Zapata's help.

Unlike Madero, who hailed from a wealthy and elite family, Zapata was a man of the people. A field hand and contract worker, he had learned to speak Nahuatl as a child. Given the support of his fellow *paisanos* (field hands), he used that knowledge to track down the legal claims the peasants had to land that was taken from them by colonial and then autocratic powers. Yet now, while he waited, he worried that something had gone wrong.

Just a month before, in Mexico City, adversaries had tried to slander Zapata and his followers, the Zapatistas. A congressional deputy, in a speech, proclaimed:

Zapata assumes the proportions of a Spartacus, he is the vindicator, the liberator of slaves . . . ; He is a great threat to society, Congressmen, he is, simply, the darkness from within the earth, and he has risen to blot out all light on the surface.

If your opponents ever slander you for liberating slaves, then you are likely on the right side of history. The newly elected Madero, though a former friend, now had no need for Zapata. In fact, he found Zapata's magnetic and controversial character a political liability. Madero recognized that he had erred in not removing all of his predecessor's men (Díaz's men) from political offices, so now he found himself in the position of needing to make concessions to them to remain in power.

Zapata called his contact, Robles Domínguez, several times to ask about the forces that appeared to be surrounding his position. After one brief call, he finally received two letters. One from Madero, terse and unfriendly, demanded Zapata surrender immediately with no concessions to the peasants he represented. Another, from Robles Domínguez, much longer, tried to mollify the situation. Zapata's biographer, Paul Hart, summarizes the scene as follows:

> Calmly, as if he were watching events unfold in some predestined way, Zapata tucked the letters into his coat, turned to a subordinate, and gave orders for a retreat. He then told a messenger, "Tell Robles Domínguez I will be waiting for him on the *cerro de aquacate* (avocado hill), and to bring his arms."

Zapata, because he knew the lands as only a peasant could, managed to escape the encircling troops—for a time. Because he refused to compromise on his devotion to the peasants, he was eventually deceived by those who were once friends and killed. He was thirty-nine. And with that, Mexico would have to wait roughly eighty years before it finally threw off its autocratic yoke to become a democratic country.

Beyond his heroism, Zapata's life and uncompromising choices embody an ethical truth of Aztec philosophy: What makes life worth living also makes it fragile. This is a core feature of their ethical "pessimism." Our friends do sometimes betray us. Our aspirations do put us into grave danger. And often enough, we are caught in the debris of our fragile environment as it fails us. None of that makes life any less worth it.

In this context it's worth returning to the father's statement to his daughter that you read in the previous chapter. In the fuller version of that statement, the father connects his view directly to the condition of life on the slippery earth, on *tlalticpac* (tlal-TIC-pak). He says,

> and now that you are of age, you've already noticed how things are. There is no happiness, there is no contentment; there is pain, there is fatigue, there is want; torment and pain dominate. The earth [*tlalticpac*] is difficult, a place that makes one weep, where one must feel pain. You will suffer. And the cold wind passes, glides by. For this is a place of thirst and hunger. This is the way things are.
>
> O my daughter, my child, hear well: the earth is not a good place. It is not simply a place of happiness or contentment. It is said only that the earth is a place of happiness-fatigue, happiness-pain. . . .

Now that the daughter is of age, she has learned the truth: everybody suffers. We may not all suffer through great tragedies, but none of us will escape lesser ones. The point isn't simply that we are going to die, but that we will feel pain, whether of a physical sort (e.g., thirst and hunger), or of a more psychological sort (such as when our loved ones die: the cold wind passes, glides by).

Unlike Stoicism or Buddhism, Aztec philosophy does not offer invulnerability as its prize. Life rains on the good and evil with the same brutality. And while it would prove foolhardy to tempt too much risk, there is no shelter that can be built to protect us from every storm.

Just as happiness is not your final goal in life, neither is invulnerability. A worthwhile life, a rooted one, is fragile. These features of the human condition, the ties between happiness and pain, between what is worthwhile and what is fragile, between luck and achievement, are threads in the same fabric. Because the point proves essential to the Aztec outlook, I want to give you a thought experiment to draw its truth a little more clearly:

You are in your late twenties, gathered with family at your grandfather's estate for the reading of his will. He was a wealthy, eccentric man, and you were always his favorite. As the lawyers announce the various bequests, you listen as houses, cars, and charitable donations are distributed. Finally, as the last item, you are left with his most prized possession—a crystal ball.

At first, you dismiss it as a strange joke, but curiosity gets the better of you. Eventually, you try it, almost playfully, asking the ball for the name of the next cryptocurrency that will skyrocket. To your amazement, it responds, and within days, you've made a fortune. With time, your wealth grows beyond your wildest dreams, and you use it to support causes close to your heart—environmental conservation, animal welfare, and other noble endeavors. Each time, the crystal ball offers perfect guidance.

Along the way, you meet someone and fall deeply in love. You decide to ask the ball a different kind of question: "Will the person I love die before me?" The ball, unwavering as always, answers "yes." You feel a sharp pang of sorrow and press further to confirm it: "Who? Me or them?" It responds without hesitation—your beloved will go first.

Faced with this knowledge, would you continue the relationship? Would you choose to embrace love, knowing it will inevitably end in loss? Or would you search for a different path, perhaps hoping to find someone whose fate aligns more closely with yours? But even if you could, would that really change the situation? If the crystal ball revealed that you would die first, would that bring comfort, knowing your beloved would suffer your loss? And what if you kept searching, looking for someone whose life would neatly end with yours? Wouldn't that turn the very idea of love into something transactional, making the person you cherish little more than a means to avoid your own grief?

My point here is simple. You wouldn't be wrong to go on loving your partner. And, likewise, Zapata wasn't wrong to fight for democracy. What makes life worth living also makes it fragile. You are not after happiness, and you are not after invulnerability. These are two core points at the heart of Aztec wisdom about living well—what philosophers call "the good." We're in a position now to understand how they unfold schematically—though we'll leave a fuller elaboration for all the concepts until later.

THE PROBLEM	We slip up, err, even in the things that matter.
THE CAUSE	We are all born unbalanced, and the sources are many.
THE SOLUTION	We must grow deep roots starting from "outside" communities and moving inward to the various dimensions of our psyche.
THE PERFORMANCE	We *do* this growing process by enacting virtues.

THE PRACTICE | We *learn* and *acquire* those virtues through exercise designed to improve our "psyche" or "soul," as opposed to physical exercises, which we do at the gym.

This sequence may remind you of the Buddhist Four Noble Truths, which similarly progress through a problem (suffering), its cause (desire), and the solution found in letting go. Their eightfold path is both the performance and practice of that solution. Stoicism offers a comparable structure: We are untranquil because we try to control what we cannot. The solution lies in becoming virtuous, and this is practiced through a series of "spiritual" exercises. Scholars have called them "spiritual" because they are mental and psychological as opposed to physical. Where the Aztecs prove most interesting is in the specific diagnosis they develop, namely that we are naturally unbalanced, and the answers they provide.

Like Norse culture, the Aztecs should be classed among the world's pessimists, if we are willing to understand that term in its philosophical and not colloquial sense. A philosophical "pessimist" is not a person or culture that dwells on negative thoughts. Rather, a pessimist holds that those who tell you "everything will turn out for the best" or that "you can master any situation" are misleading you. The Aztecs tell us, frankly, that we face impossible odds. Despite that, our lives find meaning and value in the struggle for what is good and beautiful. This outlook is most famously supported by their broader metaphysics and cosmology found in their legend of the Five Suns, which we'll review in the next section. You don't need to accept this legend to find its ethics applicable to your life, but it does provide important context. Let's begin by explaining that context with a more basic question: What is real? The Aztec answer begins in a surprisingly different spot than most "Western" approaches do.

W. V. O. QUINE was one of the most influential philosophers of the twentieth century. He taught, for most of his career, at Harvard University, and he pioneered novel positions in fields ranging from formal mathematics to the philosophy of language to ethics. In one of his most famous essays, titled "On What There Is," he begins as follows:

> A curious thing about the ontological problem is its simplicity. It can be put in three Anglo-Saxon monosyllables: "What is there?" It can be answered, moreover, in a word—"Everything"—and everyone will accept this answer as true.

Nearly the opposite could be written of Aztec philosophy. There is no way, strictly, to ask Quine's question in Nahuatl. The language lacks a term for "is." The language similarly lacks what we English speakers call "words."

As mentioned in the previous chapter, instead of words, the Aztecs had nuclear clauses—meaning that each basic component of a sentence could be its own sentence. As a result of this feature, they had no *grammatical* need for "is," "being," or similar terms that function as what linguistic experts call a "copula." While we can't translate their language without using "is" or "being," it would be a mistake to think that Nahuatl grammar implies the existence of such notions. The linguist Richard Andrews identifies the mistake at work as the "pro drop" fallacy. In Spanish, for example, the word *cantan* is translated as "they sing." The pronoun "they" is something we need to add in English; it exists from our point of view only. The Spanish speaker, however, has no need to add *ellos* before *cantan*, and doing so would even change the meaning of the statement—it would add emphasis, meaning, perhaps, "they, that group over there, sing." The same thing happens with Nahuatl. We English speakers need the words "is," "to be," and "being," but Nahuatl doesn't.

Confronted with these realities, a philosopher or anthropologist might be tempted to think that the Aztecs lacked a domain for thinking about what we call "ontology" or "metaphysics." That is untrue. They did think deeply about the fundamental character of reality. They merely did so without the use of terms such as "being" or "is." Instead, they used *teotl* (TAY-ot).

To make a first pass at the idea, *teotl* is the fundamental energy of the universe. It makes up everything. You are made up of *teotl*. I am made up of *teotl*. Our food is made up of *teotl*. Even our excrement is made up of *teotl*.

For all that, *teotl* is still regarded as divine. I mean that it commands our respect and awe as something of value beyond our merely human desires. It is not, however, a "god" in the sense that it has a personality. *Teotl* does not care about you or aim to save you from your sins. It is venerable, respectable, and reality itself, but it must develop—interact with itself in a way similar to how chemical components do—to become something that would resemble a person.

Importantly, this *teotl* does not exist outside of our universe. It is not like the Christian God, who made our universe and yet dwells in another dimension of reality called heaven. *Teotl* is our reality. The Aztecs were thus what philosophers call pantheists—meaning that they understood all things (*pan* is Greek for "all") to be god itself (*theos* is Greek for "god").

Yet, because they thought of *teotl* as a sort of basic energy, not as a person, it's easiest for us to think of *teotl* as nature. In this sense, the Aztecs held that god is nature.

That formulation, however, risks serious misunderstanding with other philosophers who stated what at first blush sound like similar ideas. In the early modern period, "Western" philosopher Benedict Spinoza (1632–1677) also proposed the idea that god is nature. How are the Aztecs different? Relatedly, given the way that the Aztecs thought of nature as something that was not fully finished, their view might superficially appear to be like that of the ancient Greek philosopher Heraclitus, who lived roughly around 500 BCE. Heraclitus is famous for the saying, "You cannot step into the same river twice." He meant that because nature, reality, was constantly changing, it would be a different river when you stepped in it again. He seems also to hold that nature is not fully finished, so, again, how are the Aztecs different?

Understanding how the Aztecs proposed alternative philosophical ideas is crucial for understanding their ethics. So let's move to unpack the Aztecs' thinking by starting with another basic feature of reality: *inamichuan* (ee-na-MEEK-wan). They are, roughly, the Aztec version of yin and yang.

ALTHOUGH *TEOTL* is all of reality, that basic energy self-expresses in more concrete form through doubling. Conceptually, reality can be thought of as a series of logical doubles: Here implies not over there, up implies not down, outside implies not inside, and so on.

The Aztecs thought of these relational pairs as the basic features of our world as it in fact exists. The Nahuatl word for such a pair is *inamic* (ee-NA-meek) and the plural of such pairs would be *inamichuan* (ee-na-MEEK-wan). As mentioned, they are a little bit like yin and yang insofar as they form conceptual pairs and balance each other, but because they are organized differently, the idea is unique to Aztec culture.

Reality, *teotl*, thus becomes our existence in this doubled form, as *ometeotl* (ome-TAY-ot) since *ome* means two in Nahuatl. The Aztecs included among these *inamic* pairs various cosmological ideas, such as east and west, day and night, dry and wet. They thus conceived of our cosmos as a vast combination of these pairs, and time itself served, in part, as an organizing principle. But it was not the only one.

The legend of the Five Suns is a series of cosmological legends that tell the story of how human beings, in our current form, came to be. The stories tell of various previous cosmological configurations in which human beings lived different kinds of lives with different kinds of food. The "sun" in each case provides the basic kind of energy for these people. And in each case a calamity happens that extinguishes all of humanity and that sun. In one story, for example, fire rains down from the sky and the surviving humans are turned into turkeys.

What the stories suggest is that each new sun emerges as a holistic principle for organizing the *inamichuan* of that cosmos. Our sun is said to be the fifth such sun. It is the *olin* (O-leen) motion sun, meaning that it is the sun of wavelike motions. Radio waves, light waves, ocean waves, even heart movements are all examples of this motion.

A general picture of the Aztec cosmos starts to emerge. At its foundation is *teotl*, an abstract, unorganized energy. For this energy to become the cosmos as we know it, *teotl* self-expresses through the organization of *inamic* pairs—complementary but opposing forces. At each stage of this process, reality becomes more specific and takes on a clearer form. Think of it like this: Just as color is an abstract concept, red is a more specific form of color, and scarlet is an even more precise shade of red. And so *teotl* becomes more defined as *ometeotl*; *ometeotl* then manifests through *inamic* pairs, and these as a "sun," and so on.

Anthropologist Alfredo López-Austin suggests that these *inamic* pairs are conceptually organized much like prime numbers. This means that there is a structure to reality but not in a fully predictable, fully determinate way. In other words, the Aztecs believed that "there is no way things are"—but not in the sense that nothing matters or that reality is chaotic.

This phrase about reality could lead to a misunderstanding with Heraclitus, the Greek philosopher. Heraclitus said we cannot step into the same river twice because everything is constantly changing. For him, there is no way things "are" because as soon as something exists, it changes into something else.

The Aztecs also thought that there is no way that things are, but with a fundamentally different sense. For them, there is no totally comprehensible organizing process for *inamic* pairs. Their relationships stabilize only for a time. *Teotl* thus never achieves a maximally specific form. After a certain point, reality is fuzzy for the Aztecs, a bit like zooming in too close on a picture. You only get pixels but not a more refined image.

To make this clearer, imagine you're planning to climb Mt. Everest. Where does Mt. Everest *begin* exactly? Is it at a particular rock or patch of dirt? Probably not. The boundary of Mt. Everest is fuzzy. After a certain amount of specificity, asking for further precision about where it begins misses the point.

This idea, that reality is never fully defined, also sets the Aztecs apart from thinkers like Spinoza. Spinoza believed that God is nature, and that nature is a substance with a fully specified form. For him, reality is not fuzzy—it has a clear, definite structure.

For the Aztecs, however, "nature" and "god" mean something very different. We humans, living under the fifth sun, have to work to give nature whatever balance and structure it has. There's no divine plan, no guarantee that a higher power is orchestrating events for our benefit. This leads to an ethical conclusion in the Aztec view: We are burdened with deep responsibility. Life's value isn't found in an eternal, perfect existence, like a heaven in another world. It's found in the quality of our struggle here on earth. This perspective can aid our own understanding of the relation between faith and reason in human life.

DURING MY time at university, I spent just over a semester in Rome pursuing coursework—an experience that has been a rite of passage for many young Catholic men over the generations. While there, I not only improved my Italian but also faced a profound struggle with my faith. Crises of faith arise for many reasons; in my case, it involved encounters with wine, women, and the works of Friedrich Nietzsche—another experience not unfamiliar to young men of my background.

Surrounded by priests and open to discussing my doubts, I was eventually given a copy of a relatively recent encyclical at the time, *Fides et Ratio* (Faith and Reason), written by Pope John Paul II. The document opens with a memorable image that encapsulates its central argument: Faith and reason, the Pope writes, are like "two wings of a bird"; without both, it cannot fly. I found this metaphor compelling and was persuaded by the overall message. It seemed to me then, and still does now, that only such a synthesis can act as a safeguard against the irrational ideologies that have caused so much harm in the past. Yet this also raised deeper, more troubling questions that have continued to challenge my belief in God—or gods.

I wondered: What good is God?

Catholics hold that God's existence can be proven through logical arguments, ones that are both valid and sound. These proofs, however, remain contentious. And so, like many before me, I found myself grappling with a broader crisis that has affected reflective individuals of faith in the "West" for some time. Put simply, modern science explains how the universe works, while existentialist philosophy provides a framework for meaning, and ethical systems offer guidance on how to live harmoniously. What we cannot find by reason alone, it appears, is a case for redemption. Without an all-powerful, all-good, all-knowing God, there is little reason to think that the broken pieces of our existence can be made whole. Bad things happen alongside the good, and not in proportion to an individual's good or bad deeds.

From a Nietzschean perspective, this line of thinking might lead you to ask, as I did: What does life look like without the possibility of redemption? The Aztec answer, like that of the Stoics and Buddhists (though for different reasons), is that you will be fine. Redemption is not necessary because everything of value is already present in the performance of a well-lived life, here on earth. In this view, a "well-lived" life is simply one that aligns with the ethical principles guiding human action. An ethical life is the highest form of existence available to us—the only life of true value. If there is a just afterlife, then so much the better. But in the Aztec framework, the essential problem—and the starting point for their reflection on how we ought to live—is a simple, undeniable truth: We all make mistakes. Given that the only meaning and value we can achieve comes from the quality of our life's performance on earth, the pressing question becomes: What are we to do about our inevitable failures?

LESSON 3

Success Is Uncertain, Slipping Is Not

In 1997, Trent Reznor, the lead singer and composer of the industrial rock band Nine Inch Nails, was launched to international stardom. He was on the cover of *Spin* magazine as the "Most Vital Person" in music. Not many people become international rock stars—multimillionaires with endless adoring fans. Yet Reznor had a problem: He was suicidal and had battled persistent depression for years. In the interview with *Spin*, when asked about the matter, he said the following:

> It's not about being content. It's about, What if everything you ever wished for in your life and never thought you'd get, you got? And it still sucked.

Failure does not often take the form we expect. Disillusionment—what Reznor expresses in that statement—is a special sort of failure, namely a failure by way of success. It typifies a core Aztec idea.

In claiming that we slip up, the Aztecs were not making the obvious point that we err. They had in mind a broader idea, namely that you and I lead our lives on the "slippery earth." They meant that even under ideal conditions, people fall into error and that wisdom begins there—in our losses.

To understand how the Aztecs approached this idea, let's look at three related points. For the first, you could turn to volume 6 of the *Florentine Codex*, subtitled *Rhetoric and Moral Philosophy*, where you'll find several common sayings that encapsulate the Aztecs' wisdom on the topic. Two of the clearest sayings follow. To make them a little more readable, I indicate the sayings by numbered square brackets, and separately indicate the glosses of those sayings.

[1] HOW'S IT GOING? BE ESPECIALLY PRUDENT, YOU GOLDEN FISH.

[Gloss] It is said in the following circumstances. If someone once lived well, but later fell into something vicious, [a] perhaps he took a paramour, or [b] he knocked someone down so that he took sick or [c] even died, and for this reason was put in jail, so at that time it is said: "How's it going? Be especially prudent, you golden fish."

The following saying clarifies and broadens the stakes of this first one.

[2] THE EARTH [*tlalticpac* (TLAL-TEEK-PAK)] IS SLIPPERY, SLICK.

[Gloss] Its meaning is the same as the one just discussed. Perhaps at one time someone had a good life, but later fell into some vice, as if that person had slipped in the mud.

If those sayings and their glosses seem odd, that's because you are reading the statements of a culture very different from ours. Let's pause to unpack them a bit.

The phrase "golden fish" is puzzling. Although we cannot be

completely confident, a plausible translation is that a "golden fish" is something akin to a divine animal. If that's right, then calling someone a golden fish is sarcastic. It's a bit like saying: "How's it going Mr. Perfect?"

With that analysis in mind, both sayings are close in meaning. The second statement tells us that everyone who lives on the earth (*tlalticpac*) is bound to slip up in some way. This could be a moral error, resulting from a vice, or just a common mistake. The first statement tells us that even (or especially) those who are perfect will fall in the mud. What it adds in its gloss is the wide range of circumstances in which one can be said to "fall" or "slip up." You might fall by [a] taking a paramour, or [b] knocking someone down (perhaps accidentally) and injuring them, or even [c] knocking them down and killing them accidentally.

To our minds taking a paramour is voluntary, and so would be worthy of blame, but knocking someone down and especially accidentally killing them are beyond what we can control. They are cases of what philosophers call moral luck, and we will return to this point soon—after we can put it in the context of the pursuit of a good life.

Aztec wisdom suggests a constraint for any plausible conception of the good life: It has to be an ideal that we (fallible and often unfortunate) human creatures can hope to achieve. Stated in a different way, the best life is one where we manage our errors and misfortunes, not one where we avoid all errors and suffering.

These reflections relate to the second feature of our lives on the slippery earth (*tlalticpac*): They are transitory. Perhaps the best spokesperson on this point is Nezahualcoyotl—or at least his legend. As part of a longer piece of philosophical poetry, Nezahualcoyotl writes the following.

> *My friends, stand up!*
> *And here they are, the princes.*
> *I, Nezahualcoyotl, am a singer.*

*Tzontecochatzin, take up your flowers and your fan,
and, using them, go dance!
You are my child,
you are Yoyontzin.
Drink up your chocolate,
flower of the cacao tree.
Now let the princes be sent away!
There is still dancing, and
there is still song, but
this place is not our home.
This is not where we live.
Even you [hearer] will have to go away.*

This view shares some similarities with the Christian Bible's verse of 1 Corinthians 15:32, "Let us eat and drink, for tomorrow we die." But the solution the Aztecs are offering isn't that one should believe in a saving god (Jesus), since for them god is just the natural environment (*teotl*). The lesson, instead, is that the human condition, life on the slippery earth, is not only one where we err and suffer misfortune, but one where death is inevitable, and life is too short. Recall that for the Aztecs our "sun" was the fifth, and that like the previous four it too will perish. Even the cosmos lives but ephemerally.

Finally, it is not at all clear that life on the earth (*tlalticpac*) will be a "happy" one. One reason for this, you saw in Lesson 1, was that happiness, understood as the presence of elevated emotional states, comes and goes. Happiness is followed by fatigue, pain by happiness, and these are basic cycles of our existence. Another reason is that, as described in Lesson 2, we cannot avoid the fragility of our experience. Zapata was not wrong to try for democracy. You'd not be wrong to love someone who would die well before you.

These three points, that we are all bound to slip up, that even our cosmic existence is ephemeral, and that happiness, or at least pleasure, comes and goes just like any feeling, form the scaffolding for Aztec philosophy. Any philosophical outlook that ignores these points, the Aztecs would say, is naive.

They are tough truths, but now that we recognize them, it's important to recognize that one of their causes is the complexity of our mind, psyche, or, to use an ancient term, "soul." The Aztecs held, roughly, that our mind is an ecosystem of sorts, which is distributed in its "thinking" throughout our body—a view that has received increasing support from contemporary scientific research. Since their insights into our embodied mind furnish the basis for the outward path, we need to develop these points.

THANKS TO the success of films like *Coco* and *The Book of Life*, many people are now familiar with the Day of the Dead as it is celebrated in Mexico—or at least, how it was once celebrated. In some ways, the holiday resembles All Hallows' Eve. It marks the time of year when it was believed that souls could cross the boundary between the world of the living and the world of the ancestors. Yet there are also significant differences. One of the most distinctive traditions is the making of *ofrendas*, or offerings, something that puzzled me as a child. If my *abuelito* (grandfather) had already passed away, I wondered, why would he need food? And why would anyone offer alcohol—an entire bottle of tequila, no less? Isn't that bad for the living, let alone the dead?

As a child, I was thinking in terms of a "Western" understanding of the afterlife—one that makes sense of Halloween, but not the Day of the Dead. The difference lies in the Mesoamerican conception of the animating forces that make up a person, forces that are often translated as "soul" but are far more complex than that single term suggests. According to Aztec belief, there were three such forces: *yolia* (yo-LEE-a), *ihiyotl* (ee-HEE-yot), and *tonalli* (to-NA-lee). To fully appreciate how these forces shaped life and purpose, it's essential to understand all three.

Yolia (yo-LEE-a)

This term was a solution to a problem. Formulated as a question, it asks: Why do humans and other animals move about, but rocks don't? Should you survey premodern cultures and their answers globally, you would see a pattern in how ancient peoples typically thought of the force or forces that moved living things—*animating* forces, from the Latin *anima* meaning "soul." If Aristotle were magically transported to modern times and witnessed automobiles driving about, he might be tempted, until told otherwise, to call them animals—precisely because they could move, seemingly on their own.

A soul, then, is that thing which explains how moving about is possible. Yet, such a notion was not (necessarily) that of a spirit in a jar, a ghost residing in our body. In the "West," "soul" typically refers to something thicker, richer, a being with additional properties. The soul carries with it our personal identity, especially by way of our memories.

The Aztec *yolia* comes close to serving in these dual capacities. It explains motion and involves our personal memories. Francisco de Molina's dictionary of Nahuatl relates *yolia* to *yollotl* (YO-lot), or heart, which has a connection with a kind of wavelike undulating motion, *olin* (O-leen). Your heart, in short, is that entity that moves you around, animates you, in the *olin* way—through the wavelike motion of your heart pumping. Additionally, because we move about for specific reasons and desires, this source of movement was also thought to be the seat of our affective states and desires. It is through this work, moving you about in pursuit of your desires, that the *yolia* becomes a storehouse for our memories. At death, your *yolia* was said to pass out of your mouth. According to Oviedo y Valdés, a local Indigenous, sixteenth-century Christian ruler, when a person died "Something resembling a person, which is called *yulio* [sic], comes out of the mouth and goes there [i.e., to the underworld]."

You may reasonably wonder why the Aztecs needed multiple "soul" types. If *yolia* explains why we move, our desires, and our memory, then what's left to explain? The answer is that the Aztecs needed to explain how we are strong or weak (*ihiyotl*) and why each of us appears to have a sort of destiny or purpose (*tonalli*).

Ihiyotl (ee-HEE-yot)

Molina, the early postcolonial linguist, groups *ihiyotl* (ee-HEE-yot) with *ehecatl* (e-HE-cat), the wind. The *ihiyotl* does not appear to map onto a specific motion, such as *olin*, but it does concern a sort of imperceptible movement like the wind's. The root, *ihi* (ee-hee), refers to a life engendering force and shares similar qualities with related notions among the Indigenous Chortí Maya of Guatemala.

Ihiyotl is a life force in the sense that it is what makes one physically strong or weak. In studying the topic, Jill Leslie McKeever Furst summarizes its connection to health and passing gas:

> The vaporous *ihiyotl* was normally contained in the flesh, but it emerged during life as flatus, a common byproduct of a healthy, well-fed individual. Breaking wind is normal, and usually the more a person eats, the greater the volume of internal wind seeking escape. The Mexica [i.e., Aztecs around Tenochtitlán] were correct: the more *ihiyotl*—spirit and breath—a person possessed, the greater the vigor of that person's life force. Conversely, people who do not eat adequately are subject to fatigue and illness and contain less life force manifested as exiting air, or flatus.

In a line, healthy individuals fart more. This is the force, then, that enters our bodies through food consumption and helps to animate us.

Tonalli (to-NA-lee)

The origins of this third and final term in this sequence are not completely known but seem to be related to *tona* (TOE-na), which means to make warm. It was seen as a force sent to a child (breathed into it) while in utero by the Lord and Lady of Duality—one name for *teotl*. When the term for this force was given a possessed grammatical form, Molina defines the resulting term's meaning as a "portion of each person, or a thing assigned by another."

The heat given off was linked to drilling, a spiraling motion. We are warm beings, after all, and that warmth was understood to move into our bodies in a spiraling way. Finally, that warmth was thought to come from the sun and imbue each child with the force of his or her life. It also contributed to the Aztecs' approach to the "parts" of our "soul."

IN PLATO'S *REPUBLIC*, Socrates articulates one of the earliest accounts of the human "soul" or "mind" as divided into parts. Socrates and his interlocutor, Glaucon, agree that if they identify two opposing intentions, then two different parts of the soul must be present. Otherwise, the same part would be acting both for and against itself. During this conversation, Socrates articulates a sort of thought experiment to illustrate this idea.

> You are lost and stumbling through a desert. It's been two days since you've had anything to drink, and you are suffering from dehydration headaches. Finally, you stumble across a puddle of water. Dropping to your knees in relief, you pause. It's obvious to anyone that this puddle is mostly mud and grime mixed with water. It is highly unlikely to be clean. Should you drink the water anyway?

My students are divided on this one. Most say that they would drink from the puddle since death by infection is likely further away than death by dehydration. Others argue that an infection would dehydrate you even more, so that it's a trap, like drinking ocean water. No unanimous decision can be made without more details. But even without those, you can understand Socrates's point. If you hesitate in this sort of situation, you can *feel* the tension in your mind between conflicting impulses: one is to drink, another is to refrain. It is from this sort of tension that Socrates concludes that our "soul" must have both a desiring part and a reasoning part.

The Aztecs likewise distinguished "parts of the soul." But they did so by identifying where the three external forces (*yolia, ihiyotl, tonalli*) were distributed, and what brought them together. These forces turned on what could be observed. For example, *ihiyotl* was introduced to the body by eating. A diminished store of *ihiyotl* was thus thought to result from fasting, which led to an experience of lethargy.

It was Alfredo López-Austin who, in his two-volume *Cuerpo humano e ideología* (*The Human Body and Its Ideology*), developed what is still the principal account of how the human body, mind, and soul were linked in Aztec thought. Because no texts survive that explain the Aztec views on this topic, López-Austin undertook his study by exhaustively examining every word in the main Nahuatl dictionaries from the early colonial period and cross-referenced relevant terms with uses in other texts available from that period. He then organized those results and presented them as data in the second volume of his work. The first volume consists of his analysis and explanation of those data. The division allows future scholars to draw from his data while disputing his analysis, but the scholarship that followed on this monumental undertaking, such as work by McKeever Furst, has expanded the analysis, not refuted it. In my own assessment, López-Austin's work is likely to prove nearly the last word on the topic—a bit as J. D.

Denniston's *The Greek Particles* has been the last word on the topic of classical Greek grammatical particles for nearly a century.

The account of the Aztec's "embodied mind" that López-Austin presents is split into two dimensions of analysis. The first dimension details the three external animating forces: *yolia, ihiyotl,* and *tonalli*. These were thought to enter or exit the human body through specific activities, including birth, baptism, food and liquid consumption, sun exposure, defecation, exercising, bathing, cutting one's hair, and a variety of what are called (for want of a better term) ritual acts, some of which involved bloodletting.

In the second dimension of his analysis, López-Austin found evidence that these animating powers were thought to be generally distributed in the human body to account for its variety of motions. They were not thought to be equally distributed, however, and this unequal distribution makes for an embodied dynamic of *inamic* (ee-NA-meek) relationships. The left, celestial side of the body was thought to be suffused with more of these forces, and the energy was collected into ten minor areas of the body. Starting from the bottom and rising, these areas were:

1. Toes
2. Ankles
3. Calves
4. Groin
5. Waist
6. Wrists
7. Elbows
8. Shoulders
9. Neck
10. Hair

Beyond these minor centers, three major centers, identified by major organs, were most suffused with animating forces: your heart, your head (it's all "mind," remember), and your liver.

To some degree, López-Austin also articulates a third dimension of analysis, namely those features of our cognition that concern our ethical life. The Aztecs conveyed important ideas using paired key terms, such as "patio and doorway" to metaphorically indicate a house. Scholars use the Spanish term *difrasismo* to describe this linguistic pattern. A famed *difrasismo* is *ixtli, yollotl* (EESH-tlee, YO-lot), which is translated as "face, heart" and signifies your character. López-Austin argues that *ixtli* in the first instance means "eye" and only in a more extended sense does it mean "face." He therefore includes a discussion of the eye (*ixtli*) within his embodied analysis, but he does not provide much support for the ethical connections at work.

That the *difrasismo* is connected to our role as ethical agents appears in many of the surviving discourses of the elders' speeches (recall that "the discourses of the elders" [*huehuetlatolli*, way-weh-tla-TOL-lee] is a genre of writing distinctive to the Aztecs). In *Discourses of the Elders*, we read the following by a daughter in response to her mother:

> Your dear face, dear heart, dear body is owed much in compensation [for your teachings].

Note how the mother treats these components, face, heart, and body, as a single unit that owed compensation. In other paragraphs, face and heart are linked with the neck, elbow, and other features of the body. For example, in a discourse in which a mother is speaking to her daughter in *Discourses of the Elders*, she advises:

> Damage not your face and heart, nor with them your shoulder, your back, your elbow, and your knee when you set yourself to sweep, to clean.

The Aztecs thought of the "face" as a seat of judgment in one way, while they used the "heart," or seat of desire, as a stand-in for all the other competing desires of the body. There is something of a third dimension at work, too, which expresses both the ethical center of your personality—your character—and the need each of us has to balance the competing claims. Keep in mind that the "face" is not the seat of reason for the Aztecs, but of judgment. Then consider the discourse of a father who, in edifying his young son, states the following:

> My blood and color, I have forged you, given you a start. Already before you and above you I stand guard. May you not be just precious metal, since you have been forged in this way. For you still come with sleep in your eyes and you will later come to discover your face.

The discovery of one's face, or in less metaphorical language, the development of judgment, is something that comes after time, experience, and reflection. One is not born with a face but, rather, finds and develops it.

For the Aztecs, then, the human embodied "mind" is an ecosystem. Cognition is not only distributed through the entire body, but the body's various areas contend and vie with one another to move us in different directions. To some extent, I think the Aztecs' approach to cognition is sensible for the modern era. But on the other hand, to say that your calf muscle or your joints "think" seems to step beyond the threshold of credibility. Yet the Aztecs meant this in a literal sense—as is amply supported by evidence—and that view is more sensible than you might imagine. If it seems outlandish, that's only because "Western" philosophers have privileged the thinking ego for the past five hundred years.

WHEN ROBOTICS researchers began programming robots to move, they initially started with a classic model of embodiment and artificial intelligence. They wrote a set of complex instructions, which detailed how the machine should respond to given stimuli. This is the approach that initially informed the movement of Asimo, a robot built by Honda. The fluid sort of movement characteristic of human walking only began to take shape recently—after a paradigm shift in the robotics team's approach. One roboticist, in commenting on the results captured in early videos, stated that the robot looked as though it suffered from "a kind of rigor mortis." The amount of computing power required to assess just how much weight to put on a leg, or how much pressure an actuator or gear needs, is enormous—reportedly requiring some sixteen times more energy than a human does. The team aiming to replicate the human gait ultimately opted for a different model of embodied computation.

An alternative approach centers on passive dynamics, which is easiest to illustrate with a glass or mug. Get a cup of some sort and place it within reach and sit down. Now, reach out and pick up that cup. Set it back down. Reflect for a moment: Do you know how much pressure you exerted to hold the cup? Which fingers did most of the work and by how much? If you had to close your eyes, could you give an exact description of where your fingers were?

Such questions all prove difficult to answer. And the reason for that is the point at issue: Our brains do not make any of those calculations consciously. That hard work is done for us through the structure of our hands themselves.

When the robotics engineer Horoshi Yoki made a prosthetic hand using the model of passive dynamics, one that can successfully grab a wide range of objects, the only input it needed was a command representing the thought "close." The prosthetic was fitted to an amputee who had relatively rudimentary electromyographic (EMG) sensors placed on the surface of their skin where the muscles and tendons that controlled their hand used to be. The user would then try to "close" their hand, acting as if they had a hand. The sensors, upon detecting this signal, would set in motion a closing action by pulling on the careful balance of robotic "bones and tendons," which diligently copied the human hand. The result was that the prosthetic hand could wrap around an object nearly as well as a natural one.

What Yoki implemented in his design of the human hand is something approaching intelligence. Your hands respond to their environment *as if* they had a mind that thought of a solution to a problem and then implemented it. This ability is why some researchers have opted to call this phenomenon "joint intelligence," meaning that your hand operates in a sort of equilibrium, which is achieved via a set of conditioned responses to environmental cues.

A few things stop us from calling a hand "smart." First, the hand has, as far as we typically conceive the notion, no consciousness of its own. And intelligence in the "West," at least since René Descartes in the 1600s, has been paradigmatically defined as a conscious activity. Second, your hand does not engage in reflective deliberation—thinking about possible courses of action on its own—even if it appears to respond as though it did. Reflective deliberation is also a conscious activity.

Were we to drop the requirement that intelligence must be defined in terms of conscious reasoning, and we arguably have in using the phrase "artificial intelligence," both barriers would fall. In their place "purposive responsiveness," that equilibrium achieved among a set of conditioned responses to environmental cues, might reasonably take a place beside the older definition of "intelligence" as, roughly, the successful culmination of reflective deliberation in response to a question or problem. In other words, a hand solves problems, even if it does not do so with deliberation or through conscious reasoning.

The Aztecs shared with many other cultures a more broadly native American view of the natural environment. Perhaps many things in nature are "intelligent," even if not conscious. A river, after all, could exhibit a sort of equilibrium as a set of conditioned responses to environmental cues. So might a mountain.

Let us again consider the Aztecs' approach to cognition. How your calf might "think" may be understood along the lines of how your hand is "smart." There is no process of making inferences at work in that activity and no implied conscious reasoning. Still, the "intelligent" way in which hands or calves or joints work can be understood and defined objectively through their ability to achieve equilibrium. This approach offers a path to understanding our surrounding natural environment as "smart." It also furnishes us with the broader sense of cognition that the Aztecs held—one in line with modern science.

ONE OF the first breakthroughs in the understanding of embodied cognition to make its way into public awareness hinges on the importance of metaphors in structuring our thinking. The linguist George Lakoff and philosopher Mark Johnson identified how advanced forms of cognition, those centered on especially abstract topics, appear to retain a connection to their embodied origins. The reason, it seems, is that our bodies schematize our thoughts and words, even if they don't totally constrain them. Lakoff and Johnson's examples, taken from ordinary expressions, are striking.

- "Time *flies*" conceives of time by way of motion.
- "Don't worry! I'm *on top of* the situation" conceives of control as an upward direction.
- "I'm feeling *up* today" conceives of happiness as moving up.
- "They greeted me *warmly*" schematizes affection in terms of warm temperatures.
- "I *see* what you mean" schematizes understanding by way of vision.

Something unique happens when language enters our process of cognition. The embodied origin transforms into symbolism. The metaphor we use to explain how embodied cognition might work for the Aztecs, then, must follow this symbolism. I've chosen to represent it in terms of a flower blooming, a ubiquitous symbol in Aztec literature—whether philosophical or simply poetic. We might think of its "blooming" as passing through three stages. First, the three external, cosmic forces, *yolia*, *ihiyotl*, and *tonalli*, enter the body and provide it with animating energy. These forces are distributed throughout the body, but, at a second stage, thirteen primary centers concentrate these forces. Of those centers, the heart, the head, and the liver concentrate the energy the most. Each area acts as its own sort of "mind," thinking in a nonconscious way, just as the hand of a robot operates using passive dynamics. Finally, at a third level, the push and pull of our many "minds," from our joints to our livers, are metaphorically represented as our "heart." Through experience and education, we form a face, a seat of judgment that guides the competing demands of our many minds—not as an external agent, but as a reflective feature of their self-reinforcing accumulation of experiences. Together, our face and heart may be taken as the center of our personality and character.

Thought thus "blooms" as it works its way up from local concerns (that joint pain in my bad wrist) to conscious awareness (that I need to move my hand) to vocalization ("ouch!") to dialogue with others who can help me to better understand the pain. This model of thinking, beginning with a seed incident that blooms into progressively more involved forms of thinking—though not necessarily terminating in conscious awareness—has received broad scientific support (even if the details of the Aztec view are not scientifically accurate). Guy Claxton, a cognition researcher, presents the emerging consensus this way:

> Many of us are familiar with this experience of "welling up"— occasionally. But my more radical suggestion is that these special moments are actually prototypical of our conscious experience as a whole. All of our thoughts and sensations well

up from visceral and unconscious origins in the same way, though we may not notice the unfurling.

This underscores López-Austin's work on the Aztecs' moral psychology—a view we now call embodied cognition—that was published some forty years ago. Contemporary science has caught up to the broader outlook of Aztecs.

In the Aztec view, our psyche is not like a rider on a horse, as Sigmund Freud suggested, or even a rider on an elephant, as the contemporary psychologist Jonathan Haidt has put it. Ideally, it is a fluidly coordinated jazz ensemble, where each player improvises in their own way, none of whom is distinctly responsible for their coordination. In less than ideal cases (which would be most of them!) the players fail to coordinate and improvise well, resulting in the screeching dissonance typical of junior high instrumentalists.

The Aztec believed that the human psyche is too complex for us to hope that it would somehow find balance on its own. Left to an untutored state, you and I are bound to lead bestial lives, to follow the path of "the deer and the rabbit," as they put it. Before we can discover how to resolve these difficulties, we need to have a discussion about balance.

SPIRITUAL EXERCISE I

The Kinder Words Practice

IN VOLUME 6 of the *Florentine Codex* there is direct evidence of the Aztecs' focus on "right speech." In one discourse, a mother tells her daughter to speak in such a way as to preserve her traditional words of wisdom "in the chambers of your heart." Right speech, for the Aztecs, is a practice meant to conserve what is good and upstanding at your core. Without a sense of what is good in life, you cannot distinguish right speech from drivel. The approach finds strong contemporary support.

The psychologist Robert Cialdini recounts a story that changed his understanding of the power of small words. He was invited to give a talk at SSM Health, a healthcare nonprofit renowned for its stratospheric performance. Yet he was told that in his presentation he would have to replace specific words.

- Instead of "bullet point" say "talking points."
- Instead of "attack a problem" say "approaching a problem."
- Instead of "beat the competition" say "outdistance the competition."

Befuddled, Cialdini asked: Why? Why would such small words matter?

The answer, he discovered, is that what crosses your lips preframes your mind. If your thoughts lead to actions, then words inconsistent with your goals will lead to actions inconsistent with your goals. After contact with the group and researching the topic himself, Cialdini stated his new view bluntly:

> I'm a convert now. My response to SSM's strict language policy transformed from "Geez, this is silly" to "Geez, this is smart."

In SSM Health's case, their goal is to improve people's lives through health and well-being. Violent language is inconsistent with that goal. So they eliminated it, or at least as much of it as they could.

There is scientific support for their approach; it wasn't mere guess work. But what SSM Health and Cialdini have rediscovered is, in fact, a bedrock practice for Aztec philosophy called "right speech." This ancient wisdom, repurposed in modern terms, rests on the Aztec belief in embodied cognition—the idea that our mind operates like an ecosystem, where even small actions, like the words we choose, play a crucial role in how we live well. The Aztec position on embodied cognition, where our many "minds" form an ecosystem of sorts, supports the view that all kinds of "small deeds," from the words we use to the small ways we interact with our environment, prove crucial for living well.

In another discourse from the *Florentine Codex*, a father advises his son on how to be prudent in public, and he elaborates the key dimensions of right speech.

> You are to speak slowly and deliberately . . . [And] guard, take care of your ears, of what you hear. Do not gossip.

In short, Aztec right speech, intended to protect and promote what is good about your personal character, has four characteristics:

- ❀ Speak thoughtfully,
- ❀ Speak truly,

❁ Speak humbly,
❁ Avoid gossip.

The last two are relatively straightforward, but thoughtful and truthful speech deserve closer examination. Thoughtful speech centers on the use of kind words. In *Discourses of the Elders*, a father warns his son that "if you make fun of people, like this, you will not come out human." This implies that kind words are necessary for maintaining a human life. A little later the father continues:

> And do not anywhere speak without consideration. Do not best people with your words and so cut off their speech. Do not talk unkindly to people, do not make them forget or fail to conserve those words which are good.

Kind words, then, are not just about avoiding insults or giving compliments—they are about addressing others with care and appropriateness. Kind words are thoughtful words.

In a world driven by social media and clickbait, advocating for kind words may seem quaint. But this principle has found practical application even in the most high-stakes situations—such as FBI hostage negotiations.

When you confront someone, it often provokes resistance. In a hostage situation, confrontation can lead to more than just resistance—it can lead to lives being lost. In any negotiation, however, it's necessary to confront the other side with evidence, which can be uncomfortable. How, then, should you approach it? Former FBI hostage negotiator Chris Voss advocates for a strategy that turns kind words into action: *mirroring*.

The academic name is "isopraxism," and it means that you should imitate the other party in subtle ways so as to put them at ease and build rapport. When the other person is being obstinate, or stating falsehoods, confronting them with facts provokes a defensive response. Instead, repeat their last three important words as a question.

Voss illustrates this with a conversation he had with Chris Watts, a bank robber who had taken hostages. Initially, the negotiating team believed the hostage-takers were working together, but through the use of mirroring, Voss broke through Watts's tough exterior. Voss recounts the experience this way:

> "We've got a van out here [in front of the bank], a blue and gray van. We've been able to get a handle on the owners of all the vehicles except this one in particular. Do you know anything about it?"
>
> "The other vehicle's not out there because you guys chased my driver away . . ." he blurted.
>
> "We chased your driver away?" I mirrored.
>
> "Well, when he seen the police he cut [i.e., left the scene]."

With that admission, that the getaway driver had cut and run, the FBI team learned that the bank robbing unit was divided. This key piece of information helped resolve the standoff without any hostages being harmed.

The Aztec outward path holds that the key to a better life is learning to master your "outward" circumstances so that you can facilitate better "inward" peace. Speaking, much like breathing, is an automatic process but one that we can control if we choose to focus on it. Right speech teaches that the words we choose shape the character we develop. Gossip entangles us in matters that don't concern us, while boastful speech blinds us to our own flaws. Thoughtful, kind words foster stronger connections, even in the most difficult situations, while truthful speech grounds us in reality. That truthful speech does not require mere truthfulness, however, and in the next spiritual exercise, after Lesson 4, we will explore what exactly is involved.

Nezahualcoyotl

LESSON 4

All Are Born Unbalanced, Some Stand for a Time

From what evidence we have, Nezahualcoyotl (Neza-wal-COY-ot / Hungry Coyote, featured on the Mexican one-hundred-peso bill) is likely to have lived a pleasant life until 1418. Born to the king of Tezcoco and a princess from Tenochtitlán (Te-noch-ti-TLAN), he enjoyed relative wealth and luxury and was able to receive the education of the *calmecac* (kal-ME-kak), the schooling system dedicated to the study of philosophy, religion, law, history, and poetry. Legend holds that this school would open doors for countless Aztec youths to enter the royal courts. But for an inquisitive boy, it was also the place for what we call "liberal studies," an education that offered space to delve into core questions about our existence. Beyond this education, he appears to have received tutoring from Huitzilihuitzin (Wee-tzil-ee-WEE-tzin), a famed philosopher in his own right.

Yet at some point in that year, at age sixteen, Nezahualcoyotl hid in a tree while he watched assassins from the ruling city Azcapotzalco (Az-ca-pot-ZAL-co) murder his father. In seconds, the color of his world changed forever.

To survive, he fled the city he called home and sought refuge in the houses of other nobles in neighboring lands. At one point, he lived in Huexotzinco (We-sho-TZIN-co), where, a generation later, philosophers would dialogue on the meaning of language and poetry. Later, he lived in Tlaxcala (Tlash-KA-la), which would eventually supply Hernán Cortés with enough warriors to overthrow Tenochtitlán (now Mexico City) and win the Spanish-Aztec war.

The textual tradition, supporting Nezahualcoyotl's legendary status, states that he wrote poetic songs during this time—what are called "flower songs" or *xochicuicatl* (Sho-chee-CUI-kat). They express his existential state of mind at this time. The first recorded statement reads as follows.

> *I was born in vain!*
> *In vain have I come forth from god's home.*
> *On earth, I am wretched.*
> *Would that I not have come forth.*
> *Would that I not have been born.*

Here is another, which, according to legend, would have been composed around the same time.

> *I am sad. I grieve.*
> *I, lord Nezahualcoyotl.*
> *With flowers and songs*
> *I remember the princes,*
> *Those who went away,*
> *Tezozomoc, and that one Cuacuauh.*
> *Do they truly live,*
> *There wherein-some-way-one-exists?*

His perspective is one of a refugee, fleeing from the safety and comfort of his home at just sixteen, now living in exile for what would turn out to be a nearly equal period of his life.

The fate which Nezahualcoyotl was dealt constitutes yet

another example of "slipping up," though in a mode quite different from the other sorts. The causes we have reviewed thus far concern the precarious nature of the cosmos, which the Aztecs thought would collapse before giving birth to another sun. Next, they held that such metaphysical incompleteness translates into an incomplete organization in our psyches. Each of us is born with a seat of desires, a "heart" they would say, but not a "face," a seat of judgment. We are thus born into an unbalanced world with unbalanced minds. But this is not all: A third form of unbalance follows from what contemporary philosophers would call moral luck.

Consider the following three cases that all involve moral luck.

[a] Suppose that a taxi driver is driving drunk, making his way through the streets of Manhattan. At the same time, an old man is walking down the sidewalk, loses his footing, and stumbles into the road. The taxi driver would have hit him, but because the driver is intoxicated, he had already veered into the empty oncoming lane. As a result, the driver narrowly misses the old man. How blameworthy is the drunk taxi driver? How bad are his actions?

[b] Suppose the same as the above, but this time, the taxi driver manages to stay in his lane, and so hits the old man. Yet it turns out, miraculously, that the old man is uninjured. How blameworthy is the taxi driver in this case? Is this scenario worse, in a moral way, than the previous? Why or why not?

[c] Suppose the same as the above in [b], but this time, when hit, the old man is seriously injured. How blameworthy is the taxi driver? Is this scenario worse, morally, than [b]? Why or why not?

The difficulty with these scenarios is remaining consistent in your logical thinking. We tend to assign blame, and assess how bad a situation is, based on the "internal" beliefs of the agent, on their motivations and goals. Yet in all three cases, the drunk taxi driver chose to become drunk before driving to whatever destination he had in mind. The driver's "internal" reasons for these cases, then, are the same. Despite this, the last case seems worse, morally, than the previous two. It's easier to assign (moral) blame in the last case, [c], than in the other cases. But the differences between the last case and the first two are purely "external" circumstances. Their details couldn't possibly have entered the taxi driver's mind before getting into his car. Do "external" circumstances, then, matter to "internal" intent?

Philosophers have worked tirelessly to make sense of our responses to scenarios like these. The Aztec's interest in them (and here this is our interest too) is simpler. All we need to recognize is that human life, the one led on the slippery earth (*tlalticpac*), is unavoidably filled with scenarios such as these.

You might slip while walking on an icy sidewalk and knock someone down, and nothing bad happens. But of course, you might knock the person down, and, because of some preexisting condition, they could be seriously injured or die from your actions. Is it just luck that you're not an accidental murderer?

You might be happily married and yet need to travel for business. By happenstance you meet your ex-lover at a hotel bar. It could turn out that because you had never really resolved your breakup, you find yourself in bed together that night. Or perhaps, because a friend is with you, she is able to intervene, and nothing untoward happens. Is it just luck that you're romantically faithful?

The Aztecs would argue that luck plays a much larger role in our successes and failures, even in our moral successes, than most of us in the "West" generally recognize. The world is simply too complex and too unpredictable for luck not to play a significant role. We come into life "unbalanced," unprepared to avoid falling. It is for this reason that the Aztec view finds its closest "Western" parallel in ancient Greek tragedy—think of Sophocles's *Oedipus Rex*.

In that tragedy, to recall, Oedipus learns from the Oracle at Delphi that he is fated to kill his father and sleep with his mother. Not wanting these events to transpire, he leaves his home in Corinth and flees to another city, Thebes. On his way, he meets a man, has an altercation, and kills him. When he arrives at his destination, Thebes, he learns the city has no ruler and it is cursed by a Sphinx. Oedipus solves the Sphinx's riddle, ends the curse, and as a prize marries Jocasta, the dowager queen. It is only later that Oedipus learns that the man he killed in his journey was his father and that Jocasta is his biological mother.

To bridge Aztec and ancient Greek ways of thinking, you could say that the basic sources for a lack of harmonic balance derive from: (1) metaphysical reasons, (2) observations about the complexity of the human psyche, and (3) observations about the role of moral luck. Even if we discard the Aztecs' view on metaphysical cosmology, the latter two remain compelling for us, as they pose no immediate challenge to the conclusions of modern science. A deeper view about ethics and our human place in the cosmos follows.

IT'S OFTEN said that people are drawn to the philosophy that suits their temperament. In my experience as a teacher, this rings true. So why should you follow the Aztec approach over that of the Stoics, Buddhists, or even Nietzsche?

You can begin to answer this by asking yourself: How chaotic do you think the world is? We all know that terrible, unexpected things happen. But how frequently do you think they occur? When they do, are they an anomaly in an otherwise harmonious universe? Or are they the natural expression of universal chaos? Perhaps your take on this falls somewhere in between.

Many of the practical philosophies that have gained traction in the "West" are built on the idea that the universe is a rationally organized system. Take the Stoics of ancient Greece and Rome, for example. They believed that the cosmos itself was a conscious, rational being that used reason to organize all events. As Diogenes Laertius explains:

> The claim that the cosmos is a living being, rational, animate and intelligent, is laid down by Chrysippus in the first book of his treatise *On Providence*, by Apollodorus in his *Physics*, and by Posidonius. It is a living thing in the sense of an animate substance endowed with sensation; for animal is better than nonanimal, and nothing is better than the cosmos, therefore the cosmos is a living being.

According to the Stoics, if the cosmos is a rational being, then everything that happens is part of a greater rational order—everything happens for a reason. If that's true, your role is to learn to accept events as they unfold. This is what the Stoics called *amor fati*, or the love of fate. Your task, then, is to train your mind to assent to reality in the right way, focusing on what is within your control and stopping harmful thoughts before they take root. For the Stoics, enlightenment comes through this kind of inward discipline.

Nearly the entire outlook of Indian philosophy also holds that the universe is rationally organized. This is true whether a school accepts the authority of the Vedas, as the Vedānta does, accepts an independent authority, as Yoga does, or rejects the Vedas altogether, as Buddhism does. In their *Introduction to Indian Philosophy*, the scholars Satischandra Chatterjee and Dhirendramohan Datta summarize the point as follows:

> The faith in an order—a law that makes for regularity and righteousness and works in the gods, the heavenly bodies and all creatures—pervades the poetic imagination of the seers of the Ṛg-veda which calls this inviolable moral order Ṛta.

It is this rational organization of the universe, especially its moral organization, that supports the law of karma. In general, the law of karma holds that all actions, both good or bad, yield their proper consequence for the individual actor—whether in this life, or the next. As a result, the path toward a good life is one that liberates the individual from her ignorance about herself and the universe. It takes practice to transform oneself, and some of the most popular techniques are explained through Yoga. For the one seeking a better life, then, the path is inward.

A few philosophers, rather notoriously, deny that the cosmos is rationally organized. The names, in the "West," most closely allied with this rejection are Friedrich Nietzsche and Niccolò Machiavelli. Both philosophers are difficult to interpret, but their bases for this rejection find rather plausible support in some of their more well-known formulations. In *Thus Spoke Zarathustra*, Nietzsche explains cosmic organization in this way:

> Indeed, the truth was not hit by him who shot at it with the word of the "will to existence" [e.g., Darwin]: that will does not exist. For, what does not exist cannot will; but what is in existence, how could that still want existence? Only where there is life is there also will: not will to life but—thus I teach you—will to power.

What Nietzsche means is this: If you want to understand how things happen in the universe, not how they should happen, then the truth is staring you straight in the face. The strong overcome the weak. Fish eat insects. Bears eat fish. Humans hunt bears. What exists doesn't only want to live, as Darwinian evolution suggests. Living beings want to exercise their capacities, to exert their will to power. Power over what? Over everything they can. The universe has no other organization. Karma is false. And Stoic *amor fati* is a consolation for the weak.

Written during the Renaissance, one of the most politically turbulent eras in history, Machiavelli's *The Prince* endorses a chaotic view on the cosmos parallel to Nietzsche's. Near the end of the work, just before exhorting the prince Lorenzo de' Medici to take up arms in war, Machiavelli explains his views on "fortune" using a metaphor charged with misogynist violence.

> I judge this indeed, that it is better to be impetuous than cautious, because fortune is a woman; and it is necessary, if one wants to hold her down, to beat her and strike her down. And one sees that she lets herself be won more by the impetuous than by those who proceed coldly. And so always, like a woman, she is the friend of the young, because they are less cautious, more ferocious, and command her with more audacity.

Violence and misogyny are endemic to both Nietzsche and Machiavelli's work, and that follows from their view of the cosmos. In their view, what there is exists largely through the force of human creation, as a result of those violent and bold individuals who hold and strike fortune down.

For both Nietzsche and Machiavelli, then, there is no path to enlightenment apart from accepting that the course of things can be explained by the strong overtaking the weak. Can you bear this truth, they challenge? If so, then you will need to learn how to exert your will to power to make whatever cosmic order you see fit. The path is not inward, but outwardly directed from whatever your inward vision dictates. *The Prince* and *Thus Spoke Zarathustra*, then, are but instruction manuals, for the art of living well is nothing other than the art of war.

The Aztecs—and I think that they are joined by some strands of Confucian philosophy—hold that neither of these outlooks are correct. The Stoics, Buddhists, and Nietzscheans have grasped only a part of the truth. As previously mentioned, we live under what the Aztecs call the fifth sun, the fifth organization of the cosmos. There is no eternally pervasive order. Whole universes arise and decline, and the next universe will not necessarily be better than the last. Nietzsche and Machiavelli would agree. But it is obvious that our cosmos, our sun, does have some sort of organization that we can know and that seems to reward the right kind of behavior. This is where the Stoics and the Buddhists have identified some truths. Combining these points, the cosmos is a system of equilibria. These equilibria collapse, as all things do, but there is beauty, goodness, and value in preserving this order as long as possible.

A great deal, nevertheless, is out of our control. And given the generally chaotic pattern of creatures fighting and dying in our world, it is naive to think that your individual efforts will be enough. We must start with the help of others and work our way toward inner stability, though this does not mean that inward, that is, Buddhist-like, practices have no role to play. The art of living well consists neither in cultivating inward peace exclusively nor in learning the practices of war, but in growing deep roots.

How you feel about the character of the world will decide which of these views you find most appropriate. In my own case, I have lived between and among worlds. It has been a life of relative calm, punctuated by chaotic upheavals. While I recognize the value of the other views, I feel at home with the Aztec approach.

And you should not conclude that the Aztecs, pessimists though they were, thought that we are fated to misfortune even after a string of bad luck. At some point in his exile, Nezahualcoyotl recognized the opportunity to take back what was his. Because his mother was of royal lineage from the Mexica nobles in Tenochtitlán, Nezahualcoyotl was able to secure their support. Then, after three years of battle, their forces fought for Tezcoco's liberation from Azcapotzalco, and they won. As a result, by 1433, at the age of thirty-one, Nezahualcoyotl had gone from inquisitive youth, to exiled philosopher, to warrior general, to a returned king in his homeland. This is how the Aztecs found themselves with a philosopher king, what Plato in the *Republic* proposes as an ideal yet distant possibility. Nezahualcoyotl excelled in his role, by all accounts, presiding over a period in which arts and inquiry flourished, and his people lived well. It is in memory of his accomplishments that you may today find an artistic rendition of his image on the Mexican one-hundred-peso bill.

The Aztec model tells us that we do not really want happiness or invulnerability. What we are after is a good life, but in a specific sense. When we survey our experience, moreover, we should recognize that each of us slips up, even sometimes when we succeed, because we are born into unbalanced circumstances. A series of metaphors suggests we might thus call the good life that we seek a "rooted life," and it is to this lesson that we shall turn next.

SPIRITUAL EXERCISE II

The Truer Words Practice

TO BE a philosopher in Aztec culture was to be a kind of counselor. In a description of the philosopher in volume 10 of the *Florentine Codex*, you will find the following lines.

> Like a watchful physician, the good philosopher is . . . a counselor and coach, fostering sound judgement in others. . . .
> Like a physician . . . she is confided in, trusted, quite affable, satisfying one's heart, making one content.

The philosopher's role was to directly cultivate the alignment of "face and heart," one Aztec metaphor for one's character. As we've seen, one of their core practices was exercising right speech, which included both kinder and more truthful words.

Speaking truthful words, however, can often be more difficult than speaking kind ones, especially when it requires us to avoid exaggeration. Most of the time, exaggeration stems from a desire to impress others. This, in turn, stems from our own inability to address the sources of our shame. Speaking the truth exposes you to vulnerability, but that is the only road to a good, rooted life.

A personal story might help illustrate what's at stake. When I moved to Boston, Massachusetts, for graduate school, I quickly realized that I was the student with no pedigree. Growing up, I lived in Caldwell, Idaho, and often spent extended periods with family in Mexico. Yet I soon discovered that Idaho was so obscure, even among well-educated Americans, that I often had to preface my introduction with a geography lesson. (Something like: If you're not familiar, Idaho is located in the Pacific Northwest, near Oregon and Washington, and my "hometown" is about thirty minutes outside Boise, the state capital.)

Rather than explain all this, I took a shortcut and told people I was last from the Dallas-Fort Worth area in Texas. It turned out that being labeled a "hick" from Texas was better than being a "hick" from nowhere. What I said wasn't technically a lie, but it was misleading. And this strategy had its costs.

The problem arose when people tried to get to know me better. Inevitably, there would be an awkward moment when they learned of my true background: "I thought you were from Texas," they'd say. While the Texas story smoothed over early interactions, it also created distance between myself and the deeper relationships I wanted to build.

The Aztecs didn't counsel mere truth-telling. They were a socially astute people and understood that communication involves more than just conveying facts, unlike some "Western" philosophers who insist that one should never lie, under any circumstances. The Aztecs recognized that we sometimes use white lies to connect with one another and to offer support.

Consider the clichéd example: If a friend or partner asks, "Do these pants make me look bad?" what they often want is reassurance. Simply responding with "yes" might be truthful, but it wouldn't fulfill the purpose of language, which is to communicate. A blunt answer would be unkind. Right speech requires more thoughtfulness. If your friend's fashion has obvious flaws, then perhaps a laugh and an honest "Yes, let's find a different style" might be sufficient. If not, then a probing question could help you understand your friend better. You might ask, for example, "What makes you say that?"

Practicing truthful speech is part of the broader practice of right speech. While it requires a commitment to honesty, it also needs to be paired with thoughtful speech. White lies are permissible, but only when they serve a supportive purpose. If you use a white lie to avoid the effort of being truly supportive, you are not practicing right speech.

These demands may seem daunting, but it is important to remember that the Aztecs advocated an "outward *path*"—they only asked for progress, not perfection. You might start by exaggerating less or by pausing before you respond. Small steps, taken consistently, are enough to live well.

LESSON 5

A Good Life Is a Rooted Life

Don Domingo de San Antón Muñón was born in the twilight of the Aztec empire, in 1579. Of noble lineage and living three generations after Montezuma and Cortés, Domingo grew up immersed in the stories of his people. From a young age, he was captivated by the legends and history of his family, whose ancestry stretched back nine generations to the 1200s, when they first settled the great city of Chalco. A gifted child, Domingo was sent to Mexico City at the age of eleven to be educated by the Dominicans, where he honed his Spanish and learned Latin. By the time he was sixteen, he had been appointed the general manager of a new church on the outskirts of old Tenochtitlán—taking on the responsibilities of a man, though still a boy. This position not only provided him with a livelihood but also gave him access to books on European history and philosophy that would have otherwise been out of reach.

Years later, in 1608, after a series of devastating epidemics, floods, civil unrest, and the publication of a history of "New Spain" that largely ignored the legacy of his people, Domingo grew concerned. He feared that the wisdom, history, and achievements of the Nahuatl-speaking peoples would soon vanish from the historical record. Determined to preserve their legacy, he set out to write a comprehensive history in Nahuatl—not just for his home city of Chalco, but for all the great Nahuatl-speaking cities.

Domingo must have realized early on that he was uniquely positioned to take on this monumental task. He possessed the rare combination of skills: fluency in multiple languages, an education that equipped him for historical scholarship, connections with both Indigenous and Spanish authorities, and access to the necessary resources. To reclaim his family's history and assert his cultural identity, he signed his work with his full name, Don Domingo de San Antón Muñón, and added two further names to reclaim his ancestry: Chimalpahin (Chimal-PAH-in / Ran with a Shield) and Cuauhtlehuanitzin (Cuaw-tle-wan-EE-tzin / Rises Like an Eagle).

It might be tempting to view Chimalpahin's self-designation as audacious, but I see it as his way of planting roots within his community while preserving its memory for future generations. In terms of Aztec thought, he was achieving "rootedness"—and in doing so, supporting others. Rootedness, for the Aztecs, was not just a metaphor for personal growth; it encapsulated a shared wisdom about how to live well. Yet, because this idea is so deeply intertwined with the community and is different from many "Western" approaches, we must take care not to impose our own interpretations on it. To explain such wisdom more carefully, we need to explore three key images the Aztecs used when they talked about the concept of rootedness, starting with the literal trees and their roots.

THE AZTECS identified two sorts of trees that metaphorically represented ideal human beings. The first was the ahuehuete tree, or as it is also called, the Montezuma cypress (*Taxodium mucronatum*).

It is unsurprising that the Montezuma cypress is Mexico's national tree. If you've ever been in the presence of a great ahuehuete, or any similarly large tree, then you will have experienced the sense of calm and awe that surrounds them. Their size, sometimes that of a full city block, is arresting. Their thick trunks exemplify what it means to be sturdy, to stand firmly rooted in the earth. And while children play in the shade the tree provides, adults often use that same shade to take a moment of repose.

The second tree is the great silk cotton tree (*Ceiba pentandra*), also called the great ceiba. The great ceiba tree, though somewhat smaller in size than its more towering counterparts, remains a striking presence, standing tall above the forest canopy. Its massive root structure is visibly anchored to the earth, giving it both stability and prominence. Among the Maya, who shared a broader Mesoamerican culture with the Aztecs, the ceiba symbolized the mythical world tree—connecting the heavens above, the underworld below, and our own world in between.

To grasp how the Aztecs viewed the ethical significance of trees like the ceiba, we can turn to the wisdom shared by elders with younger generations. One example comes from the sixth volume of the *Florentine Codex*, where a newly appointed king, after being instructed by the elders, addresses his people. In his speech, he teaches them how to live well. About halfway through his address, the king begins to describe the ideal types of men and women, resembling what "Western" philosophers might call the "great-souled" or magnanimous individual. The king says:

> And he is esteemed. In truth, he is known as a defender, sustainer. He becomes the ceiba, the ahuehuete, next to and beside which one takes refuge.

In *Discourses of the Elders* there is a similar description, wherein one nobleman admonishes another.

Images of the same ahuehuete in Santa María de Tule in Oaxaca, Mexico

And now, strengthen your heart, your body. To whom, in truth will you leave the mandate [of your office]? Whom, truly, will you observe? For you are already mother and father of the people; you already educate the people, you instruct them. You are he who has the charge, who has the shields. Great is that which you bear; great is your responsibility, because you are the ceiba, the ahuehuete.

In both passages, the charge of rulership is likened to the ceiba and the Montezuma cypress. The ideal ruler is one who is rooted firmly in the earth so that he or she can act as a shelter for others,

A ceiba tree in Guatemala

and to weather the storm of disasters that are likely to assail during the leader's tenure.

A person who can learn to take root as the ceiba and the Montezuma cypress will lead a life successfully on the slippery earth. This person will also, in another metaphor, learn "to stand on their feet." In another discourse, a father speaks to his son the following:

> It is virtuous that you take care of earthly matters. Work, labor, gather wood, till the earth, plant nopals, plant magueys. It is from that which you will drink, eat, dress. With that it is enough for you to stand [*tihcaz*], for you to live.

A ceiba tree in Palm Beach, Florida

The term *tihcaz* is from *ihcac* (IH-kak), which means to stand upright. Its context here clearly aligns the activity of standing upright, or standing on your feet, to the sorts of activities you need to do to live well on the earth. While rootedness is not explicitly at work here, the idea is that you need to be able to take a stand, perhaps as the Montezuma cypress does, by doing the appropriate work.

In another metaphor, the Aztecs spoke of leading a "true" life. A piece of philosophical poetry that was composed and recited before a meeting of philosophers and court officials in Huexotzinco (Wey-shot-ZIN-ko), where Nezahualcoyotl had sought refuge a generation earlier, makes the point. The central question at stake in the poem is how to achieve some kind of permanence on earth. Lord Ayocuan (AYO-kwan), who is addressed in the poem, is said to be acquainted with *teotl* in his form as the Life Giver. The solution he proposes is that by creating philosophical poetry you can achieve a sort of permanence on earth.

> So this is how the exalted lord [Ayocuan] comes, creating them [i.e., the poems].
> With these precious bracelet beads [i.e., the poetry] he goes on pleasing the Only Being.
> Is that what pleases the Life Giver?
> Is that the only truth [*nelli*] on earth [*tlalticpac*]?

By writing philosophical poetry, the kind that addresses the basic problems of our human existence, one is able to find "truth" on the (slippery) earth. The Aztec answer for how to live is to live truthfully. Since the passages likening the idea of nobles and rulers to the ceiba and ahuehuete trees used the language of truth repeatedly, that's not entirely surprising.

But there is another dimension to this proposal. I've translated the Nahuatl phrase "*aço tle nelli in tlalticpac*" as the question: "Is that the only truth on earth?" But big abstract concepts, like "truth," are generally metaphors taken from homier contexts. The linguistics expert George Lakoff and his philosophical collaborator Mark Johnson call these contexts "primary metaphors." To recall their points from Lesson 3, we think of "time" as a kind of motion in expressions, like "time flies." We think of "happiness" as going up, such as in the expression "I'm feeling up today." And we think of affection in terms of warmth, such as when we say, "they greeted me *warmly*."

The Nahuatl word for "truth" that the Aztecs used works similarly. The term *nelli* (NEL-lee) has *nel* as its stem. And that stem can be found in other terms that might be linguistically related, which mean a "principle, foundation, base, or root." A primary metaphor behind the Nahuatl word for "truth" might thus turn on the idea of finding a firm foundation, a firm place to stand, or take root. And this is exactly what is being asked in the poem: Is there a way to find rootedness on our slippery earth?

An abstract noun for *nelli* is *neltiliztli* (nel-tee-LEEZ-tlee), so that you could say that the best life is the life of truthed-ness. Yet, the word resides in a constellation of metaphors that turn on standing on one's own, not slipping, and embodying the positive characteristics of greatly rooted trees. This is why I think that the simplest shorthand in English to designate this goal is to call it rootedness.

Those metaphors are nice, you might now be thinking, but *how* exactly is one supposed to find rootedness? Are we to believe that everyone should be a philosopher or maybe plant nopals (edible cactus plants)? Should we all till the field by day, and dance and sing philosophical poems by night?

While the Aztec philosophers do seem to have held that creating, dancing, and singing philosophical poems were uniquely good activities, they also recognized that such a path was not suitable to everyone. That proposal, moreover, is an incomplete description of the good life, even for philosophers. So let's turn to the question of *how* to live a rooted life, which happens by way of shared agency.

. . .

SHARED AGENCY is at once intuitive and slippery. To explain, consider the following case.

> **Case 1. *Montezuma's Headdress*.** In preparation to receive the strange Castilian visitors to his palace, Montezuma has his servants adorn him appropriately, including a headdress of quetzal plumes. The two servants take the delicate headdress, lift it together, and arrange it on their king's head.

How is one to describe the actions of the servants? Did they think of themselves as part of a group, so that, if they thought anything at all, it would be: "We are going to lift the headdress"? Or did they each think of themselves more individualistically, thinking something along the lines of "I have in mind that you have in mind that I intend to lift the headdress"? That's more complex, but it's possible that it's related to the first one as atoms are to molecules.

A technical field of philosophy called action theory centers on solving problems like this one, and my favored view holds that in cases like this, you are thinking of yourself in the plural—as a "we." If you were lifting the headdress and you had anything cross your mind, it would be something along the lines of "we're lifting now." This is different from acting as an individual where you think of yourself and your actions as an "I."

This difference, between "we" thinking and "I" thinking, grounds the difference between shared and individual agency. To elaborate, consider the following case.

> **Case 2. *Walking with Someone*.** Socrates and Phaedrus meet outside the city of Athens and decide to walk together while discussing Lysis's argument on lovers. They cross the Ilissos River and eventually find a tall plane tree where they can rest and address the topic more thoroughly.

A Good Life Is a Rooted Life • 71

Case 3. *The Royal Court Crowns Montezuma*. After being nominated to occupy the role of Great King, Montezuma awakes early in the morning and performs the appropriate rituals. The last of these is a ceremony in which he receives the crown. He then goes to the royal court where the nobles both praise and admonish him. Some even chastise him. He listens attentively and replies to each admonition. He then addresses the people of his city in a grand speech and celebrations follow.

Case 2, walking with someone as Socrates and Phaedrus do, is another example of the Montezuma headdress case. It takes longer and is a more complex activity but is structurally similar. Taking a stroll with someone can be distinguished from merely walking alongside another person, as one might do in walking down Broadway in Manhattan. If you're walking alongside another person on a busy sidewalk, the two of you are doing two different activities. But if you're taking a stroll like Socrates and Phaedrus did, then you both are engaged in a single activity—you are thinking of yourself as a "we" as in the headdress case—though it's again worth noting that the stroll lasts longer and constitutes a more complex activity.

Walking with someone also differs from the group-based activity that you find in the royal crowning example (Case 3), where a political (or corporate) body engages in an official activity. While walking alongside someone may involve hierarchies, as a parent might walk with his toddler holding her by the hand as she makes uncertain steps forward, such actions do not (i) exceed the duration of the activity, and (ii) cannot exist if members of the group are replaced.

Let me explain. Suppose that Phaedrus and Socrates take a walk back into the city after a lengthy dialogue. Well, they'd be strolling together again, but that wouldn't obviously be the same stroll as the previous one. But if Montezuma and his court stopped to eat lunch and then resumed, it would be the same coronation. Similarly, it matters if one of the members is substituted for another. If Socrates were to walk back with Phaedrus's brother, Polemarchos, then the shared walking would be a different activity than if he walked again with Phaedrus. But if Montezuma replaced a noble, or even were replaced himself, the royal court would still exist. The *tlatoani*'s (king's) role continues despite the passing of an old king. To distinguish these groups' actions, let's call strolling-type actions (Case 2) those of a plural group, and royal court crowning-type actions (Case 3) those of a corporate group.

Even with these qualifications, you might ask: Are cases of walking with someone just more complex versions of two people walking side by side? I don't think so, but fortunately, you and I don't need to answer that question. We're doing ethics here, not action theory. The only thing we need to show is that the ethical evaluation is different.

TO EXPLORE the ethical dimensions of "we" actions, consider the exercise of practical wisdom in plural group (Case 2–type) deliberation. It has some historical basis in the aftermath of the Spaniards' arrival at Tenochtitlán. Cacama (Ka-KA-ma) was the young and controversially appointed king of Tezcoco, the great city that Nezahualcoyotl ruled in generations past, and his rival, Ixtlilxochitl (Esh-tleel-SHO-cheet), hoped to storm the city and take what he perceived to be his birthright with blood and fire. At some point, Cacama appears to have deliberated with some of his advisors—we do not know which exactly, so I shall take some poetic license here to focus on the philosophical point.

Case 4. *Cacama's Deliberations.* After Montezuma received the strange visitors in Tenochtitlán, Cacama worries about his war of succession with Ixtlilxochitl, specifically that matters were left unresolved. Cacama meets with trusted friends, and they decide that the best course of action is to return to Tezcoco across the lake, and to prepare in advance of Ixtlilxochitl's next move.

Let us assume that the questions they addressed roughly concerned: How can we best protect the city? Should we return to Tezcoco without Montezuma's military support since he is preoccupied? How soon will our allies' reinforcements arrive since this will largely determine whether there is any need for preparation?

In such circumstances, how is the ethical force of the group decision *not* reducible to the ethical force of the individual agent's decision? Especially in this case, since Cacama is the king of Tezcoco, how is this deliberation *not* the same thing (for ethical evaluation) as Cacama simply making up his mind?

Remember from the discussion on embodiment in Lesson 3 that reasonable expressions of value bear the ethical burden for evaluation. This means that if my actions can be reasonably connected to my values, they are an expression of my agency. That makes them candidates for ethical evaluation. Suppose that four thieves are trying to hide the evidence of a job by disposing of the getaway car. They are trying to push the car off a cliff, but the car only requires the pushing strength of three of the four men. Are they all responsible for pushing the car over the cliff even though they are not all causally needed for the pushing? How do you attribute responsibility to this group action, which is a kind of shared agency?

Four logical possibilities exist for any such scenario, and to simplify the explanation let's assume that a goal is a kind of value. First, an action could be consistent with the values of an agent. One of the thieves could want to push the car and does so. He is responsible for this action. Second, an action could be inconsistent with the values of an agent. One of the thieves could trip and push the car because he fell on it, not because he had the desire to do so. He would be considered responsible for the action, in this case, though perhaps less blameworthy. Third, an action could be both consistent and inconsistent with the values of an agent. A thief could trip and be unable to push the car though he genuinely wished to do so. In this case he would be responsible, but perhaps less blameworthy. Finally, an action could have nothing to do with any of an agent's values—whether those values are well thought out or only implicitly held. For example, while deliberating what to do, one of the thieves might stroke his chin in a habitual way. He would not be considered *ethically* responsible for this chin-stroking. When tying responsibility to the values of individual actors this way we can attribute responsibility to members of group actions. On this view, all the thieves pushing the car are ethically responsible if they want to push the car, even though they are not all causally necessary for the activity. The upshot of this analysis is that it is the *reasons* for an action that make it an ethical or an unethical one.

To show that cases of Cacama's individual deliberation are different from cases of his involvement in group deliberation, we need to identify how the reconstructed *reasons* at work in group deliberation are different from those an individual agent has or could have.

Let's start with an illustration that oversimplifies the process of group deliberation but nevertheless proves useful. Suppose that Cacama determines that he and his emissaries ought to return to Tezcoco if reinforcements are unlikely to arrive soon. His co-deliberators have the following information:

Case 5. *Collective Deliberation.*

> A. A. Cacama knows that their sworn enemies, the Tlaxcalans (Tlash-CA-lans), have forces just to the east of the city.

B. Xochicoatl (Sho-chee-CO-at) knows that reinforcements come from the east but does not know of the Tlaxcalans.

C. Tezozomoc (Te-zo-ZO-moc) knows that another group of reinforcements are coming from the north.

D. Cuauhtemoc (Cu-aw-TE-moc), having led battles to the north, knows that the terrain is rough going and so has a different mental model for troop movements in that area, but he does not know the locations of any possible reinforcements.

While no individual possesses the complete set of knowledge to make the inference, the deliberating group can combine A and B to infer that the reinforcements from the east will be impeded by the Tlaxcalans, and so be delayed in their arrival. The case is different with respect to C and D. Tezozomoc possesses the relevant knowledge about forces coming from the north, but he lacks the appropriate mental model to know that travel in that area is difficult. Only by deliberating with Cuauhtemoc, thus combining points C and D, can the group make the inference that reinforcements from the north will be delayed. As a whole, then, the group is able to infer that reinforcements are unlikely to arrive soon, and that the best course of action for fulling their obligations as political leaders of that city-state is to return to Tezcoco.

What Case 5 shows is that the appropriate inference can be made only by joining the knowledge and mental models, that is, the reasons, of the individual members. As a result, the reasoning of the group is different from the reasoning of any individual within the group. If those reasons carry ethical force, as might be thought to follow from the obligations Cacama has to ensure the safety of his city as its *tlatoani* (king), then the ethical evaluation of the group decision must be different from any evaluation of its individual members. QED.

We now have something important: *a new philosophical idea*. In addition to actions by individual agents, we have actions by plural groups. They have ethically different features, since the reasons that express the values at work are different in these cases. Now we've got to do an obvious thing and bring this distinction to bear on the performance of a good life, what the Aztecs called virtuous action.

LESSON 6

A Rooted Life Is Not a Product, but a Performance

In his autobiography, Benjamin Franklin relays the circumstances behind his falling out with an older brother that lasted most of his life. That brother, whom he admired, had started the second newspaper to appear in North America, called the *New England Courant*. The young Ben was employed there composing the typesets and then delivering the newspapers to customers. He also used to eavesdrop on the conversations of the learned men of letters who came to the shop to discuss the topics of the day. Ben was convinced that he could contribute to their discussions, but that they would not consider his views because of his youth. To circumvent their prejudices, Ben devised a gambit. He writes:

> I was excited to try my hand among them; but, being still a boy, and suspecting that my brother would object to printing anything of mine in his paper if he knew it to be mine, I contrived to disguise my hand and, writing an anonymous paper, I put it in at night under the door of the printing house.

To his great joy, his brother agreed to print the essay and it was received warmly by the group of learned men. Ben continued in this way for some time, receiving equally strong support on each occasion.

Eventually, Ben revealed his identity to his brother as the author of the many esteemed essays printed in the *Courant*. Yet, rather than react positively, his brother was angry, and Franklin recalls that it was the beginning of years of conflict. While wise enough, in the theoretical way, to grasp the points of politics at state, the young Franklin lacked the practical wisdom to anticipate his brother's reaction.

Perhaps his brother was envious of his younger sibling. He, after all, had to wait a great many years to launch the *Courant* and took on considerable financial risk to do so. Yet his younger brother merely stepped onto the stage that had been built and stole the spotlight. Franklin's brother also had a reputation to maintain at the paper. In short, the young Ben only considered the effects of his actions from his own point of view, and never considered how it might affect his brother.

The quality of this falling out between the brothers—due largely to a failure to cooperate—highlights a cultural difference between those of European heritage and those of Indigenous, Mesoamerican heritage, which continues even today. European-heritage children are raised to be more individualistic and confrontational, even in their cooperative tasks.

In a series of studies, Barbara Rogoff and her team have examined the social habits of children of Guatemalan heritage, Mexican heritage, and European heritage to learn about how they collaborated. In one study, they looked at sibling pairs (six to ten years old). Some were of European heritage and others of Mexican Indigenous heritage. The pairs were asked to plan the shortest route through a model grocery store. The task was supposed to be hard enough to prompt collaboration, but easy enough for children to solve. What Rogoff and her team wanted to observe was not whether the children would solve the problem, or how long it took them. Instead, they wanted to know: *How* would they go about solving the task?

Through detailed observations, the team made one expected finding: The children of Mexican heritage collaborated more frequently than their European-heritage peers. This aligns with the well-established understanding that Latine cultures often emphasize social interconnectedness. However, the researchers also uncovered a remarkable difference: When the children of Mexican heritage collaborated, they demonstrated what Rogoff called "fluid synchrony" at more than twice the rate of the European-heritage children.

Fluid synchrony refers to the seamless coordination of actions between individuals without the need for explicit discussion. It is similar to the way professional dancers move in perfect harmony on stage. In the task where the children were required to chart the shortest course through a model grocery store, they had to navigate obstacles as necessary. The Mexican-heritage children collaborated with such fluidity that the researchers were struck by the sight, remarking that the children seemed like "one child with four arms."

Due to this synchrony, the Mexican-heritage children were half as likely to go off-task compared to their European-heritage peers, and they exhibited overt conflict at less than half the rate. In contrast, the European-heritage children often required explicit verbal agreement to begin a task together and spent nearly twice as much time in disagreement. These findings suggest that fluid synchrony is not only effective for physical activities like dancing but also for cognitive tasks requiring cooperation.

Rogoff's team conducted numerous similar studies. In one, children of Mexican heritage were found to be more likely to assist a teacher without being asked. In another, Guatemalan mothers were observed to engage in play with their children in a way that exhibited fluid synchrony at nearly double the rate of their European-heritage counterparts.

Taken together, these studies show that the difference in styles of collaboration between European- and Mesoamerican-heritage children are scientifically and statistically significant. They show that fluid synchrony is learned very early in life, often through play. (If you are interested in viewing the videos, see the URLs in the Notes.)

These studies highlight two key lessons from Aztec philosophy about how to live. First, if you wish to cultivate a rooted life, you must learn to collaborate more effectively than is typically encouraged in European cultures. Don't be discouraged if you weren't raised this way—European-heritage children still exhibited fluid synchrony, though less frequently. The spiritual exercises of this book are meant to help you in that task (whatever your background). Second, while the Aztecs had a concept of moral "excellence" or "virtue," their understanding of its practice differs significantly from that of many "Western" philosophers. Let's unpack this point more fully.

THE AZTECS didn't use a single term to express the concept of "virtue," as their aesthetic sensibilities resisted simplifying important ideas into one word. One of the key phrases they used was a *difrasismo* (a "paired metaphor"), *in qualli, in yectli* (in CUA-lee, in YEK-tlee). Taken literally, the phrase means "the good and the correct." The first term, *qualli*, means "good" and metaphorically refers to consuming something well, without harm, since it's derived from the word *qua*, meaning "to eat." The second term, *yectli*, means "what is right or correct," in the sense of being morally straight. My proposal, supported in part by a holistic analysis (see the Postface), is that this expression serves the same role as "excellence" or "virtue" within the broad ethical framework of what we call "virtue ethics." As a result, one may *philosophically* translate the term as "virtue," bearing in mind that this English term designates an idea that unites a wide range of quite different literal terms (*aretē* in Greek, *virtus* in Latin, *de* in the Confucian tradition). Put simply, performing "virtuous" deeds, in the Aztec view, means that you are enacting a rooted life.

The Aztecs believed that achieving a rooted life—a life lived well—occurred at three levels: in the body, the psyche, and society. On the embodied, physical level, they appear to have practiced a set of movements and exercises, similar to yoga, aimed at aligning the body and the mind. On the second level, focused on the psyche, they cultivated what we recognize as virtues: courage, temperance, prudence, justice, and humility. This is part of the philosopher's task, to help instill these virtues in their students. Finally, the third level of rootedness is found in society—because we only ever take root with the help of others. This includes not just friends, family, and political institutions, but also the sacred natural environment (*teotl*).

The desire for a broader connectedness as a solution to life's problems finds expression in a poem attributed to Nezahualcoyotl. He writes:

> *In vain was I born!*
> *In vain did I emerge from the house of our lord*
> *onto the earth [tlalticpac]!*
> *I am miserable.*
> *In truth, it would be better had I not come forth,*
> *In truth, it would be better had I not been born.* . . .
> *Can we really be happy, making our way on earth?*
> *It seems we form a fellowship [in misery],*
> *and by doing so there is "happiness" for earth dwellers.*
> *It seems so for all of us who are miserable.*
> *It seems so with every sufferer*
> *living here among people.*

Here, Nezahualcoyotl questions whether our existence on earth can lead to anything other than misery. He is doubtful, but he suggests that perhaps through friendship—by leaning on others who share the same struggles—we can make our way together. It's a powerful reflection on how the solution to a basic problem of our existence requires the help of others—requires that we follow the outward path.

This reveals several key differences between the Aztec approach to virtue and that of the "Western" tradition. First, the Aztecs' concept of virtue is more expansive, incorporating the role of physical, embodied excellence. Second, it is more collaborative in character, so that the virtues themselves are conceived by way of shared agency—perhaps typified in fluid synchrony. Third, some virtue ethicists in the "West" have conceived of virtues as "products" rather than "performances." For example, when a potter creates a pot, the pot is a product—something external to the potter's activity. But when a dancer performs, the dance itself is the activity, with nothing left behind. The Aztecs thought of life as a series of performances, which could be performed with more or less virtue. Crucially, this means that virtue, like a performance, cannot be maximized. More dances do not mean better dances; only better performances (more excellent ones) mean better dances.

These differences raise two related questions. First, in the "Western" tradition, virtues are often linked to character through the concept of "habits." If Aztec virtues involve more than just individual character, what role does habit play in their understanding of virtue? Second, the issue is complicated by the fact that the Nahuatl language has no word for "to have," which is the root of the English concept of "habit." How, then, did the Aztecs discuss the idea of cultivating habits?

TO ANSWER the first question, let's begin with a more basic problem: What exactly is a "habit"? To modern readers, activities like mindlessly playing with your hair and effortful exertion in a workout routine come to mind. Relatedly, we need to identify habits as a special sort of repeated action that would not include actions such as your liver cells dividing, or your eyes blinking. The general solution we'll pursue here is to stipulate what we mean by "habits," noting that the result will be only partly related to colloquial uses. Since our goal is ethical, let's think of "habits" as concepts that need to be linked to an expression of value. Admittedly, there may be some blurriness, but not so much that there aren't clear cases. Three main qualities count.

1. Habits are not mindless routines, but practically reasonable activities that an agent could endorse as an expression of a specific value—so that it might count as a virtue—or deny as contrary to their values—so that it might count as a vice. It is unlikely that twirling your hair could rise to the level of either supporting or diverging from your values.

2. Habits are neither merely passive nor active states. Courage is a virtuous habit, which is both more involved than twirling your hair, and yet different from one-off activities, such as deciding to eat cotton candy ice cream rather than strawberry ice cream.

3. Habits are not always conscious, though they may be. It is often unclear whether someone decided actively to be courageous in a given situation or simply acted in character. This is typical of how habits operate.

For something to be a habit, in the ethical sense we're developing here, you do not need to have sat down and deliberated explicitly on your values. What matters is that you could retroactively reconstruct your actions as consistent (or inconsistent) with your values if you had to.

. . .

AS FOR the Aztecs' understanding of habits, Nahuatl has a wide range of particles and syntactical conventions to denote possession and having. Some of these, including specific instances of the *-ni* and *-yo* affixes, indicated that a person had taken on a specific trait. A philosopher, *tlamatini*, for example, is a *tlamati-ni*, a "knowledge-about-various-things-er."

In the discourses of the elders genre, there is a single, most used metaphor for habituation. The idea is that a person guards (*piya*, PEE-ya) a "word," or "bit of reputable wisdom," called a *tlatolli* (tla-TOL-lee), in the chambers of their heart. Consider the following exhortation a mother makes in summing up her instructions to her daughter.

> This word [*tlatolli*] my daughter, dove, little one, place it well within the chambers of your heart. Guard it well [*xic-piya*]. Do not forget it. For it will be your torch and light for all the time on earth.

The passage suggests a process of habituation. The mother would like her daughter to take a set of reasons, a *tlatolli*, and put them within the chambers of her heart. She would like her daughter to do this not only once, but to make it a sustained feature of her life. She must guard it (*xic-piya*) well. If habituation is the placing of the word in one's heart, then the guarding of that word is the active condition, the habit, of realizing it throughout one's life.

In Nahuatl, *piya* may sometimes mean to hold, though it more characteristically means to look over or guard. Rather than draw on a metaphor for holding, as our English "habit" does, the Aztecs drew on a metaphor from watching over and guarding. Importantly, this conception of the term fits most of the basic criteria of habituation outlined previously: Habits are not mindless, since their purpose is to retain the role of reason in action, and they are active conditions, since guarding requires constant vigilance.

A Rooted Life Is Not a Product, but a Performance • 85

Finally, habits may not always be conscious, because the purpose is to establish a set of reasons to guide action, to guide the heart as a principle of motion for the human body, and not to engage one's face—one's seat of deliberation and judgment. Another example of this idea is illustrated in a father's exhortation to his married son in *Discourses of the Elders*. The metaphors used in the text are predictably different in character, since they would have come from different speakers producing new and more beautiful metaphors, but the central point remains. The father says:

> My son, eagle and jaguar, tail and wing. Perhaps here, on your wrist and throat go attached a word or two, a bit of jade that you have guarded [*omitz-piya-lti*]?

The passage begins with two *difrasismos*, "eagle and jaguar" and "tail and wing." The former is a typical expression for the virtue of courage. The latter designates the social position of the child, he is one who serves the people, which is a way of saying he is a commoner. The next *difrasismo* uses the expression "your wrist and throat." These are not only critical areas of one's body, connecting portions, but also in this discourse appear to be a *difrasismo* for the moving features at the core of a person. Finally, and this is the critical feature for the present analysis, they are something that has been guarded (*omitz-piyalti*, o-meetz-PIYA-lti). The meaning of the passage, then, expresses the same point as one finds in the *Florentine Codex*. The father hopes that his son has taken his words and has guarded/held (*piya*) them within the most vital parts of his body.

These points suggest that while the Nahuas didn't have an exact word for "habit," textual evidence suggests they had a notion of "habit"; that is, serviceable for ethical purposes—an idea different from merely twirling your hair and which could be related to your personal values. Finally, as noted in Lesson 4, the Aztecs believed in a sense of character expressed in the *difrasismo*: *ixtli*, *yollotl*, the face and the heart. This means that we have most of the conceptual tools needed to explain their ethical outlook. We can turn now to the Aztec approach to right action—how they discerned whether an action is right or wrong—using courage to focus our discussion.

LESSON 7

Great Courage Concerns Small Things

Don Martín earned the title "don" when his father, Hernán Cortés, was named marquis of the Mexican lands by the king of Spain. Though Cortés had many children, he took the necessary legal steps to ensure that his son, Martín, would be recognized as legitimate. Yet on January 7, 1568, when Martín was dragged into a cell outfitted with the instruments of torture—the rack and the water-pouring device—it was not his father's strength that sustained him.

Instead, it was his mother's. Doña Marina, known among her people as Malintzin, had been born into royalty, sold three times into slavery, and had survived it all. Martín was her son, and though he carried the privilege of his father's name, unrest among the local powers made him a target for Spanish retribution. He had become a scapegoat, bound for punishment by European hands.

Earlier that day, in the courtroom, Martín had stood before his judges, accused of treason against the Crown. When asked if he understood the charges, he answered calmly, stating he was accused of treason, but that he was not guilty. He refused to confess.

And so Malintzin's son found himself strapped to the rack, a device designed to force confessions from even the most resolute of men. As the guards prepared him, Martín was asked one last time if he had anything to confess. His response was simple: "I have already spoken the truth and have no more to say."

The scribe was instructed to record only his words, ignoring any sounds of pain that might follow. Martín was stripped bare and bound to the rack. The levers were turned, and with a sickening crack, his joints dislocated, his arms and legs twisted beyond their natural form.

Once more, the question was asked. Once more, Martín replied, "I have already spoken the truth and have no more to say." And so the levers turned again.

Growing impatient, the judge ordered Martín moved to the water-torture device. They bound him head-down, closed his nose, and forced a horn deep into his mouth and throat. Slowly at first, then faster, water began to pour, filling him with the sensation of drowning. Death was a real possibility, as it had been for many before him. But the goal was not death—it was confession.

After the pouring had continued for some time, the judge signaled his men to stop. Sputtering and gasping for air, Martín gave the same answer, "I have already spoken the truth and have no more to say."

What the Spanish officials failed to grasp was that in the Aztec world, honor was not merely a birthright, but something earned through action. It could be won or lost, and even kings were deposed for failing in their duties. Failure to act courageously was always a source of shame.

Frustrated, the judge ordered that the water treatment continue. Again and again and again. And still Martín endured. After many treatments, his body wracked with pain, his breath ragged, he managed to whisper, "I have told the truth, and in the holy name of God who suffered for me, I will say nothing more from this moment until I die."

But even that was not enough. The judge, undeterred, signaled for two more rounds before he finally deemed the case useless.

Martín remained alive and silent. Months later, he was sentenced to perpetual banishment from his homeland—for a crime he had never committed.

This story holds great meaning for those who wish to develop good habits, for the virtue at stake here is courage. Unlike other self-improvement habits, courage cannot be hacked or shortcut. There is no easy path, no "cheat diet" or simple routine that leads to bravery. The only path to courage is through facing your fears—through enduring them, reflecting on them, and learning how to stand firm in their wake.

In the surviving documents, we have relatively robust records that detail how Aztec children learned to develop good habits, how they learned to endure pain and to responsibly enjoy pleasure. The texts show that for the Aztecs, changing your character is *not* about optimizing for the outcomes you desire, using, for example, the smallest amount of time to get the greatest result. Rather, they optimized for human psychology, learning to act *with* each other, and how to reinforce their actions through social roles. Repeated focus on small actions was the source of great courage.

In the spiritual exercises, we will explore the concrete ways the Aztecs fostered this habit. There is important conceptual work lingering in the background that we must consider before conducting these exercises, however. In particular, we need to examine how the Aztecs distinguished courageous actions from rash or cowardly actions. This broaches the topic that philosophers call an account of "right action." Metaphorically, the Aztecs called it "the middle path" or "the mean."

PRACTICAL REASONING is shot through with considerations of too much and too little. We wonder whether we are devoting too much time to office work, or whether we have dressed with too little formality for an event. We wonder whether we were too harsh in rebuking a boy who throws a rock at our dog, or whether we said too little to our friends and family about our collective mistreatment of the natural environment. Reflections on our practical deliberations, in short, reveal that whether the matter is strictly pragmatic or more specifically ethical in character, much of any assessment hinges on whether we have expressed our thoughts and actions in due measure. Instead of "due measure," we might use the phrase "apt expression"; but in the ancient world, most peoples settled on a metaphor: they called it the mean or middle path.

If we were to reconstruct what "right action" means for the Aztecs, we'd say, very broadly, that it is an action performed at the mean, and, though it is related to the concept of moderation, is a fundamentally different notion. For the Aztecs, the concept of the mean is not a simple middle point. To illustrate the motivation for this complexity, I often present my students with the following thought experiment:

> Wendell Witless is an inept villain. He plots harmful deeds, but he's terrible at carrying them out, so his actions inadvertently help people. He tries to rob a charity, but instead, his attempt boosts their donations. He schemes to start a war in the Middle East, but his interference brings about lasting peace. At the end of his long, failed career, Witless has done so many unintended good deeds that he's awarded the Nobel Peace Prize. The question is: Should he have received the prize? Are his actions moral or immoral?

The case is absurd, but it sparks genuine debate. Some argue that, despite his intentions, the world improved because of his actions, and therefore something about them must be considered good. Others insist that Witless isn't a good person, and his actions, though beneficial, can't truly be called moral. So, what's the answer?

The Aztecs believed that intention and internal character dispositions matter, but so do external circumstances. In other words, the mean of right action is doubled. It concerns both the "outer" circumstances for the realization of the action, which goes beyond mere consequences, and the "inner" circumstances that support it. To explain, let's start with the outer circumstances part. Recorded at the end of the sixth volume of the *Florentine Codex*, you will find a catalogue of common sayings. You can read there the following about the mean:

> The Mean-Good [*tlacoqualli*] Is Necessary
> Not very tattered will be the things we put on, neither quite magnificently shall we dress. We shall adorn ourselves at a medium splendor with respect to clothing.

Quite literally, *tlaco* (TLA-ko) means the middle of something, and *qualli* (KWA-lee) is the general Nahua term for goodness. What is at stake, then, is not moderation but the mean, and it is said to be necessary for life. The example concerns an external state of affairs, namely how one dresses oneself. One is urged to dress oneself with a medium amount of splendor. At work, then, is a sort of arithmetical mean. But there aren't exact quantities for "too much" splendor or "too little." The arithmetical "middle" here is a metaphor for *apt* expression in outer circumstances.

The Aztecs bolstered this idea with another that might be called an inner mean. You may witness this notion at work in the parable of the mountain and the abyss, recorded in a noble mother's speech to her daughter in the *Florentine Codex*. We discussed a portion of this passage in Lesson 6 for its articulation of habit in terms of chambers of the heart, but its broader context shows how habit is related to the mean, to a conception of right action.

> Behold, the path [*otli*] you are to follow, by which you are to live. The ladies, the noble women, the elderly women, the ones with white hair, the white-headed ones educated us in this way. Perhaps what they left was very much? For they gave us, they left, only a thought, and brief were their explanations. "Understand.

The earth [*tlalticpac*] is a place, a domain for care, for caution. This is the thought [*tlatolli*] you must understand and guard [*xicpiaca*], and by means of it make your way of life and labor. On the earth we make our way, we travel along a mountain peak. Here is an abyss. There is an abyss. If you go over here, or if you go over there, you will fall in. Only in the middle [*tlanepantla*] does one go, does one live. This thought [*tlatolli*], my dear daughter, dove, little one, place it well within the chambers of your heart. Guard it well. Do not forget it, for it will be your torch and light, for all the time you live on the earth.

You would risk overinterpreting this passage if you claimed that *tlacoqualli* (tlaco-KWA-lee) was used exclusively for the outer mean and *tlanepantla* (tla-ne-PAN-tla) for the inner mean. Yet for the purposes of clarifying the philosophical point, we can treat the terms in that way—remembering that the Aztecs never preferred one word for an important topic. In this passage, then, you'll notice that a particular word, *tlatolli*, is that which the mother wishes for her daughter to guard, to habituate [*xic-piyaca*]. The context of discussion, then, concerns the inner state of the agent and the wisdom needed to identify the appropriate form of that state. The daughter is, moreover, to lead her life middlingly, *tlanepantla*. Literally, this word means that she is to live her life for any matter (*tla-*) in the middle (*-nepan-*) space (*-tla*). The admonition directs the daughter to maintain her inner dispositions at the mean.

The historical record furnishes us with evidence that shows the Aztecs *did* have in mind an explicit account of the mean as a term for right action. It concerns both an outer state of realization and an inner state of character habituation. This double condition makes sense of the Wendell Witless case because it shows why his actions were wrong: Witless realized outer conditions well that did not issue from the right inner conditions. Some puzzles remain for this topic, which philosophers call the "doctrine of the mean." Let's consider another case.

BORN Inés de Asbaje y Ramírez de Santillana in Mexico, in 1648, she later assumed the name Juana upon becoming a nun, perhaps because the position allowed her to avoid marriage. Despite her social position, she was nevertheless able to achieve international renown for her works as a writer, poet, and philosopher.

As a child, Inés showed an unmistakable intellectual aptitude— of the sort only paralleled in the "West" by John Stuart Mill. Her father, an educated man, exposed her to history and literature early and granted her access to his library. At the age of three she could read and write Latin. By the age of five she could do accounts, and by eight composed a poem about the Eucharist. By thirteen she had mastered Greek, logic, and was teaching Latin to other (presumably older) children. Along the way, she also learned Nahuatl and would go on to compose in the language of the Indigenous people of her native land. At the age of sixteen she was sent to live in Mexico City and received more extensive tutelage. At the age of seventeen the viceroy Marquis de Mancera invited several theologians, philosophers, and jurists to test the girl on subjects ranging from scientific matters to literature. She stunned them all with her brilliance, and this added to her already growing fame.

You might not have heard of her. It was not until the Nobel laureate Octavio Paz devoted a book of scholarship to her life and work that she was revived as a figure worthy of historical recognition in the closing decades of the twentieth century. Her brilliance was largely forgotten when, near the end of her life, she sold— either voluntarily or at the insistence of the Catholic church—her library and scientific instruments, and never took up a pen again.

One of her most notable works was a response she penned in 1690 to a sermon Father Antonio de Vieyra, a celebrated Portuguese Jesuit, had delivered decades earlier. At the heart of the matter was a theological controversy surrounding how to understand Christ's loving actions. What is one to make of Jesus's actions when He washed the feet of others? Father Vieyra had argued that Christ acted for love's own sake, but Sor Juana maintained that it was evidence of Christ's love for humanity—implying a certain kind of reciprocity between humankind and God.

Sor Juana's response was published, without her consent, and caused a stir among intellectuals and the Church. The Bishop of Puebla took issue with it and wrote to her under the pen name Sor Filotea de la Cruz—that is, he pretended to be a woman so as to criticize another woman. Sor Juana took up her own pen in response, though she hesitated. In the opening pages of her reply, she writes:

> I beg you, lady, to forgive this digression to which I was drawn by the power of truth, and, if I am to confess all the truth, I shall confess that I cast about for some manner by which I might flee the difficulty of a reply, and was sorely tempted to take refuge in silence.

In short, Sor Juana was aware of the political peril her response would invite. Nevertheless, in the course of the essay she undertook to defend the rights of women to have an education and to discuss topics in theology and philosophy. Though a formal punishment does not seem to have followed, an informal punishment plausibly did: the (perhaps mandated) divestment of the instruments that facilitated her education.

The episode raises a question of direct relevance for our inquiry: Was Sor Juana courageous? Let's assume, for a moment, that Sor Juana knew a form of punishment was likely to follow her actions, and that it was the form many think constituted her "informal" punishment. In those circumstances, is it courageous to speak up for the truth when you know that doing so will extinguish your ability to ever do so again? Would it not have been better for her to let matters blow over? Was she vindicated only by historical happenstance, retroactively viewed as a hero for the cause of women's rights and intellectual tolerance? Were her actions not rash, given what she knew at the time and what was under her control? How we might arrive at an answer to these questions depends on what philosophers have called the "parameters" of mean actions.

IN HONESTY, and I expect that you feel this way too, my gut says: Of course, Sor Juana was courageous! She was standing up for the truth and justice against an oppressively sexist Catholic institution that to this day has not reformed its ways. It's foolhardy to suppose that you can disarm the powerful or persuade those who are already bigoted to change their ways in favor of what is good. Should you ever find yourself in those circumstances, the best that you can do is to act on behalf of what is right and learn to endure the consequences. Courage and fortitude are thus linked whenever you are surrounded by those who would oppress you.

But philosophy is the practice of explaining the reasons why such conclusions make sense. A gut feeling isn't enough. Those have too often led the well-intentioned into dark woods. Thus far, we know that right actions issue from the inner and outer mean, but *how* do we know that those actions are "at the mean"? The Aztecs spelled out their philosophical reasoning in three ways: through a parameters account of the mean, through their relationship to social roles and rituals, and through their relationship to humility.

The parameters argument changes the idea of a literal middle point between two extremes to one that meets any relevant parameters. Let's return to the parable of the abyss and the mountain peak. The line that I rendered in the previous section as "on the earth we make our way, we travel along a mountain peak" more literally translates to "go along an area with sheer cliffs." A mountain (*tepetl*) is never explicitly mentioned, but it seems to me the most memorable way to render the notion of a place where one is surrounded on all sides with sheer drop-offs. Still, the literal meaning matters philosophically, since it suggests that in all ways but one, you will err, you will fall off the edge. The line of reasoning at work in the literal Nahuatl statement is thus different from the earlier metaphors about a middle point between just two extremes. In the parable of the mountain peak and abyss, the many ways to err are indefinite, but there is only one right path. You might have the wrong intention behind your actions, or draw on the wrong set of habits, or act without reflection when you should have had forethought, or attempt to control what you cannot.

The further qualifications for the mean concern outer circumstances. The apt realization of our actions in the world must consider specific social roles. In an earlier discourse in volume 6 of the *Florentine Codex*, you can read how the advice given is always delivered by a father or mother of a certain station, usually a station of nobility, to a son or daughter of a similar station. When the father tells his son, "With respect to how you are to outfit yourself, to clothe yourself, do not dress extraordinarily," his advice is given in the context of a social role. While there is general advice to aim at a "medium splendor," this absolute mean is dependent on context relative to an individual's social role. Thus, two features are relevant to the outer mean: its conception generally, and its conception with respect to one's social role.

Further textual support for this notion may be found in the tenth volume of the *Florentine Codex*, which addresses "the people" of Aztec culture. A description of a noble man of middle age relays that he is

> strong, forceful, full of vigor.
> The good man of middle age is a doer, a laborer, a hard worker, industrious, and diligent.
> The bad man of middle age is slothful, negligent, slow, indolent, sluggish, idle, languid, a bundle of flesh, a human lump. He is a thief. He hides things from others; . . . he kills by conning others; he takes things from others.

Similar statements are found throughout the tenth volume of the *Florentine Codex*. The meaning is twofold. First, good adult men are those who perform their duties and roles well, while the bad ones are indolent. Second, bad adult men hardly resemble men at all. They become mere lumps of flesh. Leading a life in community with others involves conditions, and should you not observe them, you'll tend toward not leading a human life at all.

Social roles, of course, were numerous and often particular to individuals, but they included more than roles acquired through elective affiliation, say those of teacher or medical doctor. For the Aztec commoners, ordinary activities centered on the household, the family, and the broader neighborhood, or *calpolli* (kal-POL-lee). Each *calpolli* had rights to the land under its domain, and it was held in common among the individuals and families of the *calpolli* with the stipulation that they improve and cultivate it. Yet, because each *calpolli* was also part of a larger city (an *altepetl*), each individual bore those obligations too. They were required to pay taxes, according to their ability, and each was expected to engage in the sort of activities that constituted his social role. Men, for example, were expected to participate in warfare, unless they were priests or merchants. Women were to run the household and manage the finances.

At the highest level, each person's social role was to facilitate the "ordering and arranging" of the cosmos. During the inauguration of a king, a speech recorded in the *Florentine Codex* reads: "Let him bring peace, by ordering and arranging." The king is said to be arranging peace, *ivian* (i-WEE-an), for someone, *mjtz* (meetz). The context of the discussion, moreover, indicates that the person for whom the work is done is the "Old God." The widest sphere of social obligation is thus to god as nature (*teotl*), and while this is usually enacted as a citizen with other members of one's city (*altepetl*) or neighborhood (*calpolli*), strangers are also included even if they were fleeing another city.

Whether an action is right (that is, an apt expression of a virtuous character) thus turns on whether it meets the relevant parameters of a person's "inner" circumstances (the inner mean) through their realization in outer circumstances (the outer mean). Both sets of circumstances include relevant features of the individual's social role. These circumstances must also be exercised with humility—a virtue we haven't touched on yet, though we shall in the next chapter. For now, your common sense understanding of "humility" is enough: actions cannot be apt expressions of an excellent character if they are performed arrogantly. Pop culture provides a good example: The fictional character Gregory House, MD, portrayed by Hugh Laurie in the television series *House*, was often right in his assessments, and he managed to fulfill many of his social obligations to his patients, but his unflappable arrogance made almost all of his actions fall short of virtue.

Let's return again to the case of Sor Juana, using these points to help us resolve our quandary: Was Sor Juana courageous? While she acted against the wishes of officials in her immediate institution, the Aztecs would argue that the broadest circumstances for her actions, its parameters, mattered most—those concerning her obligations to her intellectual "neighbors," that is the community of scholars, and to god (*teotl*). They issued, moreover, from inner circumstances particular to who she was: an intellectual with obligations to pursue the truth, and a human aiming to guard the delicate balance among the dimensions of her psyche through virtuous activity. Her actions were right, apt expressions of virtue, since they satisfied both inner and outer parts of the mean according to the relevant parameters. Her actions might have been rash had the costs been higher. Had she reasonably expected to be put to death, for example, then it's considerably less clear that she should have proceeded to fulfill her social role obligations through public statements that risked such retaliation. Some forms of courage do require such risks, however, and to articulate the relevant points in more detail I'd like to start with a case that typified courage for the Aztecs—valor on the battlefield.

WHILE THE Aztecs and Stoic philosophers often differ, they are remarkably similar in their approach to valor in war. In this context, I think it appropriate to consider the actions of James Stockdale, a twentieth-century Stoic and Congressional Medal of Honor recipient who is best known for his actions behind enemy lines.

In his essay, "Courage Under Fire," Stockdale recalls a moment in his career as a naval pilot. He was shot down over enemy territory in the Vietnam War. Upon landing, he was captured, and the capturing forces broke his leg. It never healed so that he forever walked with a limp. He was then taken to a Hanoi torture camp, where, as the most senior officer behind enemy lines, he determined to keep as many of his men alive as possible.

His essay is sobering. In describing the process of "taking to the ropes," Stockdale relays that it is a Hollywood fantasy to suppose that most of us can endure the pain of physical torture without breaking. Don Martín's composure, it turns out, is unmistakably rare; and Stockdale concluded that he himself lacked it. The best he could do, then, was to correct for his lack of inner personal composure through strategy.

Nearing the end of his eight years in captivity, he learned of a revolt that his men were planning. Sensing something was afoot, the camp officers seized him from his cell and returned him to the torture room to extract whatever information they could from him. Stockdale knew that he would not be able to withhold enough of what he knew to save his men from a similar fate. They, in turn, would fare little better in withholding information, and so a cascade of torture and death would ensue. After enduring hours of torture, the Hanoi officers left him hanging from ropes in his cell until the next morning.

Stockdale realized what he had to do. Alone in his cell, he

swung toward the window, broke the glass, and somehow managed to pick up the shards. Then he slashed his wrists. The officers found him the next morning in a pool of his own blood.

Fortunately for Stockdale, Ho Chi Minh City had just fallen. Stockdale's wife, Sybil, had been in Paris that very week demanding humane treatment of prisoners. She was in the world news, a public figure, and the last thing the North Vietnamese needed was the death of the highest-ranking officer behind their lines. The medical staff worked to save Stockdale as life leaked from his veins. They succeeded. Eventually, Stockdale was returned home, his men saved, his limp permanent.

Stockdale was willing to die for his men and was saved by luck. The episode shows with clarity how deficient inner circumstances, paired with enough practical wisdom, can lead to an ethically right action. It also serves as a paradigm for what we mean by courage—if this kind of activity in battlefield conditions does not count as courageous, what does? This, at least, is where the Aztecs started.

AS IS TYPICAL, the Aztecs had several metaphors for "courage" or "bravery." In Nahuatl, the most apt *difrasismo* is "eagle and jaguar" (*quauhyot, oceloyotl* / ku-WOW-yot, o-sel-O-yotl). In the first discourse recorded in *Discourses of the Elders*, a father explains his actions stating "the character of the eagle and jaguar [*in quauhyotl, in oceloyotl*] has matured, has grown well in me." In a later discourse, when his son wishes to marry, the father queries his son:

> Will you burnish, will you defend what is noble [*in pillotl*], what is your legacy, what is brave [*in quauhyotl, in oceloyotl*], so that you act like an eagle and jaguar [*ti-quauhti, t-oceloti*]?

The expression "*in quauhyotl, in oceloytl*" is an abstract substantive, meaning (too literally) "the eagleness, the jaguarness." It defines the characteristic courageousness of eagles and jaguars, and of the warriors themselves who were called eagles and jaguars. In the second quotation, the son's courage is said to consist in defending what is noble, in *pillotl* (in PEEL-ot). Importantly, this nobility concerns his legacy, and not only his individual reputation.

In the descriptions of individual people, one finds the following entry under *oquichtli* (o-KEECH-tlee), literally "a man."

A [BRAVE] MAN [*Oquichtli*]

The [brave] man is tall, quite tall, small, fat, thin, quite fat, quite thin, a little like a stone pillar, capable, handsome. The man of eagles and jaguars [*in oquichquauhtli ocelutl*] is scarred, painted, strong hearted, firm hearted, rock hearted [*iolo-tetl*].

The good, the true [brave] man is one who stands as a man, resolute [*iolo-chichic*], who charges and who strikes the enemy. He stands as a man, making his heart resolute and firm, he charges, he strikes at the enemy. None does he fear. None meet his gaze.

The bad [brave] man is one who leads others to destruction by deception, who by deception puts one into difficulty. He is one who concerns himself with other houses, who shouts, who petulantly kills others, who forsakes others. He is one who pisses himself with fear, becomes terrified and urinates from fear. He puts others in difficulty by deception.

Most literally, *oquichtli* means "a man," often a "married man." Like the Greek term for courage (*andreia* / an-DRAY-a), *oquichtli* also has a metonymic function, so that it identifies what men characteristically ought to do, namely display bravery on the battlefield. This idea is made clear though the compounded, poetic phrase "*in oquichquauhtli ocelutl*" (EEN o-keech-KWAW-tlee o-SELL-ot), the eagle-jaguar-man.

This passage also calls attention to other qualities that are thought to be associated with courage. While in *Discourses of the*

Elders it is stated that the courageous person acts for the sake of what is noble, and for his legacy, here the passage adds that the courageous person is able to hold firm, to have a rock heart in the face of what is fearful. The Aztecs linked courage and fortitude. The specific term for a coward is not used in the passage, but it is stated that the bad brave man is one who is overwhelmed by fear to the point of pissing himself, and those words are linguistically linked to cowardice. Such a man also puts others into difficult straits by deception, presumably because his cowardliness makes him unreliable.

It is these further qualities, acting for what is noble, maintaining one's resolve, and proving reliable that fully encapsulate bravery. The Aztecs held that women too can be courageous. Women typically faced death in childbirth—this was their "battle." But just like men, they were thought to have courage beyond the battlefield. The following description, for example, shows that a brave woman was expected to have the same qualities as brave men.

A LADY

> The lady is a careful administrator, sympathetic, a provider, worthy of being obeyed . . . The good lady is one who is patient, who is calm, who is empathetic, humane, one who supports another, who is rock hearted [*iollotetl*], resolute [*iollochichic*] . . .

A "lady" is literally a woman (*cioa*, SEE-wa) lord (*tecutli*, te-KU-tlee). This role requires that she is to merit obedience through her ability to protect, to be patient, and to be kind. She is a reliable person who supports others, and she exhibits courage beyond the battlefield by maintaining rock-hearted resolve.

These threads weave a cohesive pattern that shows the Aztecs' core sense of courage is one typified by the activity of facing one's fear on the battlefield. Yet it is extended beyond that domain through a willingness to act on behalf of what is noble, as Sor Juana did, and to act in a resolved way as both Don Martín and

James Stockdale did. Courageous action derives from the inner state, which Stockdale realized was deficient in his case, and from a broader purpose to enact a rooted life among friends, community, and what is divine—god as nature (*teotl*).

TO BE especially clear for professional philosophers, who will be lost without it, a contemporary workup of the formula for right action that follows from the preceding runs thus:

> An action is right if and only if it is at the mean, meaning that it is (i) a virtue, (ii) expressed in good character (inner circumstances), (iii) in virtuous company, (iv) in the right role, and (v) aptly realized.

In the Aztecs' case, the "aptly" of (v) refers to the parameters imposed by the sheer cliffs surrounding one on all sides in the parable of the abyss and the mountain peak. In the same way, our actions must fit the constraints and realities of our lives.

The Aztec method for developing good habits—what we would call virtues—relies on progressive exposure paired with reflection. Great courage is built through small, everyday acts, just as prudence, temperance, and other virtues are. This approach was central to how they trained their children in various schools, a topic we'll explore further through the spiritual exercises.

If you're afraid of something specific, the Aztecs would suggest practicing by facing smaller fears in different contexts. If you struggle with self-discipline, start with activities that require small amounts of effort, something you can manage and build upon. In this way, you gradually develop the tools to handle more challenging situations. There is an affective dimension at work in this approach also. The idea is that by exposing yourself progressively to experiences, strong initial emotions—such as fear or excitement—gradually fade. Often, we suffer (or enjoy) more in our minds than we do in real life. We use our imagination to magnify the negative (or positive) consequences far beyond what we'd actually experienced.

This is why the Aztecs combined reflection with small experiences. It's how they fostered practical wisdom, which lies at the heart of their ethical thinking. Practical wisdom is a virtue you can practice, one that helps you live well, even if you don't have the legendary courage of figures like Don Martín.

SPIRITUAL EXERCISE III

The Social Vulnerability Practice

IN A discourse to his young son, recorded in *Discourses of the Elders*, a father recalls how he made enough money for the family to get by. He says the family managed

> because in the market, because among the merchandise I peddled wood, a grain of salt, a bit of chili. And I have tilled the earth for others, I have gathered them firewood. I have carried others' staffs, I have supported their scepters. In that way I filled other people's hands with a fist full of stale corn, when I had need for a little bit of grain, so that your small body would sprout, would warm. I did not abandon you. I did not forsake you. I cried much for you; I was sad. Yet, I did nothing to ruin your reputation. At no time from people's bags, at no time from their coffers, in no place from their pots did I take, did I collect, to make you grow, to raise you up. Because the character of the eagle and ocelot has matured, has grown well in me.

This passage unites several features of courage that are not often associated with one another. The first is a commitment to acting well, not on the battlefield, but in everyday life. The second is a concern for guarding what is truly valuable—not property, but rather the elements of a good life. Finally, while the father is aware of the opinions of others, his concern lies in how those opinions might affect his son. He willingly takes on a series of humble tasks to avoid the need to take from others.

We might say that the heart of courage lies in our ability to act in favor of what is right, even when faced with physical danger, and even when others might think poorly of us.

Today, we live in a society deeply concerned with how others perceive us, perhaps to an unprecedented degree. It takes courage to act well despite being misjudged—not merely because it's the "right thing to do," but because that is the path to the only kind of life worth living. In this book are two practices that can assist you in developing this kind of courage: social vulnerability practices (Spiritual Exercises III) and personal vulnerability practices (Spiritual Exercises IV).

To practice social vulnerability, you must learn not to be trapped by social categories and expectations. I'll give you some examples using gender, since it remains as significant a social category for us as it was for the Aztecs. For those who identify as men, the challenge can be put this way: Can you do "girly" things? Could you, for example, order a cosmo as a drink? Could you go to a yoga class? For those who identify as women, the challenge isn't simply to adopt "masculine" behaviors. Often, given the way our society is problematically structured, women are still viewed positively when crossing into masculine domains—for example, a woman who can chug a beer in four seconds might earn the respect of the bros at the local bar. A clearer form of challenge might be found in the no-makeup trend we sometimes see among celebrities. By not wearing makeup, a woman doesn't cross into a masculine role, but she makes herself vulnerable by defying the gendered expectation that women should always present themselves a certain way.

A friend of mine practiced this kind of social vulnerability in a memorable way. After dating a man for a few months, they went out to dinner, but the meal didn't sit well with her. She simply announced her discomfort—and then, in the car, she farted. Not the sexiest thing to do, perhaps, but her boyfriend laughed.

Something good came out of that honest show of vulnerability. They're married now.

To practice social vulnerability in the Aztec sense is to intentionally subject yourself to possible social disapproval. Start by identifying an activity that makes you uncomfortable and act on it. One of my students, for instance, had a sweater from her grandfather with the name of a sewage treatment company on it. Though the sweater was one of her favorite items, she never wore it outside her room because she feared what others might think. To begin her practice, she wore the sweater around campus as she normally would.

The second step is to identify an "affective cognition," a "feeling." The thought that helps you identify this feeling goes something like this:

They are looking at me . . . and I'm not as I'm "supposed" to be.

This is an immediate impression—what one of your many "minds" suggests, but it is not a complete thought. When undertaking your challenge, in this second step you only need to notice this cognition.

The third step is to articulate that feeling. My student, for example, realized that her worry was: "People are noticing my sweater and may think that I have something to do with a company that treated sewage, which is bad somehow." As it turned out, few people noticed the sweater, and no one seemed to care about the company name.

Finally, reassess which parts of your feeling were valid and which were exaggerated. The point of this exercise is to align your face and heart—to evaluate whether your emotional reaction truly makes sense. Your life as a whole does not worsen because of others' thoughts. But if you give in to that irrational first impression, it might.

LESSON 8

The Wise Don't Think for Themselves

Motecuhzoma (Mote-ku-ZO-ma) is known to the world as Montezuma. Though his name most literally means Angry Lord, it is perhaps better to think of his title as Passionate Lord. He was appointed to the throne at only thirty-five years of age and was universally recognized for his valor. He also appears to have had a reputation for thinking well in groups—listening, deliberating, responding, and the like.

In historian Diego Durán's telling of the postconquest era, after receiving his nomination to the throne, Montezuma faced a problem: The other key cities in the Aztec "empire" opposed his leadership. Rather than convince the leaders of those cities with words, he thought it best to circumvent their doubts. He met in secret with his advisors and they collectively decided on "sending invitations to his enemies the Tlaxcalans, Huexotzincas, Cholultecas, and to those of the Mechoacan and Metztitlan."

Montezuma's emissaries had to be brave as they traveled behind enemy lines, and they had to speak other languages, so that their disguise as foreigners would be convincing. When they arrived at the other kings' courts, they announced themselves and presented their invitations to attend Montezuma's coronation. The emissaries also promised the kings safe passage and a luxurious stay.

These kings in turn held their own councils, and while some sent emissaries, many of the kings decided to go themselves, though in disguise. When they arrived, Montezuma had them ushered into the royal quarters through a secret door and ensured they enjoyed their stay in opulence.

For the first three days leading up to the coronation, they enjoyed the local festivities, and on the fourth day, they attended Montezuma's swearing in. Durán reports that it culminated in a mushroom eating ritual. Many visiting kings, high on the mushrooms, saw visions of the future and were reportedly awed by Montezuma's presence. After this experience, sufficiently impressed by the new ruler, they returned home.

By securing the respect of his local enemies, then, Montezuma appears to have led the other leaders to overcome their doubts. He was able to secure ongoing arrangements of semi-peace with these enemy cities, and so mollified concerns about his abilities.

Beyond this point of strategic cunning, however, this episode also shows us how the Aztecs made good decisions. Buried in the series of events are details that demonstrate sound judgment—for the Aztecs—is not the product of smart individuals, but of smart groups.

While there is not a cure for bad judgment, there might be a general strategy for avoiding serious error. We can begin to develop that strategy by distinguishing between two sorts of wisdom—what in the "West" we call theoretical and practical. The former aims at understanding things while the latter takes that understanding and puts it into practice. We shall see that the Aztec understanding of that distinction was rather more blurred than parallel views in philosophers such as Aristotle.

· · ·

BEARING IN mind that the Aztecs preferred a multiplicity of terms to one term, one term they had for "wisdom" is *tlamatiliztli* (tla-matee-LEEZ-tlee), meaning "knowledge about things." Similarly, one of their favored terms for "practical wisdom" is *ixtlamatiliztli* (eesh-tla-matee-LEEZ-tlee). The added prefix (*ix-*) differentiates this term, in some passages, through its emphasis on the exercise of knowledge for living well.

The description of the philosopher in volume 10 of the *Florentine Codex* supports the differentiation of terms for "wisdom" among the Aztecs. To be clear, I do not think that the Aztecs had an exclusive class of people who identified as philosophers to the exclusion of their roles as priests. Rather, much as one finds with pre-Socratic philosophers in ancient Greece, or with philosophers during the medieval ages, these people would have been learned persons who also asked questions that we recognize as central to the activity of philosophy. Although we have read portions of this description in the *Florentine Codex* in previous lessons, it is worth surveying it in its totality to develop the current point.

THE PHILOSOPHER

1. The philosopher [*tlamatini*] is a lighted torch, a stout lighted torch,
2. a mirror, a great mirror, pierced on both sides, who uses the ink of black and red
3. and reads the illustrated books. He *is* the ink of black and red. He is a path and a leader of people, a rower,
4. a companion, a guide, an achiever, an accomplisher.
5. Like a watchful physician, the good philosopher is an estimable person
6. of trust, a credible teacher worthy of a confidence,
7. a counselor and a coach for others to develop a face;

8. he informs one's ears and clarifies, acting as a guide, preparing one's path,

9. and goes accompanying one, teaching one to know oneself.

10. Like a physician, he is worthy of being taken as an example. He effectively arranges affairs and

11. establishes order, illuminating the world for others. He knows what is above and below the earth.

12. He is serious, dignified, with whom one is strengthened, and whose descendants

13. revere him. He is confided in, trusted, quite

14. affable, satisfies one's heart, makes one content, [and] like a helpful physician,

15. empathizes with one.

16. Like a stupid physician, the bad philosopher is imprudent.

17. He claims to know divine matters and boasts falsely and vaingloriously.

18. He pretends to be wise, boasts vainly, and is disgraced.

19. He is a lover of the obscure and the edge. Like a [bad] mystery worker, soothsayer, or physician,

20. he steals from the public. Like a [bad] soothsayer, he is one who disorients others, misleads them,

21. destroys people's judgment, makes difficulties for them, and leads them into hard situations. He causes others to die,

22. destroys them, devastates land, and mysteriously ends up better off.

The passage supports two observations: (a) that the philosopher's knowledge is more general than that of craftspeople, and (b) that it concerns the highest things. With respect to (a), it is notable that none of the craftspeople in volume 10 are described principally as having knowledge indefinitely (*tlamatiliztli*), but rather have knowledge by perception (*mati*), skill (*imati*), or experience (*ixtlamatiliztli*). These linguistic differences are further developed, in point (b), through the contents of the things that the philosopher knows. He is one who is, in line 11, "illuminating the world for others. He knows what is above and below the earth." Just as Socrates was accused of claiming to know what was above and below the earth, so the Nahua philosophers were held to have similar knowledge.

Crucially, the philosopher's knowledge is also knowledge of the human personality, and his ability to aid others in developing it—this is the link between theoretical and practical wisdom. Recall that the Aztecs referred to human character by way of the *difrasismo*: the face and heart (*ixtli, yollotl*). The description of the good philosopher is accordingly divided into two portions, each signaled initially by a comparison to the ideal of a good physician, and each addresses the philosopher's role in relation to one feature of the counselee's personality. In the first portion, lines 5–9, the philosopher's activities center on helping the other person to develop a face (form sound judgments), and in the second, lines 10–14, the philosopher's activities center on guiding the other's heart (organize our competing desires).

With respect to the first of the philosopher's tasks, line 7 reads that the philosopher is "a counselor and a coach for others to develop a face." The first, taken (too) literally, means "one who enables others to take a face." The second, similarly, means "one who frees others for a face." The Aztec philosopher's role is similar to Socrates' role in ancient Greece insofar as he helps another come to understand better.

You'll find a similar point with respect to the heart. In line 14 the philosopher is "affable, satisfies one's heart, makes one content." This passage uses the stem *yol*, for heart, in its description. As the surrounding context indicates, this set of activities differs from the reflective and deliberative sort, because they concern empathy—feeling with and responding to the relevant emotions of another. The philosopher's general understanding of the cosmos and human personality thus combine to form his practical wisdom.

The sense of practical wisdom at work in the passage is further developed in the description of the bad philosopher, whom I'm tempted to call the sophist. The description reads:

16. Like a stupid physician, the bad philosopher is imprudent.

The term here translated as "imprudent," *xolopitli* (sho-lo-PEE-tlee), is often translated as "fool." Its basic meaning identifies a person who lies. The term *xolopiyotl* (sho-lo-PEE-yot) is an abstract substantive that means foolery and deceit. The overall idea, then, is that bad philosophers, like bad physicians, do not know the truth about the way things are, as fools likewise do not know, though they might also deliberately lie. The description continues in line 20 wherein the bad philosopher is described as disorienting others. In the next line, 21, the bad philosopher is said to destroy people's judgment. It is for these reasons that the bad philosopher puts others into hard places, destroys them, the land, or anything else of value. Thus, as prudence leads to the development of a personality, of sound judgment and a satisfied heart, imprudence leads to unsound judgment and the loss of one's personality and property.

We now have evidence for two of the most important virtues: wisdom and practical wisdom (prudence). You'll also notice that the primary articulation has the philosopher helping another person out; it's a description of practical wisdom that hinges upon shared agency. This is an Aztec ideal: The best deliberation happens in groups. To understand how that ideal worked, you and I shall need to address the role of ritual.

RITUALS USUALLY strike us, "Western" and "modern" people, as suspicious. The closest we come to understanding ritual is through religious activities, and in those cases, they are often bewildering. As a child, I recall asking my father why, during a Catholic mass, there was so much kneeling, standing, and sitting involved. My father joked: "So you can get some exercise." Much later, I learned that the activities were structured to preserve (enact even) the liturgical space that opens within a mass. If you are a believer, then those activities are sacred and, through their performance, you show the appropriate deference to what exceeds the profane—in part facilitating a differentiation between those two realms.

Anthropologists and historians have typically focused on the religious dimension of Aztec rituals, which often reinforces our prejudices. I'd like to set that dimension to the side. While religion was undoubtedly a facet of most Aztec rituals, it was not their only dimension. Our analysis of shared agency enables us to understand the additional way that rituals could facilitate plural group activities.

What might be called "secular" rituals pervade our contemporary lives. If you enter a restaurant (in the United States), when the waiter approaches your table and asks, "How is everyone doing?" what are you supposed to say? Common responses would be, "We're doing well," or "Great." Why not answer honestly? What if you said, "Well, I had terrible sleep last night because my roommate was loud and I'm stressed about my next philosophy exam"? If you did, you'd be breaking the social protocol, the social ritual, which in this case is an exchange of greetings, not intended to be taken literally and meant to facilitate an interaction with a previously unknown person.

That secular definition of ritual helps us understand what the

Aztecs did that was different from our society. They extended this coordinating role for rituals to nearly every dimension of life, structuring group deliberation in many ways. In a volume of the *Florentine Codex* devoted to the merchant class, ritual structures were described for how merchants prepared for travel between cities—an activity fraught with peril, from the natural to the ever-present risk of highway banditry.

The ritual begins when the leader of the traveling merchant group consults with a day-reader, who would determine which day was most propitious for departure. The night before departure, a ritual sacrifice of (likely small) animals is performed to secure good fortune. Finally, on the morning of the departure, the leader hosts a gathering for those in his surrounding neighborhoods, *calpoltin* (kal-POL-teen), to deliberate about the practical conditions of travel. He welcomes them, and they reply in kind. Then the text reads:

> And when he [the host] had thus spoken to them, then the principal merchants of all the neighborhoods, the leaders of each *calpulli* . . . responded to his words. When in the case that the host had means and invited guests, then they sat in order by rank. At one side, by the wall on the right, were the principal merchants; and on the other side, starting on the left, sat the other sorts of merchants, the sort that spies in enemy territories. Capping the ends were the youths.

The Aztec definition of "merchant" is a little different from ours. We don't group spies in the same class as "merchants," but they apparently did. The defining activity, it seems, was that these were all people who traveled to foreign places, sometimes as far as the Mayan territories.

With that in mind, you can see that the process of group deliberation is structured according to background, as the spies are separated from the trading merchants, and rank, which in this case follows both from experience and nobility. Often the elderly occupied positions of higher rank, having accrued relevant experience over the course of their lives. The youths, though not excluded from the merchant class, are positioned in the place of least importance. In the deliberations that follow, the topics range from known difficulties in travel conditions to admonitions against failing to respect the customs of other people and how to behave in foreign lands. The passage suggests that while all may participate in the group deliberation, not all opinions are equally weighted. There is a reason some people sit at the center, having developed more of the qualities conducive to excellent deliberation, and some at the ends. In sum, the purpose of the ritual organization is to recommend action for each traveler's well-being. These deliberative recommendations range over the merely practical and the more distinctly ethical, including how to show proper respect and how to conduct oneself interpersonally.

Practical wisdom exercised in groups such as the merchant activity is structurally unlike individual practical reasoning, even when this latter is done excellently. Group deliberation is undertaken with the purpose of coming to a shared decision and with the mutual awareness of all involved. Moreover, since the differences of the individual participants covers more than differences in sets of knowledge, that is, because it covers the ways in which experienced members can reason differently about the same information, the conclusions reached by the group will not be the same as those reached by any individual. And since practical wisdom for the Aztecs is an ingredient in any virtue, then all the virtues are, at least indirectly, made possible by shared agency.

Now we come to the challenge. In the *ideal case*, wouldn't it be best if just one supremely smart individual knew everything? Aren't cases of group deliberation (though admittedly different from individual deliberation) just the best we can do, given that no one is perfectly all-knowing? Why abandon an ideal account of practical reasoning in favor of optimal reasoning?

A philosophical point is at work here. Not only did the Aztecs approach practical wisdom differently than Aristotle (or whomever), my point is that they were better off for doing so. They were right. A smart individual reasoner *is not the ideal case*—at least not for an ethics that's supposed to guide *human* action. Group think—though often used pejoratively—is a good thing when done well.

TO ILLUSTRATE why group think done well is the ideal case for humans, I'm going to pull from a trove of contemporary social scientific work. We have a question here that's solvable only by running some experiments and analyzing results.

My argument begins with evidence supporting a negative point, namely that without collaboration humans are impaired in their reasoning. One of the most widely recognized cases of "feral" children dates to the 1970s, when "Genie," who had spent most of her thirteen years imprisoned in a single room, was discovered by authorities in Los Angeles. Genie was tragically impaired. Some portion of this impairment, likely, was due to her isolation. Children who are so confined are typically subjected to other sorts of mistreatment, but the formative lack of socialization looks to have played a significant role in explaining Genie's observed cognitive and social disabilities. If this analysis is roughly accurate, it shows that impairment in sociality, at least during development, results in impaired abilities to reason.

You can find data consistent with the preceding analysis, though this time in adult populations, in the mental health effects of solitary confinement. The practice in American "supermax" penitentiaries was thought "to perfect" solitary confinement. In California's Pelican Bay supermax, for example, prisoners have almost no physical contact with other humans, sometimes for years at a time, with the exception of a "pinky shake" performed through nickel-sized holes in cell doors. Such social isolation has been found to result in a new mental health disorder: Security Housing Unit syndrome. What follows is but a small sample of noted mental malaise, reporting both the percentage of that symptom as observed in inmates placed in solitary confinement and the rate at which that percentage exceeds the estimated base rate for the same symptom in nonincarcerated populations.

1. Chronic depression, 77% (3×)
2. Nightmares, 55% (7×)
3. Confused thought process, 84% (8×)
4. Heart palpitations, 68% (18×)
5. Hallucinations, 41% (24×)

Studies in Danish populations of prisoners provide additional support that the causation, if not simple, moves in the assessed direction, that is, from solitary confinement to deleterious mental health effects. After "just" four weeks of solitary confinement, the probability of being admitted to the prison hospital due to psychiatric crisis was twenty times higher than for prisoners in the general population. So whatever mental health issues the inmates suffered previously, solitary confinement looks to function as a pathogen adding further illness, rather than as a corollary effect of whatever mental state they had when entering. It is obvious that the effects of Security Housing Unit syndrome, which include confused thought processes and hallucinations, inhibit reasoning capacities. Lack of socialization, then, appears to translate into poor reasoning even for developed adults.

Similar negative evidence is available with respect to ethical reasoning. You need only venture over into the domain of personality disorders. Two well-known disorders connect a lack of social ability with deficits in ethical activity: narcissism and psychopathy. By some accounts, these are not different personality disorders, with narcissism serving as the less exacerbated form of psychopathy, and in both cases the differences between clinical and subclinical cases are often nebulous. For the present argument, then, it is enough to address narcissism, bearing in mind that what holds in this case, that is, that degraded sociality translates into degraded ethical reasoning, holds *all the more* for psychopathy.

Three features characterize narcissism. First, narcissists exhibit an unrealistic sense of superiority and grandiosity, which usually manifests in the form of self-admiration, vanity, and delusions of grandeur. What supports this view is an unstable conception of self, for while their self-esteem is high, it is also fragile. As a result, they crave recognition and validation from others. The immediate ethical implication is that this trait inhibits the narcissist's ability to accept feedback, to be humble—a notable Nahua virtue. Second, narcissists exhibit less interest in other people and suffer affective empathy deficits, meaning that they have difficulty feeling what others feel. It is rare, as a result, to find narcissists displaying genuine consideration for people other than themselves. Finally, narcissists typically exhibit high levels of entitlement. They behave as though they deserve more status or privilege than they ought, and that rules, including laws, do not apply to them. In one notable case, a clinical narcissist thought it appropriate to suggest that his luggage aboard an airplane had an explosive device in it because he wanted to delay boarding. Narcissism, a disorder that interferes with proper socialization, thus also impairs ethical reasoning.

The preceding evidence, however, has limits. Congenital and environmental impoverishments of sociality inhibit one's ability to reason practically and ethically. What the negative point does not entail is that optimal reasoning is to be found in social processes. Neither does it support the considerably stronger view that the Aztecs held to be true, namely that practical and ethical reasoning are not only developed in social circumstances, but that they are sustained and enacted in these situations.

It is easiest if we begin with cases of mixed evidence. Early studies of group reasoning found that groups outperformed individual reasoners, but these analyses unfortunately compared the output of the group to that of single individuals. The noted effect, then, may have been a function of the larger numbers of individuals in the group, and not a function of the group process itself. Later studies were constructed to avoid the confounding factor. In these studies, numerous cases favored individual activities. So there is evidence that group reasoners do outperform individual reasoners with a relevant matchup.

This outcome is, on reflection, to be expected. Group decision-making requires cohesion among members. Members must not receive a free ride, and comfort among them must exist, so that ideas can be expressed and challenged freely. Moreover, the group must possess a capacity for mutual understanding in order for the free exchange of ideas to prove beneficial. If the task proves simple enough that one person could perform it, then one would expect a group to perform no better than its most able individuals (thus rendering the group activity itself superfluous). Only with activities of sufficient complexity, then, or ones that are especially error prone, or both, should you expect groups to outperform individuals.

The social scientific literature suggests that this analysis in favor of group bonuses for complex problems is accurate. Groups are more able to identify errors than individuals are. Groups are also able to uncover solutions faster than individuals, even for apparently simple tasks. In one study, eight "turning gear" problems were presented to groups and individuals. Participants were asked, for example, to imagine a row of five interlocking gears and then asked in what direction the fifth gear would turn if the first were turned to the right. A formula expresses all solutions: all odd numbered gears turn the same direction as the original, even numbered gears turn the opposite direction. Only 14 percent of individuals discovered the rule, while 58 percent of pairs did.

Evidence for the superior performance of group solutions to

complex problems is abundant in a variety of practical fields. In creative tasks, such as songwriting, groups outperform. Most have heard of one duo: Paul McCartney and John Lennon. But few have heard of Martin Sandberg, author of multiple global hit songs, in part because he always worked in globally and ethnically diverse teams. His path, moreover, is now the norm as teams of two or more songwriters write the majority of Billboard 100 hits. The same is true for equity management. More than three-fourths of equity mutual funds are managed by teams, and gains for funds run by three or more people outperform those directed by single individuals by 60 basis points. Patent data confirm the same point, as more than half of all patents are written by teams. Moreover, when researchers evaluated the quality of those patents, they found that team-authored patents earn more citations, both overall and by subclass.

Perhaps the most compelling and most direct evidence for the value of collaboration for complex problem-solving can be found in the publication trends of scientific articles. In social science research, approximately 60 percent of papers are multiauthored, and in every one of its 54 subfields, multiauthored papers outnumber single authored papers. In science and engineering research, 90 percent of papers are team efforts, and of the 171 subfields of research, team efforts outnumber single author publications in 170 of them. In medical research the trend remains consistent, as multiauthored papers exceed that of single-authored papers by a ratio of three to one. Finally, data from a National Academy of Sciences report shows that team-based scientific work, from 1960 to 2013, exhibits an almost 100 percent increase in multiauthored papers over that period.

Such marked shifts in research require an explanation, since teams both take more time to reach decisions and cost more money to administer than individuals. A reasonable explanation, then, is that teams perform better than individuals in solving scientific, that is, paradigmatically complex, problems. The data support this inference. Multiauthored papers have higher average citations in 167 of the 171 scientific subfields, and the same is true in all 54 of the social scientific subfields. A common benchmark for excellence is when a paper receives more than one hundred citations. Team-authored papers are four and one-half times as likely to achieve this milestone in science, engineering, and the social sciences, and they are more than six times as likely to surpass one thousand citations in science and engineering. The general point, then, is clear: Collective reasoning, when practiced in well-formed groups, outperforms individual reasoning for complex tasks.

Yet, you might wonder what evidence exists that collaborative reasoning facilitates practical reasoning in ethical cases. The reply is twofold. If one agrees with the view that ethical reasons are practical reasons (and no more than that), then the foregoing suffices. But even in the case that one holds that ethical reasoning forms a special class of practical reasoning, as the Aztecs did, then the foregoing still impinges on ethical deliberation in a direct way. First, because the analysis of the nonethical dimensions of a case proves crucial for a group's final judgment. In deciding what one ought to do, for example, it is helpful to know accurately what the situation is and which options that situation makes available. Second, one should bear in mind that the line between ethical and practical reasoning is not always a bright one.

In the description of the Aztec philosopher, the relationship between knowing what is above the heavens and below the earth (theoretical wisdom) is not far removed from the practical advice that the philosopher is able to give. The terms used for both types of knowledge build on the same roots. While the Aztecs distinguished these poles of human reasoning, then, they nonetheless appeared to hold that the differences blur. Can we find contemporary evidence for this?

I think so. To explain, we need a background concept: present value. The idea is easiest to understand with money. Would you rather have $100 now or $200 ten years from now? Most would rationally choose the $100. Waiting ten years for an extra $100 is not worth the opportunity cost. Moreover, given standard inflation, that future $200 isn't worth today's $200. To figure out how much that future $200 is worth, we'll need to discount that amount back to its present value—using expected annual inflation as a baseline rate (say, 3 percent). This means that each year, we assume that the $200 is worth 3 percent less—discounting it by that amount. How much is it worth after ten years, then? The fancy name for the equation used to calculate the answer is called a "model," and the typical discount rate model suggests that the future $200 is worth no more than $148 dollars in today's value. Let's take this idea, calculating the present value of something using a discount rate, and apply it to the environment.

A now-standard example of the blurriness between ethical and practical reasons is the Stern and Nordhaus exchange over the (fiscal) value of future environmental harm. The two economists, Stern and Nordhaus, agree on the use of a standard discounting model for assessing the costs of environmental degradation, and both advocate a carbon tax as a market efficient solution. Yet they disagree on one crucial point: How much should one be required to pay, by way of tax, for these future costs? You could choose to discount those future costs heavily (7 percent or more), implying that they are not valued much today. Or you could choose to discount them lightly (2 percent or less), implying that they are to be valued more strongly today. Your choice of discount rate matters a great deal since discounting percentages compound significantly over lengthy periods, such as over the next seventy years. Critically, Stern and Nordhaus's disagreement over what discount rate to use is not a fiscal point that is altogether distinguishable from how great an *ethical* value you place on maintaining an undegraded environment. In order to complete the financial model, you must choose a discount rate, and which rate to choose is an ethical choice. The very same equation thus involves financial and ethical components, which underscores how blurry some practical reasoning gets. Even though the Aztecs never made this sort of argument, the Stern and Nordhaus exchange furnishes evidence in support of their position.

Beyond that discussion, there is direct support for the argument that collective activity facilitates ethical reasoning, and these considerations form the second stage of reply. It has been found, for example, that it takes only the support of one other person to embolden someone to speak out against an ethical wrong. Notably, the Milgram experiments illustrate this concept's dark side. In these experiments, two-thirds of subjects were willing to shock, repeatedly, a person whom they thought had also volunteered for the experiment, and who was vehemently protesting, at the polite request of the person running the experiment. In another version of the study, the "two peers rebel" condition, obedience dropped to 10 percent when two experimental confederates refused to comply with the request to continue the shocks.

Studies on deliberative democracy also provide evidence that deliberative discussion in groups changes the minds of participants on ethical and political (where those are distinct) topics. In experiments on deliberative polling, participants are surveyed on their views on a range of topics before and after a weekend of small group, moderated discussion, accompanied with a plenary conversation with a panel of experts. In a 1996 deliberative polling event held in Austin, more than half of the participants changed their positions both on specific policy items and general concerns, including the following:

- The agreement that "the biggest problem facing the American family" is a "breakdown of traditional values": decreased by 10 percent;
- The agreement for the view that the "biggest problem facing the American family" is economic pressure: increased by 15 percent;
- The preference for a "flat tax" decreased by 14 percent.

It may be that these changes, and the many others recorded, are not changes for the better, but participants in these studies are much better informed, which plausibly contributes to better overall judgments. The participants also report a greater level of respect for one another's beliefs and the circumstances that inform them. Finally, because the events are carefully structured, participants engage in reasoned discussion, drawing inferences from the newly available cognitive repertoires their interlocutors make available.

These points all support the claim that collaborative intelligence facilitates better *ethical* reasoning. Aristotle was not right in his formulation about the ideal case of human reasoning, that a single intelligent person could do it best, and we have the evidence to prove it. In such cases of group-based reasoning, however, humility emerges as a capital intellectual virtue— something totally absent in Plato and Aristotle's account of practical wisdom.

RAY DALIO is the now retired chief executive officer of Bridgewater Associates, which is among the world's largest hedge funds. He is a billionaire who made his money through intelligently reinvesting other people's money. But his life wasn't always a picture of success.

In his book, *Principles*, a sort of manual of practical wisdom, Dalio recalls an early career error that almost cost him everything. He was monitoring the level of debt in the United States and how emerging markets were likely to default on what they owed the US government. When the defaults began, given his understanding of past history, he expected a depression to follow and appeared twice on *Wall Street Week*, the main financial show of the time, confidently declaring that this was the direction of the market. He summarizes the results of his bets as follows.

> I was dead wrong. After a delay, the economy responded to the Fed's efforts, rebounding in a noninflationary way. . . . The stock market began a big bull run, and over the next eighteen years the U.S. economy enjoyed the greatest noninflationary growth period in its history. . . . At one point, I'd lost so much money I couldn't afford to pay the people who worked with me. One by one, I had to let them go. We went down to two employees—Colman [his closest friend] and me. Then Colman had to go. With tears from all, his family packed up and returned to Oklahoma. Bridgewater was now down to just one employee: me.

The firm that emerged from that experience is the Bridgewater that the world remembers. But it was born from Dalio's serious, nearly obsessive reflection on what he had done wrong and how he could have acted differently to avoid those errors.

> In retrospect, the mistakes that led to my crash seemed embarrassingly obvious. First, I had been wildly overconfident and had let my emotions get the better of me. I learned (again) that no matter how much I knew and how hard I worked, I could never be certain enough to proclaim things like what I'd said on *Wall $treet Week:* "There'll be no soft landing. I can say that with absolute certainty, because I know how markets work." I am still shocked and embarrassed by how arrogant I was.

A hedge fund must, consistently, make the right decisions for its clients. The vice that nearly ruined Dalio's life was arrogance—an overconfidence in his position, even if it was backed by reason.

Dalio's experience directly aligns with the Aztec ideal of humility as a capital virtue. Yet, since it has no place at all in "Western" accounts of practical intelligence, such as Aristotle's, it deserves a bit more development.

TO ARTICULATE why the Aztecs thought humility integral to practical wisdom, it might be helpful to begin with the term itself: *tololiztli* (to-lo-LEEZ-tlee). In a mother's exhortatory speech to her daughter, recorded in *Discourses of the Elders*, she instructs her daughter:

> And lower your head [*xi-tolo*], humble yourself in public. Next to the people, be respectful and reverential. Do not go in front of and on top of them but live with tranquility and calm. Love other people, implore them, sigh with them.

Broadly, Nahua humility is a part of a family of notions that consists of three further crucial dimensions: performing one's social role, accurate self-estimation, and heeding council.

Chapter 20 of volume 6 in the *Florentine Codex* is entirely devoted to humility and explains how performing one's social role is a dimension of humility. The opening description is of a father admonishing his son, "that [he] should look to the humble life, to the bowing, to experienced skillful knowledge of oneself in order to please the gods and humans on the earth." Toward the end of his discussion, the father explicitly connects the topic of humility to one's social role.

> Oh my son, my dear son, take this [word] to heart. In what manner do you act? Perhaps you will be able to do something, and yet it will be without purpose? Perhaps He By Whom We Live will yet designate you for some role? And if you happen to be assigned to a role on the earth, how will you act from your heart? Do not praise yourself. Do not take your role lightly or claim it all for yourself. Do not be vain, proud [*ti-mo-pouh*], or presumptuous.

What is at stake in these lines is the father's wish for his son to put a reason, a word, in his heart—to take up good, purposeful habits. He underscores the point that humility, so understood as a character virtue, concerns one's social role. When you act with humility, you take part in the cosmos, guided by the one god, He By Whom We Live.

With regard to the second feature, accurate self-estimation, it is easiest to recognize this in tension with its opposite, which engenders a range of vices from what we colloquially call "narcissism" to "low self-worth." Perhaps most prominent among the terms used for humility's vice is the vice of pride, which literally means the counting (*pouh*) of oneself (*mo*) as more important than one is. Among the common sayings recorded at the end of the same volume of the *Florentine Codex* is one that reads:

HE ESTEEMS HIMSELF; HE HONORS HIMSELF.
This saying was declared of him who was not great in making friends by talking, and [yet] valued his words excessively. He did not cause himself to be demeaned either by way of laughter, or by joking. In this case it is said: He esteems himself excessively, he honors himself exceedingly.

The explanation is careful to distinguish a person who loses reputation through misbehavior from one who loses it by making a fool of themselves through pride or arrogance.

The final dimension of humility concerns the ability to heed appropriate council, which is directly related to practical wisdom. Numerous common Aztec sayings attest to the centrality of this notion. One reads as follows.

I HEED NO MOTHER, NO FATHER.
This saying was declared of him who was admonished many times, and he did not heed them, he absorbed nothing of its

reason [*tlatolli*]. Then it is declared: "He learns not from his mother, his father. He wishes to live only by his own accord."

The person in this case fails to accept a good reason, a *tlatolli*, supported by traditional sources indicated by the *difrasismo* one's father, one's mother. Instead, this person lives in his own self-made spotlight, independently on his own accord. A similar statement is recorded in a saying just prior to this one in the *Florentine Codex*. It reads:

I MAKE THE ASH HEAP, THE CROSSROADS [TAKE THE ROLE OF] MY MOTHER AND FATHER.

This statement was declared of the women or men who remained somewhere on the road [*otli*]. In nothing do their mother and father advise them. Only by their own accord do they remain somewhere on the road, only by their own accord did they take themselves there.

At stake in this passage is the wrong path, the path in opposition to having a place in society. Your ability to heed good council is what keeps you on the right path.

THE AZTECS had a sense of practical wisdom expressed by the term *ixtlamatiliztli* (eesh-tla-matee-LEEZ-tlee). And they thought that in all cases—and this is especially true in the case of practical wisdom—the virtues were enacted best by way of shared agency in groups.

It's worth connecting these ideas with those about the mean for right action. Practical wisdom identifies both the means to accomplish a goal, such as traveling safely to another town, and the mean as apt expression, so that your actions are not awkward. A second point follows. Because practical wisdom identifies what apt expression for a virtue is, it's involved in all the virtues.* The overarching point, however, is straightforward: Since practical wisdom is conceived by way of shared agency, and since practical wisdom is implicated in all the virtues, shared agency suffuses all the virtues.

These points, when taken together, imply that Aztec ethics is *structurally* more socially centered than Aristotle's, for whom the lone person of practical wisdom forms the ideal. Aztec ethics are even more socially centered than Confucius's virtue ethics, because rituals, in the Confucian tradition, aim to facilitate *individual* character development but are not the ideal mode of performing deeds. Aztec ethics also challenges Stoicism, Buddhism, and other philosophies, which hold that by working on your own, individual inner self first, you'll find a way to happiness and fulfillment. That view makes sense only if practical wisdom is understood as an individual activity. For the Aztecs, such an individualistic approach is fundamentally limiting. An important "spiritual" exercise follows from the Aztec's paradigm shift in virtue ethics, which we'll address next.

---

* A fuller discussion of this point is reserved for Appendix II, which is somewhat technical.

SPIRITUAL EXERCISE IV

The Personal Vulnerability Practice

THIS SPIRITUAL exercise involves what might be called "personal vulnerability." Unlike the social vulnerability exercise (Spiritual Exercise III), the focus with this practice is not on social categories. Rather, it's on how you think about yourself as a person. Are you an athlete? A chemist? An entrepreneur? A writer? Those are categories of self-conception. They're also where our deepest vulnerabilities lie.

Below is a poem, attributed to Nezahualcoyotl, written when he was supposed to be fleeing his home after his father's murder.

> *In vain was I born!*
> *In vain did I emerge from the house of our lord*
> *onto the earth!*
> *I am wretched!*
> *In truth, it would be better had I not come forth,*
> *In truth, it would be better had I not been born.*

While we'll never know with certainty whether Nezahualcoyotl penned these exact lines, they express the emotions he would likely have felt as he fled home under perilous circumstances. He was, at this point, a refugee, not a prince. The life he had imagined for himself and was trained to pursue, namely a life in a royal court, was no longer relevant. His life had lost its purpose.

The vulnerability at stake in this circumstance does not concern trauma but an ingrained personal judgment. It concerns how you think of yourself and about the vulnerabilities at the core of your identity. I'll give you another story to put flesh on the bones of the practice. And to be appropriately vulnerable, I'll tell you one about myself.

I'm a professional philosopher in the university system of the United States. This means that I'm supposed to be able to research, get my work accepted at peer-reviewed public conferences, and get it published in peer-reviewed journals. The core of who I am is wrapped up in this profession. Three years into graduate school, I had not figured out this process. I was supposed to be smart. But I couldn't get anything accepted into conferences, much less into peer-reviewed journals. My wife started graduate school two years after I did. Yet she earned a spot at a peer-reviewed conference her very first year. She succeeded while I was still struggling.

I took the advice of "keep on keeping on," and after much trying, I finally landed . . . a commentary . . . on another graduate student's talk. The mountain of rejections was difficult to handle, in part because conference applications, at the time, only opened twice a year. Failures would thus linger for months.

Eventually, I knew I had to let go of the idea that I knew how to write philosophy. Instead, I set myself the task of reviewing a stack of journals to figure out commonalities among all the publications. I worked as a sociologist, analyzing what was being published, how common certain topics were, and so forth. Then, after an embarrassing amount of time doing meta-work, I discovered that philosophers make only about fifteen publishable types of arguments. And only four of those are both accessible to graduate students and regularly appear in print. Of those four, two look to be the most regularly published. I focused my efforts on just those two formats, and it worked.

In brief, I ate humble pie—a critical part of the Aztec conception of wisdom—and restructured the core of my identity, which required courage. Unlike the social vulnerability challenge, where the difficulty turns on how other people think about you, the difficulty I faced turned on how I thought about myself. I changed my activity, then, not to please another so much as to advance toward a goal meaningful for me. This is the idea of personal vulnerability.

There is a specific train of thought at work here. It goes something like this:

> I'm supposed to be an x.
> X's are people who do y.
> But I'm failing **at** y.
> So I must **be** a failure as an x.
> And because of that, I **am** a failure.

These thoughts lead to an insidious spiral. Remember, your many minds need coordination. I'm not going to say that you shouldn't think of what you are doing as failing. It was crucial that I recognized that I didn't know how to write professional academic papers. It was crucial that Nezahualcoyotl recognized that he had to live a different sort of life—one for which he had no training. Neither of us could have managed without those realizations.

What you need to stop is the *slide* from *outcomes*, what you are failing *at*, to states of being, to who you *are*. The challenge, in a question, is: Can I think through the facts of this matter and let the irrational first impression go? Here's another way to practice this: Can you tell your own shame story (as I did above)? Maybe not to someone else, but at least to yourself?

Once you can recognize shameful past events as just events, without a value judgment, you can learn to accept them as they are. You can see failure not as a wholly good thing, but a natural part of life. Facing failure is hard. Facing failure that concerns the most intimate aspects of your personality is exponentially more difficult. But you must do it. You must find the courage to face the sources of your shame, and then reckon with them.

LESSON 9

Willpower Is Three Things, Not One

It had been nearly fifteen years, in 1479, since the Mexica, the Aztecs of Tenochtitlán, had destroyed the city of Chalco. They had disbanded their royal houses and excluded the Chalcans from participating in political discussions at the council that included the other major cities of the central basin.

The youth, living now almost a generation later, wanted to return to a state of self-governance—or at least to one where they had some say in the affairs of their city. In open, communal discussions they debated what to do and how to change the mind of King Axayacatl (Axa-ya-CA-tl / Face of Water). One man, Quecholcohuatl (Ke-chol-CO-wat / Flamingo Serpent), had an idea.

A member of a troop of dancers, singers, poets, drummers, and actors, Flamingo Serpent decided to perform the piece that we now call "The Chalca Woman's Song." It is a poetic song at once sexually explicit and ripe with political implications. He adopted the persona of a female prisoner of war, who laments her fate at having lost her honor in the aftermath of defeat, just as Chalco had lost her position relative to Tenochtitlán. She tries to seduce her captor and ends the song with an offer: She would come to live with her new master willingly, provided he treated her with respect.

At one point during the song, Axayacatl, clad in the vestments of a great king, left his place in the audience and began to dance with the performer. The Chalcans thought this was a good sign, but at the end of the song, he retreated suddenly to his chamber and sent a messenger asking for the lead performer, Flamingo Serpent. The young man, Flamingo Serpent, paused before he crossed the threshold; it might prove to be his last free moment of life. Then he entered, kneeled, and made the customary gesture of taking earth and touching it to his lips. He addressed the king with formality to further signal his humility, but it all proved unnecessary. Axayacatl, who had thoroughly enjoyed the song, took him to bed with his wives, and made him promise to sing only for him in the future. He then granted the Chalcans what they wished, and the former rivals were given a seat at the council.

Flamingo Serpent's story has long intrigued scholars in the field of Mesoamerican studies because it provides some evidence for understanding homosexuality in Aztec culture. The Aztecs did not have, as we do, a view that one's sexual orientation is something that is supposed to be stable over a lifetime. They do not even seem to have had a notion comparable to our idea of sexual orientation at all.

But the story is interesting for another reason: It demonstrates the great weight the Aztecs placed on enjoying significant moments in life. The king of Tezcoco, Nezahualpilli (Neza-wal-PEE-lee / Fasting Child), son of Nezahualcoyotl, seems to have reversed a legal judgment for a woman who dishonored him because her husband composed a song of great beauty. The Aztecs in Tenochtitlán did not normally drink alcohol. But they suspended their ordinary custom banning the consumption of alcohol for special occasions, such as weddings, and for specific festivals. In short, the Aztecs advocated neither a life of self-indulgence, nor asceticism, but one of balance.

This insight informs their broader view that temperance, the virtue of having appropriate willpower, is not one thing but three. To explain, let's start with a story.

SOME TIME ago, my home's basement was flooded with about two inches of sewage water. The main pipe at a central intersection had clogged so that all the households in my neighborhood had sewage backing up from pipes into their homes. In our case, it flooded from our basement sink and drain.

I rushed downstairs into the poo-water repeatedly to save as many of our belongings as I could. It was a rancid and highly disagreeable affair. Doing so required the kind of willpower we call on in situations of high emotional intensity—what we might call *drive*.

A quite different form of willpower is involved in working out daily. I dislike doing squats in the morning for my exercise routine, but not so much as running into poo-water. The difficulty involved in doing squats involves knowing that I must continue to do this moderately disagreeable activity several times a week, *forever*. There is thus a meaningful distinction between these high-intensity and high-consistency forms of willpower, so that we have both *drive* and *durability*.

A third sort of willpower is involved in willing *not* to do something, which we might call *discipline*. This is the kind of willpower at work in Mischel and Shoda's Stanford marshmallow experiments. In these, researchers placed a marshmallow in front of a child between the ages of three and five and asked them to wait until the researcher returned. If the child successfully resisted temptation for that period, they would be rewarded with another marshmallow. The researchers hoped to identify whether this ability to exhibit discipline resulted in different life outcomes for the children—whether the marshmallow resisters would do better in school, make more money, and have better romantic lives. To some degree, all those points turned out to be true. We'll see that the Aztecs had practices seemingly designed to inculcate discipline in terms of the ability to "resist" temptation better. The mental tools necessary to enact these three kinds of willpower are in harmony with the Aztec's view of our body as an ecosystem of many "minds." The advice given by elders, as recorded in their discourses, includes a broad range of practices to help us increase our willpower intelligently. Their general conception of the virtue for willpower, which covers drive, durability, and discipline, is called "temperance." So understood, temperance is close to many "Western" discussions of "moderation," even if it is broader. In a departure from these discussions, we'll see that temperance additionally concerns a realm of activity beyond the activation of willpower and self-denial. It also requires a bit of "balancing" indulgence.

"WESTERN" PHILOSOPHICAL convention expects a single Nahuatl term for the virtue of "temperance." One of the most commonly used in the discourses takes the abstract form *iximatiliztli* (eesh-mee-ma-tee-LEEZ-tlee). Professional philosophers might define the Aztec account of "temperance" as:

> an experientially informed and skillfully executed prudential restraint with respect to the wide range of spheres in life where this might be appropriate, coupled with sensitive enjoyment in apt circumstances.

I know, it rolls right off the tongue. What the Aztec view has in common with "Western" articulations, as one might find in Aristotle or the Stoics, for example, is the need to restrain oneself and not give into whatever one desires. The Aztec view differs in not being restricted to mere "bodily" pleasures, in its execution by way of social roles and rituals, and in its modulation with respect to apt circumstances.

Given that the Aztecs conceived of our "mind" as located directly in the organs of sensation—so that the eyes understand in their way, the ears in another, even the skin in its own way—their moral psychology has no mind-body split, as preoccupied Aristotle and the majority of European thinkers who followed him. It would make no sense for the Aztecs to conceive of a mental restraint exerted upon "bodily" pleasures as Aristotle did. Yet the Aztecs did also consider eating, drinking, and sexual activity to be important domains in need of prudential restraint.

In the noble father's admonition to his son in the sixth volume of the *Florentine Codex* where he gives his speech on the abyss and the mountain peak, he broaches the topic of gluttony in the following way.

> Listen! Above all you should be temperate in drink and food, for very many things pertain to it. Do not eat excessively, beyond the amount of food necessary. But when you undertake something, when you perspire, when you work, it is necessary that you break your fast. Additional prudence in this respect is this: when you are going to eat, do not be hasty, do not be thoughtless . . . Do not gulp down your food like a dog. . . . [Otherwise] because you were acting as a glutton, you may fall to the ground [choking] when you were attempting to eat. You would be acting intemperately, and by the same stroke become a ridiculous spectacle.

The father goes on to exhort his son to exercise this virtue in all domains of life: "Go on living with temperance on earth, for you have just heard, there the mean is necessary." The same root form of the term "temperance" (*ixmimatiliztli*) appears here in the general context of leading a life on earth.

Two further points are notable. First, the father explicitly connects this virtue to the mean. Temperance thus facilitates the apt expression of an action. Second, toward the middle of the longer quoted text on gluttony, a *difrasismo* appears that is one expression for practical wisdom. Temperance is thus a virtue wherein practical wisdom plays the role of identifying the mean.

The Aristotelian conception of temperance relates only to food, drink, and sex, for which a rational "mind" needs to exert control over body. It thus fails to address a whole range of other activities that the Aztecs considered to be in need of discipline. For example, the Aztec father urges his son: "Be temperate [*timjmatiz*] in your travels. Peacefully, carefully, calmly, with deliberation you are to go." Because the Aztec notion concerns prudential discipline quite generally, the father applies it to sleeping in, staring at other people, gossiping, ostentatious dress, and idleness. Aztec temperance does include discipline in sexual activity too. In the speech recorded just before this previous one in the *Florentine Codex*, the father says:

> Although she is your partner, your body, when you are going to live with her, when you are going to bed with her, it must be as with food, which you are not to eat hastily; that is to say, do not live lustfully; do not simply give in.

The son is to exercise sexual discipline even with his own spouse, just as one restrains oneself in not gulping down food. What that means varies by personal traits and social role. As the father explains, Aztecs thought that an ordinary man could use up all his "substance," meaning life force, in sexual activity, becoming "old and wrinkled," but rulers had more such substance, and so were permitted to have multiple wives. Nevertheless, a certain sense of discipline was thought necessary even in the case of kings.

Furthermore, in keeping with their emphasis on the collective, the Aztecs thought that social rituals modulated the discipline you might need to exercise in a given situation—for instance, when drinking alcohol.

In the series of discourses that follow the appointment of a new king (*tlatoani*) at the beginning of volume 6 of the *Florentine Codex*, the new king addresses his people and unequivocally condemns alcohol, calling it "the origin, the root of vice, of perdition." This statement may have introduced a new law, likely for Tenochtitlán. Even in the relatively restrained discourses of volume 6, a passage about a marriage ceremony describes how old women guarded the room of the newly betrothed by conversing and "becoming drunk." In other recorded texts there are descriptions of the drinking games played during the celebration of the Four Hundred Rabbits, showing that drinking to the point of inebriation was expected. For example, the fifth chapter of volume 6 begins:

> Fifth chapter, which tells how many kinds of drunks there were. And it was said that wine was known as the Four Hundred Rabbits. One drinker might not harm, not belittle his spirit. . . .

The festival described in these passages is devoted to a god of alcohol, Four Hundred Rabbits, and it took place on the day sign of Two Rabbit. The merchants were supposed to drink during their celebrations, and the passage details various games. In the Eagle Feast, all were expected to drink, though the women only drank *chicha*, a different from of alcohol than "wine" (*octli*).

These contradictory views on alcohol consumption likely turn on the need to celebrate certain cosmic forces, and the need to celebrate important milestones in life, such as the successful completion of merchant traveling, or a marriage, or a funeral. This means that the occasions for indulgence would be relatively infrequent. Nevertheless, they form an important feature of temperance for the Aztecs.

In our modern society, we gather together and drink on appropriate occasions. We might think of this as a suspension of the rules of ordinary life—or at least a departure from them. But for the Aztecs, the "rules" are not so much suspended during these occasions as completed. For example, they held that you are supposed to get drunk during a wedding, as our lives offer only a few occasions for real joy. Only the foolish would abstain at these times. Rather than conceive of such indulgence as a suspension or departure from ordinary life, the Aztecs understood these actions as the sort that completed an act of balancing. They would, for example, fast before feasting and live a sober life before becoming drunk at a wedding. The two extremes balanced each other and gave their lives a feeling of rhythm.

In sum, the Aztec sense of temperance requires that we act according to our social roles in our drive to do certain things, our durability to continue doing them, and in refraining from others through discipline as the occasion permits. Practical wisdom determines what the apt expression is, given one's particular social role, but it is also informed by a sense of justice, which is our topic in Lesson 10.

SPIRITUAL EXERCISE V

The Consistency Practice

FORMING A consistent habit like working out in the morning relies on durability (low-intensity willpower). The Aztecs trained their children in this sort of activity by having them practice daily sweeping. In the third volume of the *Florentine Codex*, we read that while training at the *calmecac*, the school for the royal courts,

> it was brought about that everyone swept when it was yet dark.

Everyone was to partake of cleaning—not a terribly onerous task, but one that needs daily execution, that is, high consistency. Of course, the Aztecs had rituals to facilitate the regular achievement of such goals: They performed it with friends and sang while working.

There are simple ways to adapt these insights to our lives. You may have heard the advice that you should make your bed every day, a recommendation often attributed to Admiral William McRaven. The practice facilitates the development of willpower durability. A more Aztec approach would involve simple social exercises that connect you with others. You could, for example, wish each of your friends and family a happy birthday when your social media apps remind you. It is not a hard task, but life's circumstances are such that it is easy to let such things slide, and learning to assess and correct one's lapses will facilitate the development of willpower as consistency.

Next, the Aztecs would advise that you should experiment

to find the best way to "hook" new practices consistently into your life. The Aztecs had structured rituals in their society to help them do this. But in our modern world, we need to do this structuring ourselves.

Let me give you some examples. I have a daily to-do list, written on paper, which I check off. My wife finds my low-tech approach unnecessary and prefers to use cell phone reminders. She adds items to her Google calendar and then she acts on them. A student of mine found that he could build new consistent social habits if he interrupted his toothbrushing routine—that was his "hook." He would pause after putting toothpaste on his brush, wish people a happy birthday via his phone, and then continue. Odd, surely, but effective in his case.

The purpose of this exercise, after all, is to learn how you can start building these "moderate effort" practices into the things you already do regularly. Then you can add more as you are able. Record your successes and failures. When you fail, determine the cause and adjust for it. This is the meta-skill that will help you improve your willpower's durability.

LESSON 10

Justice Is a Path; Fairness Is Accounting

We do not even know her original name, but she proved to be the most important woman, possibly the most important person, in the events that led to the fall of Tenochtitlán to outside powers.

Since the Aztecs often didn't give children full names until their personalities were better known, she was probably called Daughter Child. Just as the Romans called their children by prosaic names, "Sextus" for the sixth born, and "Octavius" for the eighth, the Aztecs sometimes used "Middle Daughter," and "Elder Daughter." They also used more affectionate names, such as "Little Old Woman," and more poetic ones, such as "Deer Flower." But "Daughter Child" is a likely name, and as good a guess as any.

Daughter Child, then, was born to an Aztec nobleman of Coatzacoalcos (Coat-za-co-WAL-cos), close to modern day Veracruz, but her mother was of low-class standing, perhaps even a slave. Daughter Child was born royalty, as a result, but at the lowest and most vulnerable rank. When the Mexica, the Aztecs from Tenochtitlán, came to overtake her city, it is likely that political officials tried to prevent war by offering tribute. The people of Coatzacoalcos might also have fought and simply lost. Either way,

Daughter Child was given away as a war prize to the Mexica, who then transported her to a coastal town, where she was sold as a slave to the Chontal Maya for what was likely some cloth and cacao beans.

Her name would then have changed from Daughter Child to a slave's name—we do not know which. And in the town of Potonchan, she probably worked in the house of a noblewoman, grinding corn and making tortillas. Years passed, and as she matured, she likely also filled the role of accompanying some nobleman in his bed.

Then one year, some strange white, bearded men encountered her briefly. The next year, they returned. When they approached using the nearby Rio Tabasco, they attacked with a large dog and exploding metal balls. Initially the Chontal Maya sought to befriend them, but later sought to expel them, after recognizing how dangerous they were. This last move, however, proved disastrous, and the Chontal Maya lost some 220 warriors in a few hours while attempting to fight men on horseback, who were clad with metal armor. The Maya retreated and then sought to make peace. As was customary, they paid the bearded men tribute, including twenty slave girls. The woman, born of nobility in Coatzacoalcos, already twice a slave, was included among them—in part, because of her notable beauty.

Now living with the Spaniards, her new name was "Marina." After a bit, she learned that she could converse with Jerónimo de Aguilar, a Spaniard who had been shipwrecked among the Chontal Maya for four years, and who served as Cortés's principle interpreter. Ever a survivor, and always of sharp mind, Marina also learned that the bearded men called themselves *cristianos*, that there were some five thousand of them now in the Caribbean, and that they were searching for gold.

Eventually, Cortés's expedition headed far enough west that they left Mayan lands. They even sailed past Marina's home in Coatzacoalcos and arrived at an area that would come to be called

Vera cruz. Two canoes piloted by natives approached the fleet, and Cortés summoned Aguilar to translate for him. To Cortés's frustration, Aguilar could make no sense of their language. It was, of course, Nahuatl, which is not even in the same family of languages as Chontal Maya.

Recognizing this as her moment, Marina stepped forward. Of course, she could have remained silent. Who would expect a slave girl, traded for her beauty, to take on the role of translator? But she stepped forward anyway and began to translate Nahuatl into Chontal Maya for Aguilar. Aguilar then translated into Spanish for Cortés.

Realizing the need that he had, after that exchange, Cortés promised Marina riches if she would continue in that role. Marina was far too wise to the world to believe in the promises of yet another man. I find it implausible to suppose, then, that she agreed for that reason. Initially, I expect, she thought to secure her safety. Later, she found herself leading a revolution against the very people who had sacked her city and sold her into slavery.

Within days of that exchange, the Spanish did something the slave woman probably did not expect: They bestowed on her an honorific title, *doña*, so that she became Lady Marina. Among the Aztecs with whom she spoke, she was called Malina, since Nahuatl lacks an "r" sound. Yet to recognize her honorific status, they too added "-tzin" at the end. Thus, when she knew Spanish well enough to dispense with Aguilar's help, she was addressed directly as Doña Marina among the Spaniards, and Malintzin among the Aztecs.

The company marched on to Tenochtitlán, the capital of the Mexica. There Malintzin, working with Cortés, eventually negotiated the surrender of their great king, Montezuma, and the capitulation of one of the world's great premodern empires. Afterward, she negotiated for peace and acted as the translator for the first-ever philosophical exchange between Spanish priests and Aztec philosophers.

Hardly anyone in the history of Mexico's conquest has a more contested status than Marina. I was raised on stories about her in Mexico, and perhaps you've heard the same ones. She was always portrayed as a traitor to the Indigenous people, but I think that's a mistake. It wasn't until decades later, in texts written by Chimalpahin, that we have evidence of Indigenous people thinking of themselves as different from the Europeans.

Marina, rather, saw herself as something like a wife to a rising leader (*tlatoani*), who sought to make war against the people who had wronged her and so many others in the basin of Mexico. And given that Tenochtitlán was only toppled with the help of tens of thousands of Tlaxcalan warriors, she would have seen herself as part of an alliance that happened to use the help of the *cristianos*. For the historian, these details help to contextualize and complicate the history we've received. For the philosopher, they raise a deceptively simple question: Was Marina just in her actions?

Justice is a complex topic, often murky, and it plays a different role ethically than politically. What do we mean when we say we are treating other people fairly? You already have a rough understanding of this. Plato rather memorably points this out in his short dialogue, the *Alcibiades*. In this dialogue, Socrates gets Alcibiades to recognize that he understood the rudiments of justice even as a child. Here's the exchange.

> Soc.: But before that you were a child, were you not?
> Alc.: Yes.
> Soc.: I well know, however, that at that time you supposed you knew.
> Alc.: How do you know this so well?
> Soc.: When you were a child, I often heard you, when you were throwing dice or playing at some other kind of play at your teacher's or elsewhere, instead of being at a loss about the just and the unjust things, you rather spoke in a very loud and confident way about one or another of the children

> being wicked and unjust and behaving unjustly. Or am I not speaking the truth?

Alcibiades of course agrees. And if you've ever spent any time around children playing games, you know "that's not fair!" is one of the most common grievances you'll hear. At stake in these cases is a specific kind of justice that some scholars have called "character justice" to distinguish it from "political justice." Character justice is the sort that an individual, as opposed to an institution, can exhibit. It has a variety of forms, including fair treatment, law abidingness, and appropriate observance of social norms. Some scholars call the possession of all such qualities "general (character) justice." We'll adopt this terminology, so that the kind of character justice that is at stake in the Alcibiades passage is a fair treatment of others.

The Aztecs, likewise, recognized "character justice" in a person's capacity for fair treatment. Here, for example, is a description of a hardworking merchant woman who

> became wealthy and achieved honor; she prospered in marketplaces as a seller of merchandise; as one who served and showed pity for others.

Beyond demonstrating that some women could lead a life outside the house and in the marketplace, the description also shows that the Aztecs clearly had a conception of justice when it came to economic exchange, and this woman was recognized for acting justly. She shows pity for others by treating others well.

This is the sense of justice that stands in rather stark opposition to the actions of a druggist (pharmacist) that psychologist Lawrence Kohlberg popularized in the following thought experiment:

> A woman was on her deathbed. There was one drug that the doctors thought might save her. It was a form of radium that

a druggist in the same town had recently discovered. The drug was expensive to make, but the druggist was charging ten times what the drug cost him to produce. He paid $200 for the radium and charged $2,000 for a small dose of the drug. The sick woman's husband, Heinz, went to everyone he knew to borrow the money, but he could only get together about $1,000, which is half of what it cost. He told the druggist that his wife was dying and asked him to sell it cheaper or let him pay later. But the druggist said: "No, I discovered the drug and I'm going to make money from it." So Heinz got desperate and broke into the man's laboratory to steal the drug for his wife. Should Heinz have broken into the laboratory to steal the drug for his wife? Why or why not?

Kohlberg, rather infamously, used this thought experiment to assess his subject's levels of ethical development. The right answer, he thought, was "No. Heinz should not have broken into the laboratory." But our interest hinges not so much on Heinz, but on the druggist. A 500 percent markup, from $200 to $1,000, is surely enough profit. Unlike the successful Aztec merchant woman, this druggist is acting unfairly. He lacks the justice of character that concerns fair treatment.

The Aztecs would add a further dimension to this sort of accounting exercise, a dimension that depends on an agent's social role. The matter is clear in a discourse recorded in the *Primeros Memoriales*—an earlier, smaller draft of the *Florentine Codex*. This specific discourse is an upbraiding one, rather than an exhortatory or admonishing one; in it judges scold people of all stations for various forms of misconduct. The first judge begins his speech by targeting certain midranking lords who are supposed to guard their reed mat and seat (political office). He says the following:

> These are your duties, you who are lords; you are to accuse, induce, educate and edify the people. But no longer do you talk,

do you awaken, do you live for it. You sicken the lord, the king. But now while he still fulfills his obligations to you, you who are lords forget your duties.

These lords have their own superiors and have displeased them, but the judge begins by first recalling some of the specific obligations attached to the lords' social role. They are to educate and inform the people, edifying them. The lords have failed in this obligation and so have sickened their superiors. The judge, who is the person imbued specifically with the practical wisdom to discern what is just in Aztec society, charges them with failure to act justly because they have not fulfilled their role in the city-state (*altepetl*).

Understanding your role in broader society brings us to the general view of character justice that would include all such desirable qualities—what the Aztecs called the path (*in ohtli*). In the first discourse recorded in *Discourses of the Elders*, the father who is instructing his son in how to live revisits the topic of virtue. After having discussed various specific virtues and vices, he turns to an articulation of what a vicious life is, characterizing it as a life not on the correct path—or at least, not on the correct path for humans.

> He [i.e., the vicious man] no longer follows the path [*in ohtli*], the principles. He no longer listens well to the good word, that which elevates one, which explains. Only without reflecting does he walk. He flees constantly, falls suddenly. . . . No longer with tranquility, no longer with joy does he rise, does he go to bed, for thus he hastens like a rabbit, like a deer . . .
> And so will he become food for the dogs, because he made himself a rabbit, he made himself a deer. Because by his own accord he made himself, he habituated himself into vice, into wickedness.

The path of the rabbit and the deer is described literally as the negation of the virtuous path. One can fall out of the ranks of humanity through vicious action. The way this happens is through acting on one's own accord, without regard for the concerns of others or the foundations of society. These foundations, the context makes clear, are the knowledge and rites of tradition, and so constitute the path, *in ohtli*.

So understood, the path (*in ohtli*) comes surprisingly close to the way that Plato and Aristotle speak of justice as *dikē* (DEE-kay)—as "general character justice." The primary difference between the Aztec and "Western" view of this justice is that the Aztecs thought of justice not only as following the laws of a city and treating other fairly, but also by following the social rituals that were needed to harmoniously coordinate people's actions. It is in this sense that general justice is a path, while fairness, understood only as giving to each their due, is a more restricted quasi-accounting principle. This general conception of justice, moreover, governs the appropriate rituals that give temperance its balancing rhythm.

MANY OF the practices that the Aztecs used to inculcate courage overlapped with those that fostered temperance. Just as courage requires repeated exposure, so too does temperance. To practice that temperance, or willpower's durability, the Aztecs developed practices around managing sleep: awaking early to sweep before dawn, and remaining awake until midnight to accomplish specific tasks, such as collecting firewood.

There's a general point to be made about cultivating all of these habits, namely that once you are on the path, it's easier to stay on the path. Losing your good habits makes it harder to act well. That's not how we typically speak of "justice," but it's worth thinking about it this way, and in particular how the Aztecs defined "justice" more broadly.

The Aztecs thought it foolhardy to suppose that people would always act with restrained discipline. Their balancing rituals suggest they held that a life led *only* with restraint was not well lived. Temperance for the Aztecs is thus conceived of as balanced action related to one's social role. This means that a person should fast before feasting, and that both *should* be done. It also means that children shouldn't participate in drinking alcohol, but that adults probably shouldn't refrain if the festival is the right one (and they have no personal history with alcohol that would prove problematic). Knowledge about exceptions, or the balance of restraint and indulgence, is regulated by justice—which requires that you stay on the path through observing your social role and treating others fairly. That fairness, the judges remind us, requires that inequities in exchanges are also to be restored, and the burden to maintain them falls on those who have the appropriate social role to fulfill.

Wrapped up in that definition of justice are all the virtues that in "Western" philosophy are called "cardinal" virtues, in the sense of "important" or "principal" virtues. The term "cardinal" is now archaic enough that some of my students suppose that I'm speaking about birds when I raise the topic. It was the Stoic philosophers, after Aristotle, who organized virtues this way and it resolves a theoretical problem: If a right action is measured by whether or not it is in accordance with the virtues, and there are infinitely many virtues, then how can you know that you have acted well? Philosophers call this the "enumeration problem."

The Stoics thus organized virtues into four domains—justice, courage, temperance, and prudence (practical wisdom). By utilizing these limited classifications, there's no need to worry about an infinite number of new and ever-changing virtues.

While the Aztecs did not have an explicit theory of cardinal virtues, nonetheless their notions of virtue seem to fall largely into five main groups: prudence, humility, courage, temperance, and justice. Friendship may be considered an additional virtue, given the role of shared agency in these others. A parallel argument could thus be made in the Aztecs' case so as to avoid the enumeration problem. But the Aztecs also held that how we act according to core virtues differs across our various types of relationships. Their view, as is now familiar, thus bears a social dimension not present in the Stoic views.

Returning to Daughter Child, Malintzin, I suppose that she acted under morally burdened circumstances—ones that, if they did not quite rise to the level of a tragedy, and perhaps they did, surely had no obviously good answer. Life on the path requires fair assessment, and in this case likely calls us to renounce simple accusations. In any case, our assessment must include a fuller understanding of the relationships involved and we have yet to discuss this specific class of virtues for the Aztecs. We'll turn to it in Lesson 11.

SPIRITUAL EXERCISE VI

The Intensity Practice

IN SPIRITUAL Exercise V, we saw that the Aztecs had their young students practice daily sweeping to boost their willpower's durability. The third volume of the *Florentine Codex* also details how they performed a wide variety of disagreeable tasks, from exposure to extreme heat and cold, to physically stressful activities such as carrying heavy logs. Principal among their training activities was rising early in the morning before dawn. Interestingly, Marcus Aurelius, the Stoic philosopher and emperor of Rome (121–180 CE), also commented on early rising:

> At daybreak, when you are loath to get up, have this ready in your mind: I am rising to act as a human.

Regardless of the culture, it appears that the practice of early rising is felt to be disagreeable. It is also identified as a fulcrum point by which a person could practice facing something undesirable but which permits the achievement of something else reckoned to be of greater worth. When you are exposed to intensely disagreeable situations, you eventually adapt.

For those of us who are not morning larks, a simple way to cultivate *drive*—the intense will to accomplish something—is to commit to waking up early for five consecutive days. If you are a morning lark, you might try another Aztec practice, such as cold exposure, by taking a cold shower.

I took part in this practice alongside my students, reviving Aztec wisdom through early rising. While I am supposed to have outgrown that "night owl" phase of life, I still prefer the evening lights to the morning dawn. All the same, I typically rise by 5:30 a.m. It is never an enjoyable experience, but I set my clock even earlier, to the slot I used in university to complete my study of ancient Greek: 4:30 a.m. What I (re)discovered were my own psychological inflection points—particular moments in the process that were hardest to move through. Organized temporally, they are:

1. Getting out of bed itself,
2. That dizzy feeling after standing up,
3. The cold room (I live in New York),
4. The nausea to follow.

The temptation to return to bed was strongest at points two and three, while point four made me question the wisdom of rising early at all.

Initially, a loud alarm clock released enough cortisol to prick me out of bed, but I realized that after a few days I would adjust and sleep through the alarm (to my wife's annoyance). Better solutions involved preparing at night for the following day. I set up the coffee machine to run earlier, have a bit of bread ready for the nausea, have my clothes closer by my bed to brace me against the cold, and involve my pets to make the morning happier.

That exercise is but one path to cultivating the meta-skill, the habit, that forms a facet of temperance. As with many Aztec practices, it requires you to observe yourself in the third person as a social scientist might, moving from that outward view inward. Specifically, it requires documenting and assessing impediments to acting as desired, and then identifying remedies through further experimentation. While not all challenges that require drive (intense willpower) can be approached this way, how valuable would it be to tame even a few of them? If you could pay a magical creature, a genie for example, to resolve a few of these, how much would you be willing to spend? That tells you the value of this practice in terms of cold, hard cash.

LESSON 11

Love Is What You Do, Not What You Feel

At about the age of seven, Nezahualpilli (Neza-wal-PEE-lee / Fasting Child) was called into his father's bedroom. The old king, Nezahualcoyotl, knew that he was nearing death, and so he took his son into his arms and

> covered him with the royal vestments that he himself was wearing. He then ordered the ambassadors of the kings of Mexico and Tlacopan who assisted in his court to come in. . . . And he said to them: You see here your prince and natural lord, who although he is a child, is wise and prudent, and he will keep you in peace and justice, conserving you in your rank and command. And you will obey him as lord vassals.

Nezahualcoyotl ensured that there was no doubt about his successor, and the young child was able to govern first with assistance, and then on his own in Tezcoco.

Nezahualpilli's reputation grew with age so that he was regarded only second to his father for his ability to compose philosophy, wage war, and govern. Nezahualpilli was also renowned for his difficulties in love. Despite his status and power, finding love, and (especially) sustaining it, proved difficult. Having matured into a man, then having successfully waged battle with his allies from Tenochtitlán, Nezahualpilli recognized that he had succeeded in all ways but one: He remained a bachelor.

To remedy this situation, he effectively held a contest. He had the princesses and daughters from various palaces sent to his own, so that he could choose a wife. It was a move that is echoed today in reality TV shows like *The Bachelor*. One can only imagine what feats were involved in trying to capture the heart of the only bachelor king of ancient Tezcoco. Tellingly, the legends state that the contest produced results even worse than our own televised shows.

The woman he chose for a wife, Chalchiuhnenetzin (Chalchiw-ne-NE-tzin), meaning Jade Doll, was the daughter of the ruler of Tenochtitlán. She was sensual and, we are told, prone to carnal delights. As a young woman,

> she began to show a thousand weaknesses. And whenever some gallant youth or gentle lord appeared to meet her taste and type, she secretly ordered him to come and take advantage of her. And then, having satisfied her lust, she had him killed. Later she would order a statue, or a portrait made of him, and, having adorned it with rich garments, jewels of gold and precious stones, she put it in her own room. And there were so many statues of those whom she had killed that they rounded almost the entire room. And when the king [Nezahualpilli] went to visit her and asked about these statues, she replied that they were her gods.

Eventually Nezahualpilli discovered the truth. The evidence was clear, and even the servants knew of the queen's affairs. Since no one was taken to be above the law, Nezahualpilli submitted the matter to court, and found himself compelled to execute his own wife.

The execution soured relations with Tenochtitlán, since Jade

Doll was a princess from the city just across the lake. And Nezahualpilli was forced yet again to find another wife.

Even the Aztecs, no less than us, found love difficult. In some ways, these stories recall the trials of European nobility. Jade Doll caused as much trouble as Anne Boleyn. But the Aztecs also had a different conception of love and healthy relationships than their European contemporaries, or than any of us have today.

Aztecs do not appear to have shared our contemporary views on love and romance. They did not believe in perfect soulmates who complete us, who will make us want for nothing, and who we will find through an unquestionable heightened romantic attraction. Instead, Aztecs believed that romantic love, especially in marriage, was a set of practices enacted through rituals. Feelings support those activities.

To put it memorably: love is not what you feel; it's what you do.

These active rituals also formed a bulwark against the ill effects of love as an emotion. That many have killed for love only means that the same emotions that compel the better angels of our nature can also compel the demons inside us. Everyone, then, can learn from the three kinds of ritual practices the Aztecs had that sustained their love along ethical lines: daily rituals, romance rituals, and intimacy rituals. Let's start with a relevant philosophical concept: virtues of relationships.

PHILOCTETES, as Sophocles depicts him in the play titled *Philoctetes*, was dealt a poor hand by fate. To recall, Philoctetes was bitten by a snake. His pain was grievous. His cries of agony prevented Odysseus and his men from making prayers to the gods. So, in response, Odysseus and his crew threw Philoctetes off the boat and abandoned him on an island with only Heracles's divine bow to use in hunting for food. The magical bow was reputed never to miss its target.

After nearly a decade at war with the Trojans in Ilium, Odysseus returned to the island to retrieve Philoctetes's divine bow. They wanted to end the war and decided to use the magical bow to do it. Also, if possible, they were to retrieve Philoctetes. Odysseus realized that Philoctetes would not trust him and sent someone else to talk to him: Neoptolemus. Given his wartime objectives, Odysseus told Neoptolemus that he must first make friends with Philoctetes and then take the bow by a trick (*dolō*). The basis of mutual friendship as depicted here, then, is mutual trust, and it is this trust that Neoptolemus must abuse to gain the magical weapon. An additional dimension of dependence beyond mutual trust emerges through Philoctetes's reliance on others to achieve his own tasks—to exercise whatever virtues he possesses as an individual. The venom's pain, we learn, occurs in waves and lasts for some time. It incapacitates Philoctetes, and he is wracked by agony. After such bouts he must sleep to recover his strength. As a result, he cannot safekeep his belongings during these episodes, so that if others are present, even his basic survival requires the aid of another.

Neoptolemus recognizes the measure of Philoctetes's dependence and concludes that he can identify nothing good (*kalos*) in his deceptive actions in stealing the bow from Philoctetes. He decides to return the bow and to convince Philoctetes to join the other men. Yet he succeeds only with divine assistance, which is a poetic way of displaying how the circumstances of that war—precipitating the need to save men in battle and the need to honor a friend—could not be rationally solved.

Among the lessons to be learned from Philoctetes's tragedy, the one that matters for us involves the status of friendship as a special sort of shared agency—highlighted in Neoptolemus's refusal to take advantage of Philoctetes's dependence. Let's start with the core ethical points that articulate what friendships (whether "Platonic" or romantic) are, how these relationships are sustained, and why they are fundamentally unlike other sorts of relations that we might have with people.

To begin, friendships require us to care for the other's good, which is why Neoptolemus decides to return the bow, and so are different from wanting only companionship. Deep friendships develop through shared intimate moments—usually involving vulnerability. In Philoctetes's case, this transpires after his bouts of pain. Deep friendships go beyond loving the other person only for the excellence of their character, since they often include commitments to the other person even (or especially) during their lapses of character. Neoptolemus does betray Philoctetes's trust, after all. Finally, they require you to think of the other's life as a whole—what would be best for them?—and to act on that. Though this view does entail some obligations—for example, when a friend gets married you will need to show up to the ceremony—but if you were *only* to act out of obligation, the relationship would crumble.

Most important for ethical considerations, friendships involve activities that cannot be enacted by an individual. Loyalty may be thought a virtue of a relation because one cannot be loyal to an object. Mutual loyalty, moreover, is both necessary for a strong friendship and yet extends beyond the control of any one agent. Mutual trust, which sustains such loyalty, is similar. Either person may destroy that trust. It takes only a moment's reflection to recognize that you can only practice these virtues—loyalty and trustworthiness—in strong relationships. They are the virtues that sustain it. How else, for example, could you practice forgiveness?

To develop the characteristics of such deep friendships, it is important to identify the specific class of actions that fall under the umbrella of "shared agency." Consider the following tale of romantic friendship from Shakespeare's famed play *Othello*.

Othello discovers that Cassio has the handkerchief that he gave to Desdemona on their honeymoon, and he comes to suspect her infidelity. Iago later inflames his worries further, so that Othello one night enters her room in an attempt to smother her, ruining their relationship.

This is an example of relational agency. Just like "ordinary" friendships, romantic friendships are sustained through *mutual* loyalty and *mutual* trust. What ruins the relationship in the case of this Shakespearean drama is Othello's deficiency of trust, which vitiates its mutuality. Relational agency differs from other sorts of shared agency (plural group and corporate group, as discussed in Lesson 5) in key ways. Recall the example of walking with someone (plural group agency), which is a temporally continuous act over a definite span of time. Unlike a stroll, relationships are spatially indefinite and spatially discrete, meaning that they may happen anywhere and even over unconnected spaces. Recall also the example of a royal crowning (corporate agency), where a group participates in a shared activity. Unlike the members of a king's court who can be replaced, the individual members of a friendship matter, that is, they are not replaceable.

Friendships, then, form a special sort of relational agency. Romantic relationships also form a special class for relational agency, and for our purposes, we'll consider the cases in which these romances are also friendships. Like plural group and corporate group agency, relational agency can be helped along with ritual practices, such as the mutual celebration of milestones and achievements, or the mutual grieving around death and disaster. These and similar rituals are those that the Aztecs used to sustain their romantic relationships.

IF YOU'VE ever been in a committed relationship, then you know that daily living involves its own sphere of concerns. You need to move beyond mere attraction to the practice of living together well, but this can be a murky affair. The Aztecs had their own set of rituals to facilitate this dimension of romantic life.

Most of the surviving records of daily ritual involve women, since the domestic sphere, which covered most romantic activity, was theirs. The activities of the men, as far as we can reconstruct them from traces in written records and related art, concern their roles in warfare or as merchants. Our discussion is thus tilted along this gendered axis largely because of the materials that have survived to become the historical record. A few cases of direct interaction between husband and wife are recorded, but not as many as those that focus on the couples. The Aztecs understood each of us to act by way of our social roles. Love was no different. One won't, then, find much advice for how to treat one's partner that doesn't also involve how to live with them in a household.

The story of a sweeping romance—one literally tied to the activities of a sweeper—provides a doorway into Aztec loving practice. Chimalaxoch (Chimala-SOCH) was part of a group of rescued captives and was brought before the ruler Quinatzin (Qui-NA-tzin), whose reign began in 1300. In the *Codex Chimalpopoca* (Chimal-po-PO-ka / Smoking Shield) we read the following about their encounter.

> When the ruler saw her, he fell in love with her. Then he wanted to go to her and cohabit with her.
> But she refused, telling him, "Not yet, my lord, for I am fasting. That which you desire may be done later, for I am a sweeper, a woman in service. The vow I make is for just two years, finished in two more years, my lord. Please give the word to have them prepare for me a little altar of beaten earth, so that I can make offerings to my god, offer up my sacred cup, and do my fasting."
> So the ruler Quinatzin gave the order for an earth altar to be made.... When the earth altar was finished, they left the young woman there, and she fasted. And when she had done her fasting, the ruler Quinatzin took her as his wife.

The story underscores the way that the Aztecs understood attraction to be related to love. They had a concept of love and of marital commitment not unlike ours. The conditions for restraint, however, are culturally unique. Chimalaxoch had taken on a "sweeper's vow" that required fasting. Such sacred vows were something that not even a ruler would (or could) undo. Respecting that vow proved the starting point of their relationship. Later, given the social structures they occupied, marriage proved possible.

Although the story doesn't center on it, Chimalaxoch would undoubtedly have also performed actual sweeping. This was a prototypical activity of women in a household or a temple. Textual evidence for this is abundant, including the moment in the *Florentine Codex*'s discourses of the elders when a father reminds his daughter that she should "[s]eize the broom: be diligent with the sweeping." Women and young children were supposed to sweep their courtyards and homes before dawn. The "true woman" holds vigil and sweeps. And the practice continued well into the Christian era, with the historians Durán and Mendieta both recording similar accounts.

The act of sweeping, for the Aztecs, removed *tlazolli* (tla-ZOL-lee), a concept meaning "filth" in both a moral and physical sense, from a household or sanctuary. Brooms were kept outside the house to avoid contamination within. But the imagery was also one that directly connected to women's fertility and sexuality. Huitzilopochtli (Weet-zil-o-POCH-tli), the main god of Tenochtitlán, is said to have been conceived when his mother kept a bit of trash that should have been swept up. And the goddess Tlazolteotl (tlaz-ol-TAY-ot), the goddess of erotic love, carried a broom as her symbol. A woman who was a good sweeper was a woman who kept her house in order and who organized her desires.

In the same discourse where the father tells his daughter to take up the broom, he also tells her that to live well and maintain a good household she should also wake early, hold vigil for the gods, apply herself to the spindle, present herself well, and prepare food. A separate text reads that even noble women took special care in overseeing the preparation of food for banquets. As the

Aztecs saw it, these were all features of a well-ordered house and well-maintained romance.

In a discourse covering the marriage of a younger couple, a man is admonished similarly in his role as a merchant. It reads:

> Exert yourself with the staff and carrying frame. Place the strands of chili, salt cakes, nitrous soil, and strings of fish on your back; travel from city to city.

As his wife is to rise early and take care of the household, so is the husband to rise early and peddle his wares in the marketplace of his city or another. He organizes what is physically outside the home, while she organizes what is within.

We can take from these rituals an understanding of the way that Aztec couples showed, on a daily basis, how they loved one another. As with almost all aspects of an Aztec person's life, they acted by way of rituals. And because these were effective rituals, they worked to coordinate their love in a positive and mutually beneficial way.

There is social scientific evidence that supports the Aztec view that romantic relationships are sustained, in part, by regular, mutual support. The evidence suggests that it is, in part, the *ratio* of positive expressions toward your partner that matters—at a rate of five compliments to one criticism. In the workplace, a ratio of three to one has been found necessary to maintain a positive environment. The trick, of course, is that the praise must be directed at actions and not at personality traits, since the latter may prove corrosive. Praising a person's personality, telling them that they are beautiful or smart for example, inflates their ego and makes them less resilient in the face of failure. Praising an action encourages more of the right action.

The Aztecs' many, daily acts of devotion functioned like these acts of positive expression toward a partner. Such acts foster a loving relationship in part because they serve as positive affirmations.

Service to your partner, when noticed, enriches your bond. Establishing rituals around these acts of service helps to make them easier to perform consistently and ensures that the parties involved notice and acknowledge the actions performed. Unacknowledged services nurture resentment, after all, rather than gratitude. The Aztecs, of course, extended their rituals beyond the small, daily, and admittedly rather unromantic. They had romantic rituals too.

SCHOLARSHIP ON Aztec sexuality varies rather significantly due to the quality of surviving documents and the vastly different views held in different Aztec cities at different times. The documents we do have from the early colonial period around Tenochtitlán (now Mexico City) support the view that for any but high nobles, sexual expression was thought to have its exclusive outlet in marriage.

A cautionary tale, recorded in the *Florentine Codex*, tells of two old women with white hair who were arrested for adultery. In justifying their actions, they claim that their husbands were too old and sluggish. They caution all men, stating:

> Ye men, ye are sluggish, ye are depleted, ye have ruined yourselves impetuously. It is all gone. There is no more. There is nothing to be desired. But of this, we who are women, we are not the sluggish ones.

In this passage, the women chastise the men who were too impetuous in their activities, and thus depleted themselves. The older women are justified in looking elsewhere. The story underscores the Aztecs' practice of restraining sexual activity until marriage, and even limiting it within—at least for commoners. Romance, however, was more actively and widely developed through ritual practice.

One of the cuter episodes recorded in a surviving text is a description of how young boys and girls would meet and engage in a hand-holding ritual. While the youths were socially divided into those who attended the *telpochcalli*, the school for trade and war, and those who attended the *calmecac*, the school for royal court preparation, all attended the *cuicalli* (kwee-KAL-ee), the singing house.

While there, the youths would dance and sing, learning the songs of their culture to pass on to the next generation. They also were permitted to mingle. Dúran records the following:

> If a boy became fond of one of the girls (whether or not she was of his neighborhood) while holding her hand at the festival, he promised her that when the time came he would marry her. . . .
>
> The promise made there [between the boy and girl] was to marry in due time, and thus, every time he came to that place, [the boy] sought her out and made it a point to hold her, and no other, by the hand, and she felt the same about him. In this way they went along and endured until their time came. This was when he had reached the proper age or had performed some noble feat.

Among the Aztecs, there were accepted pathways for youths to show each other affection and to make that affection known to others, and one of these was to hold hands at the monthly festivals. It is worth noting too that it would not only have been the youths who would dance in these festivals, which occurred outside the *cuicalli*. People of all ages and from all walks of life would participate, so that the married couples could rekindle their mutual interest also.

If you've ever been to a party in Mexico, among other Mexicans, you'll know that they still dance, sing, and eat at festivals— whether national holidays, birthdays, weddings, christenings, or even just the arrival of a long-separated family friend. Dancing is still an inclusive practice, so that the young and old alike enjoy participating. I think it's worth noting that it's at these fiestas, exclusively, where I've seen my father (of British heritage) dance. So, while single people connect at such events, the fiestas encourage community connection more broadly.

Several smaller practices are wrapped up in events like these where the Aztecs sang and danced in groups, and there is considerable evidence supporting their positive effects. Focusing initially on singing in groups, studies have found that choral singing improves lung function, increases your pain threshold thereby reducing the need for medication, alleviates irritable bowel syndrome, and calms heart rates while boosting endorphin levels. A meta-analysis even found that singing in groups could help patients with acquired brain injuries, such as Parkinson's or strokes.

And the positive effects go beyond the physiological. Singing in groups elevates a participant's mood for a significant period, enhances their sense of purpose and meaning, and helps to promote trust among members of the choir. Importantly, these effects are the result of singing in *groups*, not solo singing.

The benefits of singing naturally extend to gesture, movement, and dancing. Studies have confirmed that dancing elevates mood and self-esteem. Dancing also coordinates partners and brings them into sync. Studies have shown that dancers remember significantly more details about their dancing partner than control participants who did not dance.

There is also scientific evidence to support the benefits of holding hands. While the reasons are not fully clear, when romantic partners held hands, their experience of pain, induced in a laboratory setting, say through submersion of a hand in ice water, is reduced. There is evidence that holding hands improved conflict resolution in couples. This isn't too surprising, if you consider the broad range of evidence supporting the importance of ongoing touch between couples, which does everything from increasing positive moods to regulating emotions.

We'll get to the many practices that you could implement

following this evidence in a moment. For now, let's turn to the last Aztec practice concerning intimacy.

PERHAPS YOU'VE heard of the thirty-six-question quiz that Mandy Len Catron popularized in her essay "To Fall in Love with Anyone, Do This." The social science behind it derives from the late 1990s work of Arthur Aron, at SUNY Stony Brook, and his national team of collaborators, and while it doesn't automatically make people fall in love, it does lead to a deeper sense of intimacy. Questions are structured along an access of increasing intimacy that follows through three different stages. Here are some sample questions from each stage.

STAGE 1
Given the choice of anyone in the world, whom would you want as a dinner guest?
Before making a telephone call, do you ever rehearse what you are going to say? Why?
If you could wake up tomorrow having gained one quality or ability, what would it be?

STAGE 2
Is there something that you've dreamed of doing for a long time? Why haven't you done it?
What do you value most in a friendship?
What is your most treasured memory?
What is your most terrible memory?

STAGE 3
Make three true "we" statements each. For instance, "We are both in the room feeling . . ."
Complete this sentence: "I wish I had someone with whom I could share . . ."

Tell your partner what you like about them; be very honest this time, saying things that you might not say to someone you've just met.

The central point behind this set of questions is to establish intimacy through vulnerability. Most of us are unwilling to be vulnerable quickly, so the questions give you and your partner a direct shove in that direction. The Aztecs understood this same principle and developed a ritual to support it.

The ritual involves four days of seclusion for a newlywed couple. It's helpful to recall that while some Aztecs would have met in the *cuicalli* and held hands, even in that case real intimacy might have been difficult to develop before marriage. In other cases, where marriages were organized to bring prominent houses together, there is little reason to expect that the couple had even met on more than a few occasions. The new couple was thus in need of a ritual for intimacy.

To set the stage, let's start with the marriage ceremony itself. The *Codex Mendoza* records the arrangement vividly. At the bottom of the page in the codex, the bride is carried into the marriage home, flanked on both sides by torch bearers. The old men are seated on the left, the old women on the right. In the middle is a pitcher of pulque (an alcohol similar to tequila) with a cup, and above are baskets and plates of food. At the top of the page, the couple are pictured after the completion of the ceremony with the wife on the left (with the old men) and the husband on the right. They are seated on a reed mat in front of the hearth where copal, a sacred incense, is burning. During the ceremony they literally "tie the knot," as they tie the man's cape and the woman's blouse together, symbolizing their union. The organization of the ceremony achieves a harmonic balance among related pairs (*inamichuan*).

After the ceremony, the elders get drunk on the pulque and sequester the newlyweds in a room for four days. The purpose was

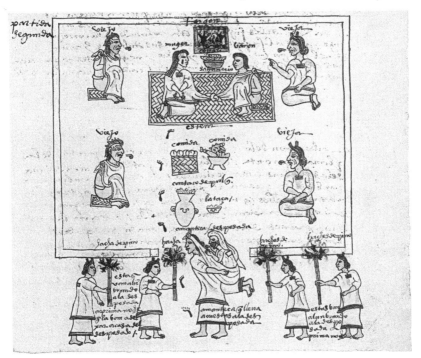

for the couple "to do penance and fast for four days before cohabitating," and so was not a sequestering for sexual purposes. While this ritual served a cleansing role, it also allowed the couple time to build their relationship undisturbed by the outside world. It was, in short, an intimacy ritual, but it was not a sexual one. The new couple could now work together in public and private to ensure the success of their joint household. And while they wouldn't have pursued a course of thirty-six questions to fall in love, the ritual permitted the partners an undisturbed period to talk, listen, and understand each other deeply. At the close of the four days, the straw mat that they had used would be shaken out in the courtyard (eliminating any *tlazolli*) and then laid in their home where they would sleep.

Just how much intimacy did the Aztecs allow in their

relationships? The answer, according to surviving documents, isn't certain. But if we turn to a story about another woman named Jade Doll (not to be confused with Nezahualpilli's ill-fated love), we are met with evidence that suggests rather strong bonds. In one telling of the story, Moquihuix (Mo-KEE-weesh), the king of Tlatelolco, which went to war with Tenochtitlán and lost, discusses the war with his wife, Jade Doll. Durán records their exchange, beginning with a dream.

> Our chronicle says that while she was asleep she [i.e., Jade Doll] dreamed that her private parts spoke, wailing, "Alas, my lady. Where shall I be tomorrow at this time?" She awoke with great fear and told her husband what she had dreamed, asking him to interpret this dream. He answered by telling her what he had decided to do about Tenochtitlán, and said that her dream might be a prophecy of events that could take place on the morrow.
>
> She wept bitterly over her husband's prediction, saying: "Lord, it is a terrible thing, that which you have begun! Have pity on the women and children who will perish because of you! Think of the deaths that will occur on both sides! Remember that you have small children, and consider that you and I shall be needed by them. They will become perpetual slaves if we are conquered."
>
> King Moquihuix arose from his mat and sighed, showing that he repented of his warlike intentions. However, he excused himself by saying that his advisor Teconal had been the instigator of the rebellion and that he, Moquihuix, was not powerful enough to stop it now that it was underway.
>
> The queen answered, "How is it, sir, that being the lord and ruler of these people you cannot calm their hearts? Give me permission to speak to them! They may listen to my womanly words and make peace with Tenochtitlán, then our past friendship will be renewed. Do not be a coward, speak to them. Go

see your brother Axayacatl, pacify him and embrace him. Do this for me, give me this satisfaction."

Given the inconsistencies among the different versions of this story, we can't be certain about what exactly transpired. But we know that an exchange, such as this, where the queen corrects the king—though in the privacy of their bedroom chamber—is consistent with the Aztec outlook on marriage. The intimacy couples developed was a deep bond reliant on mutual respect and openness to criticism.

It's worth noting that cross-cultural studies of peoples' experience with love do vary. Typically, they fall into either the individualist or collectivist spectrum. People in the United States are more likely to approach love individually, strongly valuing personal attraction, while citizens of China are more likely to explain their experience of love in a collectivist way, valuing a partner's ability to sustain a household and engage with their extended family. Important across the spectrum is the presence of affection for the other person, one form of which is intimacy. To some extent, intimacy crosses cultural boundaries. Time spent strengthening and renewing it is thus time well spent.

THUS FAR we've witnessed how Aztec romantic and sexual traditions hinge on balanced, but not fluid, gender roles. No space has so far been given for same-sex relationships, though we have seen evidence for it. In fact, if we are to believe Cortés, the Aztec model we've established here was perhaps more of an exception, since he stated that "they are all sodomites and practice that abominable sin." His purpose, after waging a war of aggression against the Indigenous population, was likely a self-legitimating one aimed at impugning the Indigenous population. Although Cortés was thus an unreliable chronicler, other sixteenth-century historians were aware of a wide range of ambiguity around same-sex relations. Antonio de Herrera, for example, writes: "Some say that in Mexico they killed those who performed the nefarious sin, while others say that it was not taken seriously enough to legislate against it." Similar caveats apply to nonbinary and gender-fluid persons, those given the names *patlache* (pa-TLA-che) and *suchioa* (su-CHI-wa), for example. Also, the pleasure-women (*ahuianime*) similarly occupy the less well-understood role of sex worker.

Still, the accounts we do have present the typical model of romantic life for an Aztec couple. We have substantial evidence that women were largely raised to manage the affairs of a household within the above articulated role. In the *Codex Mendoza* is the following image. It depicts a mother speaking to her thirteen-year-old daughter, who is grinding maize to make tortillas. Since the daughter is using a flat *metatl* to make those tortillas, we know that it's likely depicting everyday life for the "real housewives" of Tenochtitlán.

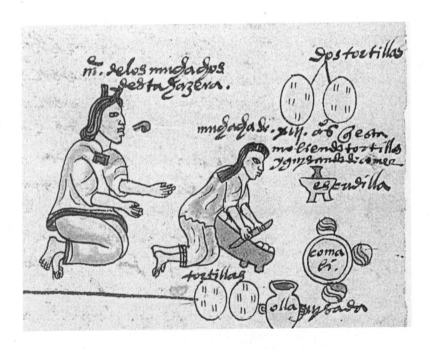

What the Aztecs teach us about love is that ritual sustains it. We've reviewed three types:

1. Daily rituals that typically involve the service of one partner to another.
2. Romance rituals such as the hand holding, group singing, and group dancing that transpired in the *cuicalli*.
3. Intimacy rituals such as the four days in seclusion that newlywed couples practiced even before having sexual relations.

One of the advantages of Aztec society's pervasive use of rituals was how they set clear expectations. Rituals ensured that even the smaller actions would be acknowledged and made it all but impossible for partners to avoid activities that could foster a closer relationship with each other.

Because they hailed from a society in which a person's individual emotions were not valued as highly as the social bond formed among partners and family members, the Aztecs took the practice of love to center largely on what you *do* and not how you *feel*. In that sense, it is an "unromantic" view of romance, but is, more importantly, an imminently practical one. That same outlook sustained them even in the hardest of circumstances, namely tragedy, as we shall see in Lesson 12.

SPIRITUAL EXERCISE VII

The Craving Practice

UNLIKE PRACTICES meant to cultivate drive and durability, resisting a craving depends on exercising discipline. Most global cultures center one key practice to facilitate this activity: the fast.

The Aztecs practiced fasting for a variety of occasions—from personal vows, to training in schools, to preparation for a feast. In all cases, the fast remained closely tied to their idea of temperance (moderation) as balance. If you plan to "party hard," then the Aztecs would commend that you provide yourself with a set of days or weeks of sober, clean living to balance that activity.

Today, some of us undertake "crash diets" before vacations, which highlights a cultural difference between our modern society and Aztec society. Especially in the United States, our approach to food often revolves around bodily shame. We rarely see fasting as part of a balanced, healthy lifestyle—but perhaps we should. If we embrace the Aztec perspective fully, we might even consider the enjoyment of feasting as equally essential to living a good life.

The Atamalqualo (a-ta-mal-KWA-lo) festival provides a glimpse into how fasting was practiced, or at least idealized, by the Aztecs. A passage from the *Florentine Codex* describes the tradition:

> But when it was the time of fasting they call Atamalqualo, they tasted nothing at all. Some ate at midnight and then waited to eat until the next. Others ate at noon and waited until the next noon to eat.

This particular form of fasting may not be advisable for many people today, especially for health reasons. However, we also know that the Aztecs often fasted for months or even years, especially when preparing for a significant life stage. In these cases, fasting was more about reducing the amount and type of food consumed, rather than abstaining entirely from nourishment.

Modern fasting practices, like those popularized by Michael Mosley, MD, follow a gentler approach. His recommendations include:

- You may drink whatever liquids you deem suitable (provided they do not add calories).
- You should aim for 800 calories a day.
- You can decide whether you would like to take those calories all in one meal, or in several bits throughout the day.
- Be sure to take appropriate vitamins to supplement what you might not consume otherwise.

This type of fasting builds willpower as discipline by cultivating the meta-skill of reflection and response. It also introduces you to discomfort, allowing you to learn how to manage and overcome those feelings. Repeated exposure, paired with reflection, strengthens your virtue over time.

If you've never fasted, and you decide to give this a try, you'll experience something obvious: hunger. The purpose of the practice is to learn to deal with that sensation. You'll observe that hunger comes in waves, varying in intensity, rather than a continuous buildup of discomfort. These waves often align with times when you would normally have a meal, and they subside on their own.

Personally, I find that the easiest way to manage hunger is to graze on my 800 calories throughout the day. I prepare small portions—100-calorie bags of nuts or edamame—so that I know exactly what I'm consuming. My strongest cravings typically come just before bedtime, but when I'm deeply engaged in an activity or in a "flow state," I feel no cravings at all.

To fully embrace the Aztec approach to fasting, however, you should prioritize balance. A fast should ideally precede a feast, and perhaps follow it as well—especially if you've overindulged. For the Aztecs, fasting and feasting were related like *inamichuan* (interdependent opposites) and were meant to be experienced in sequence.

The intensity practice, consistency practice, and craving practice all build the same meta-skill: the ability to place yourself in challenging situations, observe your response, and then progressively adjust your environment or support systems to achieve a better outcome. This is a core component of leading a life along the outward path.

You might also discover through these practices that, sometimes, an intense practice can be easier than a more moderate one. For example, I find that fasting—consuming only 800 calories a day—is easier than trying to limit my intake of sweets. Fasting is a high-intensity activity that occupies a central place in my daily routine, allowing me to resist other temptations for the day. To avoid sweets during a normal day, my best strategy is simply not to have them in sight.

The reverse can also be true. After my early twenties, I struggled to make time for the gym. My preferred workouts involved high-intensity weight training and required careful scheduling. As this routine became harder to maintain, I found that substituting low-intensity calisthenic exercises at home was much more sustainable. While I'm not in the same shape I was in my youth, this "second-best" option has proven far more manageable over time. Sometimes, the simpler approach yields better results.

I think of this kind of substitution as adjusting the intensity switch. The reason you're not succeeding in a willpower task could be that you're trying to achieve it through the wrong level of intensity. Try switching that up or down.

LESSON 12

You Cannot Prepare for Tragedy, but You Can Learn to Live After It

The year was Two Reed, which is 1299 in our common era. Chimalxochitl (Chimal-SHO-cheet / Shield Flower) and her people had journeyed from what is now the American Southwest six generations before, seeking lands where maize would thrive and droughts seldom turned the soil to dust. Mexico's central basin proved to be such a place, though when they arrived, they found the best lands claimed by others.

For a time, they survived as mercenaries, fighting and bleeding in battles not their own, earning the right to settle, to hunt their deer, and sow their maize. Yet after a season of hard-won stability, Shield Flower's father, Huitzilihuit (Wee-tzil-EE-weet / Hummingbird Feather), believed it was time for their people to live free and independent.

He did what one must, in those circumstances, and taunted the area's leader to provoke a war. But fate had other plans. Hummingbird Feather was deceived and defeated in battle. Both he and Shield Flower were taken as captives to Culhuacan (CUL-wa-can) where they were humiliated. Forced to watch his daughter paraded naked through the streets, Hummingbird Feather begged Coxcox (COSH-cosh), the king of the Culhua people, to give her clothing. But the king denied him coldly stating, "She will remain as she is."

The aftermath was even worse. Shield Flower's hands and feet were bound. Meanwhile, Culhua warriors scoured the marshes for survivors. One by one, the fleeing warriors were captured, and many, weakened by hunger and despair, pledged themselves to a life of slavery for reprieve. Yet Shield Flower refused to remain bound and shamed before her people. She was determined to protect their honor and their legacy.

She asked the guards for chalk and charcoal, and they mocked her as she struggled to mark her body in the ancient way. Then, with fierce resolve, she rose and called to them, "Why do you not sacrifice me?" Then she taunted them, telling them that they had no courage, that they dishonored themselves by delaying. She was ready; the gods were ready. Why, then, were they not ready?

Shamed by her words, the Culhuacans took her out and placed her on a pyre. With the flames crisping her naked flesh, she stood tall. And through her tears she screamed at her enemies: "People of Culhuacan, I go to where my god lives. My people's descendants will all become great warriors. You will see!"

Such were the events that mark the beginning of the people that the world has come to know as the Aztecs. Shield Flower's descendants did, eventually, build an empire as great as any in Europe by the time Columbus set sail in search of India, and they were great warriors.

This historical moment challenges how we modern people understand tragedy—the kind of circumstance in which there is no obvious good choice. Most of us don't like thinking about the topic and any sacrifice it might involve. Occasionally, we'll try thinking about its positive dimension, heroism, usually as portrayed in a film or televised series.

One antidote to this habit that has caught on is the Stoic practice of *memento mori*, which means "remember that you will die." The idea is that you should meditate on the inevitability of your own death, rather than push aside the feelings of anxiety that it produces. Two principal features are thought to result from this somber activity: First, by reflecting on your death, you will be enabled to return to your life in a purposeful way; and second, by thinking through your fears, you will come to recognize that they are not as scary as they seem.

For the Aztecs there is something missing in both these approaches, whether you are steadfastly ignoring the possibility of tragic circumstances, or unflinchingly gazing into the abyss of your own death. They wisely knew this: You can't honestly prepare for tragedy. The only thing that you can learn to do is deal with the fallout. You can learn to grieve well. And unlike the "Western" responses to tragic circumstances, this is something you need to practice with other people, guided by meaningful rituals.

THE RITUALS that other cultures use to mourn the passing of their beloved can seem bizarre to us. It's thus helpful to recall some of the reasons we have for what we now do—especially in North America. We didn't always bury our dead after embalming them. That practice seems to have become the norm only after Abraham Lincoln's death and burial. In recalling the events after Lincoln's assassination, the historian Ronald White writes the following:

> In the days after Lincoln's death, preparations began for a vast public mourning. Arrangements were made for the long train ride home to the prairies of Illinois. Lincoln's casket would retrace the exact route where cheering crowds had greeted the president-elect on his way to Washington four years before. On Tuesday, April 18, it seemed that all of Washington stood in line outside the White House to pay their respects to the dead president. After waiting hours, they entered the east Room to pass the president's open casket, finding him dressed in the black suit he had worn at his Second Inaugural.

For Lincoln's corpse to maintain composure during these showings, the latest, state-of-the-art techniques for embalming were used—the very ones that have been subsequently refined and are now standard practice. They aimed not only to preserve the president's body, but to vivify it for display. Only if fortified in this way, it was thought, would the president's body survive over many weeks during the long train ride from Washington, DC, to Illinois.

The modern practice of embalming for vivification and display, then, is of comparatively recent history. The motive, however, proves nearly universal. It is to honor the dead and help those in grief through the mourning process. The same motives are at work in the Aztec grieving and mourning rituals.

Although we have records for the mourning practices of ordinary Aztecs, the most detailed surviving records describe the deaths of the illustrious. Diego Durán, for example, records how Nezahualpilli (Nezahualcoyotl's son) mourned the loss of Ahuitzol (a-WEET-zol), the king of Tenochtitlán, in 1502. When Nezahualpilli arrived at the city, he cut past all the lords and ladies in the palace on his way to visit the body, prioritizing the late king. Upon arrival, he gave a spontaneous and eloquent speech, some of which follows:

> The city has been steeped in darkness since the sun has gone down, the sun has been hiding since your death. The royal seat is without light because your majesty and grandeur illuminated it, threw light upon it. The place, the chamber, of the omnipotent god is now full of dust, of refuse, the chamber that you ordered swept and kept clean, for you were the image of this god and you governed his state, pulling out the weeds and thorns that appeared in it.

After this speech, he delivered gifts to the corpse to carry with it into the afterlife. All the citizens likewise came to pay their respects and to offer small objects to facilitate the king's journey.

Afterward, the body was raised up and paraded through a set of ceremonial stations that culminated in moving the body to a pyre. There it was burned so that the smoke could facilitate the transition of the *yolia*, or "soul," to the land of the dead.

Typically, four days after that initial ceremony, a family in mourning would make effigies and then burn those at dusk. Then, we know that at least for the wives of kings and fallen soldiers, they would begin an eighty-day period of deep mourning. They did not wash their clothes or bathe, and they were not expected to participate in the typical activities of their social role. At the conclusion of this mourning period, the women would take part in a cleansing ceremony. A priest would attend to them and, while making a prayer, scrape the accumulated grime from the women, literally casting away their tears. The women would then go to the temple to pray and make offerings. Durán observed that

> with all these ceremonies they became free of weeping and sadness; mourning was over. They returned to their homes happy and consoled as if nothing had happened. Thus, they were free of sorrow and tears.

You and I are likely to be skeptical that the women were "totally cured" of grief in this way, but we have little reason to doubt that the ceremonies did help in the grieving process. Society was arranged to acknowledge and accommodate their grief. Their reprieve from duties would be a kind of "grief pay," where, while mourning the loss of one dear to them, they were not required to go to work. The Aztecs took mourning far more seriously than we do.

The "soul" of the deceased was thought to begin a four-year journey at this time. Recall, for a moment, the primary external forces thought to animate the human person (from Lesson 3): *yolia*, *ihiyotl*, and *tonalli*. The first of these preserved the memories of a person over this time and was then released in the smoke of the body burnt on a pyre. In Mictlan, the Land of the Dead, the soul would pass through eight deserts and eight mountains, past a serpent, and a blue lizard. Then it would arrive at a place of obsidian winds, which were as difficult to cross as you might imagine. The gifts that the corpse received would assist in this long journey. After crossing through the winds, the *yolia* would arrive at the place of the dead, nine tiers down from the earth. The Aztecs believed that a little yellow dog would accompany the dead through this portion of the journey. Once a soul arrived at this ninth tier, the dog would take the lead, as the soul could not complete this phase on its own. It would carry its master across the waters into the place of mystery where the *yolia* would finally dissipate, returning to become one with the divine energy.

The Day of the Dead, in Mexican culture, is a celebration to remember those who had passed. After a four-year period following the death of a loved one, , and we can all engage in a similar activity of remembrance a family no longer needs to make offerings to sustain this soul. In this way, a family can pay their respects and mourn in a sequence of obligations that decrease in intensity as the years pass, allowing space both for emotional connection and for the need to move on.

PHILOSOPHERS ARE not theologians. We go as far as reason lets us walk, and that stops just short of redemption. If belief in God can save us and redeem the earth, then what philosophy offers is but a consolation for our existence. And yet, I think it offers strength enough—enough to face the tragedies we meet, enough to see that in those moments our lives and actions carry value.

If the Aztec philosophers are right, then you are not after happiness, but a life well lived. You are not after invulnerability either, but instead a life of meaning and worth. Finally, you do not need eternity to seal that sense of purpose into your ways; the immutability of our actions—their performance on the world's stage—suffices. You achieve such a life, a rooted one, by following the outward path in the performance of virtuous activities. This is a life wherein you attempt to facilitate the ordering and arranging of the cosmos, the natural environment, your society, your social groups, your community, your family, and the many minds of your "soul." This endeavor is a fight, a struggle, against a landscape overrun with chaos, and you will never win. But in this struggle, there is still beauty to be had and value to be won.

We cannot know for certain if an afterlife exists, even if our more sober reflections on the state of mathematical and physical sciences suggest that such concepts are unlikely to be true. Still, reflecting on the afterlife might help us to lead our own lives better here on earth. And it was this notion that animated Socrates at the final book of the *Republic* to speak about a likely story, a myth that concerned a man name Er, who, according to the legend, died and returned to living to teach us all what was in store afterward.

The essential part of Er's story concerns Odysseus. It begins thus: After having lived for 1,000 years, all the souls who are worthy of returning to the earth are taken to a field, at the apex of the heavens, where they may each choose a daimon—a sort of fairy godmother, who will look after them in the next life. Each chooses according to their character and every soul must stand in line waiting until their number is called. The number they are given is assigned by chance—literally by the fates.

The first soul is lucky, but of bad character, so he chooses a daimon that will lead him to become a rich and powerful tyrant, but he fails to see the ways in which his life will also lead to tragedy, to his children's deaths and to his eventual betrayal. Being of bad character, he blames the fates rather than take responsibility for his lack of foresight. Other souls, having met tragic ends in their previous existence, opt for an animal's life instead. We are told that the soul of Ajax chose to return to life as a lion and that Agamemnon chose to return as an eagle. Odysseus is the last soul to choose, having the worst luck dealt by fate.

Yet, from memory of its former labors it had recovered from love of honor; it went around for a long time looking for the life of a private man who minds his own business; and with effort it found one lying somewhere, neglected by the others. It said when it saw this life that it would have done the same even if it had drawn the first lot, and was delighted to choose it.

Plato's *Republic* closes with this image. It is meant to inspire us to lead better lives, arguing that if we understand well how things are and live accordingly, with virtuous characters, that we can beat fate itself—leading a happy life in all circumstances.

The Aztecs would never have written such a tale. Their wisdom knows a deeper truth: No excellence can raise you past your fate, beyond the risk of slipping up, beyond the grasp of luck and pain. The mirror the Aztec sage holds up shows only what you are. She offers neither the promise of eternal life upon uncertain shores nor redemption for the trials of the earth.

I need not write another tale to answer Plato's myth. I've written it already, in countless forms, through many of the lessons we have shared. Shield Flower was not broken by capture. Emiliano Zapata was not wrong to try for democracy. Don Martín's worth was not diminished by the torture he endured. You would not be wrong to love your partner, even knowing they would die young. Nezahualpilli was not wrong to seek love with Jade Doll, though she betrayed him. Nezahualcoyotl was not undone by exile. And Chimalpahin lived well while bearing the weight of his people's history across the chasm of cultural oblivion.

We cannot defeat death nor master fate, but we might still fulfill our destiny in arranging and ordering, in making something beautiful of ourselves, our families, our communities, and our natural environment. This performance, brief and fragile, will stand, a value uncorrupted by death, undiminished by time.

POSTFACE

An old philosophic practice has it that a "preface" is to be distinguished from an "introduction" insofar as the former succinctly summarizes the contents of the book and the latter begins the explanation itself. This is the purpose that G. F. W. Hegel had in mind with his Preface to the *Phenomenology of Spirit*, and W. V. O. Quine still supported it in the mid-twentieth century in his *Set Theory and Its Logic*. Though a useful practice, even those within philosophy now hardly recognize it. Rather than attempt to resurrect it, which is likely to invite confusion, I have decided to mold a postface into serving this role. The first chapter of this book, Lesson 1, serves as the introduction.

This book is intended for a public audience, and success for such an aim means that I've helped you live better. By summarizing the book's statements here, I also aim to help you navigate the contents. For those of you who are researchers engaging with the diverse disciplines this book touches on—anthropology, history, linguistics, social psychology, and various branches of philosophy—my secondary goal is to clarify the approach I've taken, so we can engage more productively in academic discussions. I leave the detailed debates to the scholarly journals, as many of the arguments presented here are abridged.

Please note that this section contains few references, as the supporting evidence has already been provided throughout the book. What follows is primarily a series of summaries that highlight the core arguments. Let's begin with the meta-philosophy that underpins this work.

LIKE MANY Indigenous peoples, the Aztecs have been largely ignored by professional philosophers and silenced in broader public discourse. The academic "decolonial" movement seeks to address these epistemic and ethical injustices. I think that a decolonial metaphilosophy is crucial for the proper reconstruction and revival of their historical views. This approach requires an epistemology—a framework for understanding knowledge and its justification—that I term "soft realism." It is a "realism" in recognizing that there are objective truths at stake, but "soft" in acknowledging that historical and philosophical inquiry is less likely to produce consensus when compared with fields such as logic or mathematics—and even there, significant divergences occur. A reasonable pluralism of views follows, but I think that our conversations can engage productively if they are guided by four cognitive values: (1) holistic coherence, (2) groundedness, (3) fruitfulness, and (4) accommodation.

Even for a philosopher whose work is as well-documented as Aristotle, textual gaps exist that cannot be cured without recourse to holistic considerations, that is, to considerations of overall coherence. C. D. C. Reeve puts the point succinctly:

> An Aristotelian text often admits of multiple interpretations. Consequentially, holism soon becomes a reader's default position. His art becomes one of assemblage—of selecting supporting texts in such a way that collectively they all but interpret themselves.

The needs that motivate Aristotelian holism are felt ever more strongly with Aztec philosophy. My work develops what might be called the tradition of Mesoamerican Humanism. While this has never been a fully self-conscious school, notable scholars include Ángel María Garibay K., Miguel León-Portilla, and Librado Silva Galeana in the Hispanophone world, as well as Jacques Soustelle and Michel Launey among Francophone scholars. The core of this sensibility is that one prominent strand of Aztec philosophy resonates with scholasticism but diverges enough to be considered dangerous by sixteenth- and seventeenth-century clergymen.

Two key areas highlight these differences: metaphysics and ethics. Metaphysics, the branch of philosophy concerned with the nature of reality, was central to Aztec thought, as it was to Aristotle (with his concept of *ousia*, beingness) and Aquinas (with *esse*, to be). However, the Aztec conception of *teotl*—the fundamental force or principle behind reality—bears a closer resemblance to the "troubling" pantheism of Spinoza, where "god" is synonymous with "nature."

As for ethics, the Aztecs developed a type of virtue ethics that received some praise from early clergy, yet it diverged sharply from "Western" traditions. Unlike Aristotle or Aquinas, who positioned "happiness" as the ultimate good in human life, the Aztecs prioritized a different goal. They spoke of something akin to order and balance, variously described as standing on one's feet or (in English) being rooted. Their virtues, too, had distinct formal characteristics and content, and were markedly different from their scholastic counterparts.

While holistic considerations help guide how we approach texts and assess their relevance, all interpretations should ultimately be grounded in evidence—which is not to say that what counts as evidence will go uncontested. This is our second cognitive value. Ideally, this evidence should be drawn from multiple sources and withstand scrutiny for logical coherence. Additionally, interpretations should be approached with charity, meaning that they should align, as far as possible, with our present scientific understandings and humanly shared common sense. Attributing implausible or foolhardy views to ancient peoples, when other reasonable interpretations are available, risks perpetuating the colonial silencing that has persisted for centuries.

Third, any philosophical reconstruction of an ancient culture's thought should serve contemporary philosophical purposes. In other words, it should engage with questions and problems that philosophers consider significant. If Aztec philosophy prompts us to reevaluate a deeply entrenched philosophical problem, that too is a sign of its fruitfulness. This criterion ensures that no position is dismissed outright; only those that fail to contribute meaningfully to philosophical inquiry are set aside.

Finally, if two or more interpretations emerge that seem to be in competition, the one that accommodates more evidence and proves more philosophically fruitful should be regarded as the superior approach. If one approach, for example, insists that certain words are merely emphatic, while another approach finds a way to make sense of those words as meaningful, then the latter approach is on better grounds because it accommodates a broader range of evidence. It's worth noting, however, that the Aztecs likely had multiple philosophical schools, and what I reconstruct here is but one perspective. Other interpretations may well coexist peacefully with the one I advance. With this broader framework in mind, let's turn to the more specific formulations at the heart of Mesoamerican Humanism.

AS I SEE IT, Mesoamerican Humanism is built around six key principles. The first is that the approach to studying the Aztecs should not differ from the methods used to study classical Greek or Roman antiquity—unless there is a clear reason to justify such a divergence. It is baffling to me that some scholars publish work in this field with only a superficial understanding of the language.

Second, syncretic materials should be treated as legitimate subjects of reflection, each considered on its own terms. For example, Aristotle's *Nicomachean Ethics* and *Eudemian Ethics* share many overlapping chapters, yet scholars don't feel compelled to merge the arguments or translations between the two unless their research specifically requires it. Similarly, although the *Magna Moralia* is likely not Aristotle's work, it remains worthy of consideration for constructing a holistic interpretation.

These points lead to the third tenet of Mesoamerican Humanism: It places a strong emphasis on textual evidence when assessing Aztec philosophy. This approach is not suitable for all Indigenous peoples, and methodologies that prioritize artifacts or oral traditions may reach conclusions that differ significantly from those I advance. The "soft realist" approach embraces these potential divergences.

Fourth, Mesoamerican Humanism recognizes that language influences thought but does not strictly determine it, especially in philosophical matters. Aristotle wasn't merely "reading off" his metaphysical views from the structure of Greek grammar, though his analysis of being was likely facilitated by the language. Among the Aztecs, Lockhart distinguishes between what he calls Stage 1 (precontact), Stage 2 (minor adjustment after contact), and Stage 3 (grammatically altered Nahuatl) forms of Nahuatl. He does this by reflecting how the language evolved under colonialism and European influence. Most of the texts of interest to philosophers date from Stage 2, and while some linguistic shifts are evident, they are not as pronounced as in Stage 3. Therefore, a Mesoamerican Humanist must be cautious when mixing evidence from different linguistic periods, as philosophical works after 1640 are likely quite distinct from earlier ones.

Fifth, this tradition accepts that Ixtlilxochitl's colonial-era histories are valuable for philosophical inquiry, as well as some select historical purposes. Without Ixtlilxochitl's histories, there would be little evidence to support the legend of Nezahualcoyotl. But just as philosophers take Lao Tzu's *Tao Te Ching* seriously, despite the legendary aspects of his life, the supposed writings of Nezahualcoyotl may also possess philosophical consistency worth exploring. Even if these works reflect a postconquest "mestizo" tradition, they still hold potential for philosophical insight. This book only uses Nezahualcoyotl's legend, and other legends from Ixtlilxochitl, insofar as they support the philosophical outlook articulated here.

Finally, Mesoamerican Humanists regard the *tlamatinime* (plural of *tlamatini*) as "philosophers." Though Pythagoras coined the term "philosophy" in the "Western" tradition, most modern practitioners do not strictly adhere to his definition. Given the honorific status of philosophy, and the tendency to view cultures without it as "less developed," it's important to adopt a broad interpretation of the term. By calling the *"tlamatinime"* philosophers, I mean only that they engaged in reasoned reflection about humans and the natural world in pursuit of a better life. I do not imply that they formed a distinct class of professional philosophers, separate from their roles as priests—just as we don't exclude figures such as Augustine or Thomas Aquinas from the philosophical canon. Nor do I suggest that these people self-consciously understood their role as philosopher to be different from that of other knowledge workers such as doctors or lawyers, for then Thales, Heraclitus, and Parmenides would also not count as philosophers.

While more needs to be said about metaphilosophy and the Aztecs, we have enough to begin developing a more detailed account of the Aztec philosophy itself, beginning with their discussion of "being."

IN *AZTEC PHILOSOPHY*, James Maffie argues that *teotl* is the closest concept we have to a "basic" notion of reality in Nahua thought.

Unlike "Western" metaphysics, which often revolves around the idea of "being," Aztec metaphysics operates differently. Building on Maffie's work, I introduce findings from linguistic scholars that deepen our understanding of this difference.

First, linguists Richard Andrews and Michel Launey, working independently, discovered that Nahuatl doesn't use individual "words" in the way that English or other "Western" languages do. Instead, Nahuatl is structured around what Andrews calls "nuclear clauses" and Launey refers to as "predicates." A key example is the Nahuatl word *michin*, often translated as "it is a fish." However, this translation reflects the way English speakers think, not the way Nahuatl works. In English, we need to add "it is," but Nahuatl has no such requirement. Andrews compares this to how English speakers wrongly describe languages such as Spanish as "pro-drop"—implying that Spanish "drops" pronouns when they aren't needed. In reality, Spanish simply doesn't require a pronoun like "they" in the phrase *cantan* (which we translate as "they sing"), just as Nahuatl doesn't need "it is" before *michin*.

Launey builds on this by asking whether Nahuatl's grammar is truly unique. He argues that it is, at least to some extent. While other languages, such as Russian, also lack copular phrases (like "it is"), Nahuatl stands apart because it possesses a set of additional grammatical features that Launey identifies. He lists ten such features, and if a language has no copula and a significant number of these features, it can be classified as "omnipredicative."

This system of classification offers a range of possibilities. One language may exhibit only two such properties while another language could, conceivably, exhibit all of them. We can call languages that exhibit only two or three such properties "weakly omnipredicative" and those that exhibit all of them "maximally omnipredicative." Russian *may* be an example of a weakly omnipredicative language. Nahuatl, Launey argues, exhibits all such properties so that it is maximally omnipredicative.

This means that Nahuatl gets along just fine without a notion of "being" as it functions in English or ancient Greek. The term *teotl* thus operates in a grammatical domain quite different from Quine's discussion on "being" in "On What There Is" or Aristotle's discussions of *ousia* (beingness). If ontology is the study of what there "is" in the wake of Aristotle (in favor or against his view), then Aztec philosophy charts a conceptual course that is altogether diagonal to that discussion. The texts we have available to us exhibit no sense of "being" in the relevant philosophical sense—from the point of view of the Nahua speaker. Theirs is thus a metaphysics but not an ontology. Now that we have these rather abstract, metaphysical points outlined, let's move to Aztec ethics in a way that draws from them. And to recall, my purpose here is to summarize the key philosophical points that the book itself makes, in a nutshelled way. The justification for them is made in the book's main text.

AZTEC ETHICS is a kind of philosophical "pessimism." That doesn't mean the Aztecs ruminated about negative thoughts or held that only bad things would happen. It means that they tried to focus on the world, as accurately as they could, to better understand how to take the next step. I imagine that their first lesson for our culture would be that you're not really after happiness, you just think that you are. If that's true, and let's suppose that it is for the moment, then you are prompted to ask, "Well then, what are we after?" Philosophical pessimism focuses on uncomfortable truths so that we can figure out what our next steps should be.

Similar to the legends of Ragnarök in Norse mythology, the Aztecs held that our cosmos would come to an end. They retell this ending in the Legend of the Suns. A "sun" for the Aztecs was more than a physical body in the sky. It represented a total cosmological order. They held that prior to our sun, there were four other suns, each of which had "humans" of a sort. The myths state that those suns had different types of motion than our sun does and their "humans" dined on different sorts of "food" than we do—implying that their basic source of physical embodiment was different from ours. Our fifth sun is the sun of wavelike motion, and our humans dine on corn as their primary source of sustenance. Just as the previous suns and previous peoples perished, so the Aztecs held that our sun and our people would perish.

They held this pessimistic view for metaphysical, cosmological, psychological, and ethical reasons. The metaphysical reasons that support Aztec pessimism turn on their discussion of "matching" relations (*inamichuan*). They held that these organized the world but had no totally predictable order. By implication, they took reality to be unfinished, after a point. To use a modern example, when you "zoom in" on a photograph too far, you get nothing but blurry pixels. Likewise, the Aztecs thought that when you try to describe reality with progressive precision you end up with "blurriness." For example, there is now an entire industry devoted to helping foreigners climb Mt. Everest so that they can take photos of having scaled the highest point on earth. Yet if you asked anyone where exactly Mt. Everest begins—which rocks or earth formations mark its starting point definitively—none could answer. The boundary is vague, and that vagueness just is part of Mt. Everest. It is in this sense that the Aztecs held that there is no way that things are.

Because there is no (total) way that things are, there are no principles that could govern the totality of our cosmos and ensure that its organization lasts eternally. Rather, the principles are bound to establish perishable orders. One sun will rise because of its unique principle of organization, such as wavelike motion, and that principle will in turn be the source of its decline, making way for another sun. This cosmological reason for "pessimism" is mirrored in our human psychology.

The Aztecs believed that the human mind wasn't a single, unified entity. Instead, it was made up of smaller, semi-independent "minds" or centers of thought. This is similar to what modern philosophers call the modularity of mind. You might have experienced this when you've driven to work on "autopilot," only becoming aware of where you are once you pull into the parking lot. One part of your mind was paying attention to the road, while another was focused on the music you were listening to. Psychologists call this "goal-directed automaticity," and it's possible because we don't have just one centralized decision-making process. This also explains why we sometimes act in ways that seem irrational or thoughtless, like missing an exit or blurting something out without thinking. Just as there's no guarantee of a permanent order in the cosmos, there's no guarantee that our minds will stay organized and coherent all the time. There are principles for organizing it, however, and these make up the subject matter of Aztec ethics.

Given that reality is unfinished, that the cosmos is perishable, and that there is no guarantee that our many "minds" will organize themselves appropriately, the Aztecs thought that the best we could do, that our best method to avoid slipping up, was to learn to gain support from our friends and family, from our communities, our cities, our nations, and our natural environments. We should learn to grow "deep roots" in these areas, learn to stand on our feet, and live in the truth. They held that this was our best pragmatic option and that it outlined the conditions for living a human life—one led in human society, unlike the lives of wild animals, such as deer and rabbits.

They also knew that this outward path was a fragile venture, that it exposed us to the further risk that our closest friends and most cherished family could fail us, and that we could fail them too. They knew that in some cases either luck or misfortune could be the source of ruin. For example, I know someone who won a state lottery, but instead of bringing happiness, the sudden wealth ruined his relationships. Another friend was happily married and had a child, but when that child tragically passed away, the couple couldn't recover and eventually divorced. In both cases, the same principles that helped these individuals build their lives also became the source of their downfall—just as the cosmic principle that causes a sun to rise is also the cause of its collapse. These are the ethical reasons behind Aztec "pessimism."

If the Aztecs were right—and I provide evidence in this book for their psychological and ethical claims—then luck and misfortune are permanent and pervasive features of human life. They're permanent because there's no way to live as a human and avoid them, and they're pervasive because they affect even our most important life plans and our very sense of goodness. But the Aztecs didn't reflect on these truths to feel despair. Instead, they used these insights to help guide their next steps. Even if we can't control everything and our best efforts depend on some degree of luck, the Aztecs nevertheless thought that there was beauty and goodness to be achieved in our struggles.

PHILOSOPHERS OFTEN describe "the good" as the ultimate goal or goals that guide our actions in life. Some, like G. E. Moore in the twentieth century, have argued that there are things that are "absolutely good," meaning they are not good for someone or good in a particular way, but good, full stop. Plato appears to have suggested this in some of his works as well. I do not believe, however, that the Aztecs held this view, partly as a consequence of their metaphysical outlook.

They held that certain things were worth pursuing as human beings given our specific circumstances on the "slippery earth." This involved ordering and arranging, learning to live with others to avoid falling, to live in the truth. As part of the tradition of scholarship I'm developing, I've decided to use the Nahuatl term *neltiliztli* (truth) to cover this constellation of concepts. In English, I think the best conceptual translation is "rootedness."

This idea of a relative good—something that guides our lives but is not absolute—contrasts with how the Aztecs approached the notion of right action. If we ask whether it's permissible to kill another person or harm the natural environment, we're focusing on what's morally right. The Aztecs discussed right action in terms of "the mean," which refers to finding a balance between too much and too little. Some have misunderstood this as promoting moderation, but what the Aztecs were really getting at was the need to consider the appropriateness of an action in its specific situation—taking into account all the relevant factors.

These distinctions, between absolute and relative goodness, and between the good and the right, do not yet settle whether the Aztecs were deontologists, consequentialists, or virtue ethicists. I think they were the last of these, and that position determines, in a holistic way, how certain terms ought to be translated into English.

BECAUSE THE philosophical study of the Aztecs is nascent, philosophers must strive to translate terms from a foreign language and fit them into a conceptual map that is fraught with its own peculiar history. The English "virtue" derives from the Latin *virtus*, which is derived from the Latin word *vir* or "man." In Latin, *virtus* is a kind of "manliness." This is how Roman translators of Greek philosophers, such as Plato and Aristotle, thought they should treat the Greek term *aretē*, which is typically rendered "excellence" in English. The mismatch of terms is confusing. What the Greek authors meant to identify were those desirable qualities of character that constituted the achievement of a good life when you performed them. The Roman authors used manliness as a metaphorical stand-in for that notion.

To claim that anything the Aztecs wrote has something to do with this peculiar thread of (mis)translation in the "West" is puzzling. What could possibly warrant this identification? The answer is that our philosophical goal is to translate terms into their appropriate conceptual terrains, not merely to match words from dictionaries. One way to conceptually translate is to identify whether terms in one conceptual terrain serve a similar purpose as terms in another. It is this approach that has led me to conclude that Aztec ethical philosophy—at least the one strand I develop in this book—is a virtue ethics.

Deontological ethics seeks to constrain our pursuit of the good, however we conceive that, by way of an appeal to a conception of right action that is logically prior to the good. For Immanuel Kant, the most famous proponent of a modern form of deontology, this requires that you submit your intended action to a thought experiment to determine whether it is permissible. Not only does the existing literature of Aztec ethics lack any such thought experiment, an equivalent of Kant's tests for universality, the evidence we do have instead commends the pursuit of the good directly. A father tells his son, for example:

> Take care of worldly things. Work, labor, gather wood, till the ground, sow cactuses, plant magueys. It is from that which you will drink, eat, dress. With that it is enough for you to stand, for you to live.

The father does not first ask his son to ensure that his actions are morally right; rather, he directly encourages the pursuit of the good. This suggests that Aztec ethics prioritize the good over the right, meaning their ethics are not deontological.

Could Aztec ethics be consequentialist? Consequentialism focuses on maximizing positive outcomes, often defined as pleasure. What separates consequentialism from virtue ethics is that it focuses entirely on external reasons for action—reasons based on the outcomes of actions rather than the motivations of the person acting. Yet not only do the existing texts lack any exhortations to maximize outcomes, but they also appeal to mixed reasoning. In describing the man who does not follow the path, the father not only argues that such a person comes to destruction (a consequence) but also that "he made himself a rabbit, he made himself a deer." This means that he failed to meet the conditions necessary to live a human life. Stated differently, the reasons a person has to follow the outward path are those that enable them to live a human life, whatever other (external) consequences follow. The Aztecs appear to have accepted both sorts of reasoning (internal and external) and are thus not advancing a consequentialist ethics.

The challenge with virtue ethics is that it forms a quite broad category. It includes Aristotle and Confucius, but also Machiavelli and Nietzsche. This poses conceptual puzzles. Whether *de* (power) in Confucian philosophy ought to be treated as "virtue" tends to meet difficulties precisely because the "virtue ethics" camp is so broad. Aristotle's virtues are character based while Confucius finds an additional role for ritual (*li*) in fostering them. Nietzsche, as Swanton develops his position, advances a virtue ethics that could avoid character discussion altogether. Is there anything else one can say that's meaningful about virtue ethics, and where do the Aztecs occupy a place in the (quite) broad tent?

At its core, virtue ethics distinguishes between "the good" and "virtue," though they are closely related. Virtues constitute the good largely by way of its performance. To explain this, we can distinguish between two types of actions: productive and performative. A potter makes a pot—this is a productive action because the pot exists as a product outside the action itself. But when a dancer performs a dance, the action itself is the goal—nothing remains afterward. Virtue is like the dance: It constitutes the good through its performance.

Consider going on holiday. If you enjoy golf, and you play golf during your holiday, the act of golfing constitutes your enjoyment. Similarly, virtues are actions that constitute the good as they are performed. Your life, then, is a continuous series of these performances. It is this relationship that I take to be at work between statements of "virtue" (*qualli*, *yectli*) in Aztec philosophy and statements about the good—ordering and arranging, standing on your feet, taking root in a community, and the like. My approach, moreover, adds layers of insight where other scholars see only intensifiers—that is, words used for emphasis. And to recall our metaphilosophical framework, this makes it more accommodating. As for where the Aztecs stand in this broad tent called "virtue ethics," I think one of the more interesting features is that they have an approach that is even less character centered than Confucius, giving a role to ritual in the constitution of virtues, but not totally absent a notion of character as one finds in Nietzsche. To elaborate, we need some new concepts.

THE AZTECS teach that you are not after happiness, and you are not after invulnerability. Instead, you are after a meaningful and worthwhile life, a rooted life, wherein you cultivate strong relationships. The outward path is the "how" of that pursuit. The specifics involve a discussion of terms that are dangerous because we need to use "Western," modern words to describe them, and we will be tempted to think that we understand what they mean. The Aztecs' use of these terms, however, draws on a reservoir of concepts that transform their meaning. Principal among these are a philosophical sense of "habits," "shared agency," and "rituals."

A person may have a habit of mindlessly twirling their hair, or of goal-directed automaticity in driving to work, or of being courageous in standing up for what's right. The philosophical problem consists in spelling out how the last case (standing up) matters for ethics but the first two (under most circumstances) do not. The Aztec approach is to tie habits to what we would call expressions of value. A habit of twirling your hair probably isn't an expression of value, so it's not going to count as an ethical habit, even if it is a psychological one.

The Aztecs thought that ethical habits were ideally exercised with the help of other competent people. In philosophical terms, we act best through "shared agency." If you find yourself in Times

Square of New York City and you are walking with another person to a Broadway show, your stroll is an act of shared agency. The other people walking around you are not part of that stroll and so you share no agency with them—they are mere passersby. You have shared agency when you are thinking of your activity in the plural: "We are strolling." For the Aztecs, your ethical actions ideally happen this way, and this strong social component distinguishes their philosophy from other ethical philosophies.

Shared agency also introduces a practical problem: How do you coordinate the activities of all the group members? The conductor of an orchestra uses her baton to coordinate the players. The Aztecs used "rituals" for this purpose. Having spent twelve years in Catholic education, I tend to associate "rituals" with religious practices, and indeed, the Aztecs viewed them this way as well. But for them, rituals also served an ethical function, ensuring that the actions of the group were harmonized and that shared agency could unfold smoothly.

These concepts, from habits to ritual, help us understand what is different about the Aztec approach to virtue ethics. Among "Western" philosophers it is Aristotle who most notably develops a virtue ethical framework. "Virtue" is an excellent quality of a person's character, and he thought the most important such quality was prudence, which is wisdom in practical affairs. If you are a person of practical wisdom, he reasoned that you would know when courage required you to fight and when to run away. With practical wisdom you would know how much you could indulge in your favorite foods or when you should be more moderate. And if you were prudent, you would know when you are acting fairly and how to make up for mistakes. The human ideal for excellence, "virtue" in the philosophical sense, is thus a single wise individual.

The Aztecs instead thought that the ideal for human excellence was a person of practical wisdom who worked well in a practically wise group. Prudent people deliberate well in groups, and this shared activity is structured by rituals to ensure that all can participate as appropriate. No one human person will ever be in a position to know everything that wisdom requires, and this means that prudence requires the humility to accept that you do not know something or have reasoned poorly. Friendship, for similar reasons, enters as a virtue needed to act well in our groups. And the remaining virtues—courage, moderation, and justice—are by turns suffused with the dynamics of group agency.

These points complete the ethical framework I have drawn from the Aztec texts. I have tried to ensure that my analyses align with the metaphilosophical criteria I've outlined in this Postface and for that reason can serve philosophical scholarship productively. But my main hope is that this work will help readers live better lives, as this—whether in the case of the Aztecs or any other tradition—is the ultimate purpose of ethical study.

ACKNOWLEDGMENTS

A book like this one does not emerge quickly or by dint of an individual's effort. It emerged only through the help of many supporters for the idea that animates it. Early supporters include Sally Davies, at Aeon, who first reached out to me to publish essays on Aztec philosophy for public audiences. The BBC World, including Ana Pais and Laura García, later covered my work and agreed to include it in ongoing video segments. Esmond Harmsworth saw a practical and literary gap that this could fill and bet his time and reputation to support it.

 Among the philosophical contributors to the book, I must thank James Maffie for clearing a path before me in the field of Aztec philosophy, and for drawing my attention to the ways in which anthropologists and historians have conceived differently of the ethical domain. I owe additional thanks to Alejandro Santana, who both encouraged my research in the beginning, and who gently clarified the differences between the Aztecs and Aristotle on a range of topics. Thanks are also in order to Peter Adamson whose honesty about my initial account of shared agency forced me to rethink the topic, making it significantly better, and to Daniel Haybron for indicating the way in which my work would rather surprisingly connect with recent ethical research on group deliberation. Ian James Kidd and Sergio Gallegos both probed me along the way about the categories used to describe Aztec ethics, convincing me that they (the Aztecs) support a kind of pessimism. I owe special thanks to ongoing discussions with Alexus McLeod on collective virtues in Confucian thought, and for discussions about Mayan philosophy. Stephanie Rivera-Berruz and Leah Kalmanson helped this work by diligently commenting on an earlier formulation of the doctrine of the double mean in Aztec philosophy. In this vein I must also thank Agnes Curry and Andrea Sullivan-Clarke for facilitating the development of my first ventures into the Aztecs' views of our cosmos. Sofia Ortiz-Hinojosa has long been a friend in this emerging field, commenting in private and public sessions on most facets of my research that has appeared in print. My research is better for those comments in uncountable ways. A final scholarly thank you goes to a few of my fellow Nahuatleros, who helped in assessing my translations of difficult passages, or in finding crucial textual evidence. This group includes the late Miguel León-Portilla and David Bowles.

There are many more who supported my work academically, but I must thank numerous members who supported the broader development of the project. Andrew Fitz-Gibbons, Mecke Nagle, and Nikolay Karkov who supported this research in a department of philosophy. Unlike almost any other department in our nation would, they arranged to grant me the time needed to get it done. Alane Mason, Mo Crist, and YJ Wang at W. W. Norton helped guide this work from a bundle of scholarly ideas into something a public audience would want to read.

Una gracias sinceramente a mi familia. Thank you especially to Jeff and Nora Purcell, Hugo Rangel Roman, and Hugo Rangel Vargas who were willing to accompany me as I trekked back to Tenochtitlán and other archaeological sites while I conducted my research. Thank you also in helping me to find several texts that proved difficult to locate, without which this book would have suffered substantially.

Finally, I must thank my wife and fellow philosopher, Elyse Purcell, who not only supported me through the process emotionally, but also actively contributed to its development. Thank you for gently inquiring further about several of my inchoate ideas, a few of which I retained out of stubbornness. Thank you also for your own invaluable research on relational virtues, which proved to be the final critical component in my study of Nahua ethical philosophy.

APPENDIX I

WHAT'S IN A NAME (AND HOW DO I PRONOUNCE IT)?

Nahuatl has no standard orthography. This means that the same words may be spelled differently, even in the same work (and this is especially true of the *Florentine Codex*, which was written by four different informants, and later amended by Bernadino de Sahagún, a Franciscan friar, priest, and ethnographer).

To enable the reader who has no Nahuatl knowledge (which is almost everyone) to more easily identify the original terms, this book has preserved the form of the quoted text for analysis. Those equipped with Nahuatl, of course, will have no difficulties whether a standard orthography is chosen or not. As an example of the orthography used in the study, consider the term for "good," which is written both as *quall* and *cualli*. If at one point a quoted text uses *qualli*, then the discussion to follow will spell the term in that way. If later, another text were to use *cualli*, then in the discussion that immediately follows the term, it would be spelled in that way.

What follows is a list of standard orthographic variants, indicating which morphemes are equivalent, and which are merely treated equivalently.

i, y, j	These are equivalent and used without difference. They have the sound of an "i" whether short or long.
v and u	These are also equivalent and sound like a short "u."
o and u	These are also used interchangeably, but their sound may vary: short "o," "y," or "u."
s and x	These are equivalent and have the sound of "sh" in English.
ç	This sounds like a "z" or a "c" when it comes before an "e" or an "i" respectively.
ya, yia	These are transcribed as equivalent, but they are pronounced differently, just as they sound.
oa, oua	These are transcribed equivalently, but they are pronounced differently, as one might expect.
ll	This is pronounced as a double "l" in English.
tl	This is a single phoneme, pronounced by holding one's tongue at one's teeth and blowing air slightly out the side of one's mouth.

tz	This is a single phoneme, and one should pronounce both consonants.
/k/	This morpheme appears as either "c," if not following a consonant, or as "qui" if following a consonant. The reason is that Nahuatl prohibits more than two consecutive consonants.

Additionally, one should bear in mind that spellings vary quite widely, either due to transcription errors, or because some letters are not standardly recorded. As an example of the last case, a "y" often will not be included in the spelling of a term if near an "a." The word *piya*, then, which means "to guard," is often transcribed *pia*.

Finally, and this is especially important for an Anglophone audience, what's the best way to handle the "tl" endings that are ubiquitous in Nahuatl? The easiest course for anyone who is not going to practice pressing their tongue against their teeth and blowing air out the side of their mouth is to ignore the "l." The term *teotl* is best pronounced TAY-ot, and not TAY-ō-tol. Simply dropping the "l" comes much closer to the Nahuatl pronunciation and remains entirely within a native English speaker's wheelhouse of phonetic competence.

APPENDIX II

ARE ALL THE VIRTUES ONE?

My argument in this book is relatively straightforward. I contend that a prominent strand of Aztec philosophy, when suitably reconstructed, not only offers us a better way to live, a set of "spiritual exercises" that we can use in our daily lives, but also a better ethical framework for thinking about our lives and our relationships to others. I advance the argument that the Aztecs' "outward path" is relatively superior to other virtue ethical articulations, such as Aristotle's, in its fuller account of how those virtues operate. Yet, for the Aztec framework to rival one such as his, it must be different at a more fundamental level. How do we best understand that difference?

In contrast with familiar "Western" (Aristotle) and Eastern (Confucius) flavors of virtue ethics, the Aztec view is more socially centered. The Aztecs had a conception of the virtues that operate by way of shared agency and knew that rituals play the ethical role of coordinating these group actions. You may witness the difference shared agency makes in virtues of relation, which include those needed to sustain friendship and love, and in virtues of plural groups, which include temperance and practical wisdom (prudence). Unlike Aristotle or Confucius, the Aztecs held that the paradigm case of practical wisdom is deliberation in good groups. Now, if practical wisdom is carried out by way of shared agency, *and* practical wisdom is part of all the virtues, then every feature of Aztec virtue ethics is infused with that socially centered dimension. In Lesson 8, we surveyed the evidence that practical wisdom for the Aztecs is indeed conceived to function best in groups. We even found scientific evidence to support this view.

The key claim of this book (regarding ethical theory) thus rests on a "unity of virtues" thesis, namely that practical wisdom, so conceived, is indeed part of all the virtues. I gave several examples of this, but not an explicit argument. I've also left the exact character of this "unity of virtues" thesis unclear.

The purpose of this appendix is to clarify what is meant by "unity of virtues," since it is not used uniformly among philosophers. My position is that implicit in the Aztecs' statements on ethics is a set of logical relationships that entail support for the view that the virtues are reciprocally supporting. That notion is a special form of the unity of virtues thesis, and it is worth disambiguating their view from similar "Western" theses.

In ancient Greece, Socrates appears to have defended a stronger unity of virtues thesis than the one the Aztecs held. He defended a view in which there is only one virtue, namely practical wisdom, and that the supposed others are but facets of it. Aristotle explicitly rejects this view, and his reasons follow from his understanding of the virtues themselves. Since some virtues involve emotions and desires, while others constitute exercises of practical intelligence, they cannot all be of the same variety. Because the virtues, according to the Aztecs' conception, also have more than one basis for operation, including the intellectual, affective, and socially coordinated, they too are committed to the rejection of Socratic unity.

What is at stake, then, is a weaker claim of the unity of virtues thesis, namely that they are reciprocally entailed. Aristotle puts the matter as follows.

And so, it is clear from what we have said that we cannot be good in a global sense without practical wisdom, nor practically wise without the virtues of character.

Moreover, following this line of reasoning we might also meet a dialectical argument that someone could use to claim that the virtues exist in isolation from one another. For the same person [the dialectical argument goes] is not best suited by nature for all [the virtues], and as a result he will already have acquired one virtue when he has not yet acquired another. This could happen with the natural virtues, but with those where one is called good simply, it is not possible; for each of the virtues will be present at the same time one virtue, practical wisdom, is present.

In so many words, this means that for anyone to possess practical wisdom (*phronēsis* / fro-NAY-sis), they must also possess the other virtues of character. The reverse also holds (logicians love biconditionals), namely that to possess the other virtues of character, not as natural virtues but as real ones, a person must also possess *phronēsis*.

There are two important ethical claims here, both of which require evidence. Let's start with the way in which practical wisdom (*phronēsis*) requires the other virtues. Aristotle's reasoning posits that *phronēsis* requires the other virtues because the possession of the virtues of character enable you to discern the right goal for your life. You might have good strategic reasoning, but unless you also have a sense of courage, temperance, and justice, there is not a lot to keep you from scheming to live well by defrauding others. The other reason *phronēsis* requires the other virtues turns on the way that it is the only virtue that is global in scope. The scope is global because *phronēsis* aims to coordinate your actions through your complete life. This global quality means that only practical wisdom facilitates the achievement of the good life, and not this nor that more specific end. If practical wisdom did not have this global scope, then, for example, it might enable an agent to act generously with money that has been already promised elsewhere to repay a debt. At the same time, practical wisdom is rather empty without those more specific contexts, such as aiming to be responsible and pay back one's debts.

Aristotle's arguments explicitly work to distinguish his reciprocity of virtues thesis from the single virtue thesis that Socrates appears to have held. The depth of detail in Aristotle's account helps us recognize how similar reasons hold in the Aztecs' case, since the exercise of practical deliberation presumes that agents have been brought up well, and the globality requirement is a logical implication for any agent's coherent pursuit of the good life. Yet the Aztecs' view adds an additional dimension to the scope of practical wisdom. For in their line of reasoning, none can perform the virtues without a clear sense of one's appropriate social role and pertinent social rituals. The relational entailment at work in Aristotle's thesis is thus extended further in scope for the Aztec understanding of virtue ethics.

Turning to the reciprocal argument, that is, that all the other virtues (of character) require practical wisdom, Aristotle provides two reasons to suppose that it is true. The first turns on the reasoning at work in the quoted text just provided, which distinguishes between natural and "real" virtues. Natural virtues are those that Aristotle recognizes we have from birth. We note that some people are, for example, more generous or more brave by nature, while others are less so. The difficulty with these character traits, Aristotle notes, is that unless they are tutored by practical wisdom, they are apt to be misused or to appear only intermittently. You might give money, for example, to a friend who will misuse it, or you might act with the mere feeling of bravery when fighting a battle for a country that has waged an unjust war. Aristotle's second line of reasoning is that practical wisdom discerns the mean for right action among the character virtues, discerning what is neither excessive nor deficient in the expression and realization of a feeling in action. This implies that the proper exercise of the other character virtues is defined in terms of practical wisdom. Stated differently, it is *phronēsis* that makes the reasons right.

The Aztecs' argument is not exactly parallel to Aristotle's. You won't find any passages in the surviving texts before the 1640 period where a distinction is drawn between natural and real virtues. Where you do encounter discussion of natural talents, you tend to find that the Aztecs viewed these as gifts to be used well. Like Aristotle, however, they did argue that practical wisdom enabled an agent to discern the mean, and so to avoid falling into an abyss. Thus, insofar as the other virtues are to be exercised at a mean (*tlacoqualli, tlanepantla*) of affection, and social expression, they too require practical wisdom. Moreover, the Aztecs held that it is practical wisdom that discerned what was apt for one's social role, as in what is right to wear, and how to partake in social rituals, as in what might be considered moderate drinking at a fiesta.

Though not exactly parallel, and not for the same reasons, the foregoing shows that both Aristotle and the Aztecs are committed to the reciprocity of virtues thesis. One reason some commentators, in Aristotle's case, have been hesitant to ascribe the thesis to him is that it might appear to make the achievement of the virtues impossible. Surely no one can possess all the virtues. How then, if the thesis is accurate, could a virtue ethics so conceived be action guiding?

The answer is revealed when we see that the worry conflates the reciprocity of virtues thesis, and what might be called the perfection of virtues thesis. This latter view holds that to possess all the virtues, one must do so completely or perfectly. If perfection were true, then Aristotle's position, and by extension the Aztecs', would face a serious challenge. Happily, there is no reason to identify these two claims. You may possess a virtue without possessing it completely, and Aristotle himself speaks of the acquisition of virtue itself as an activity that is scalar in character.

To sum up, the argument of this book advances the claim that practical wisdom is both (a) ideally instantiated in well-functioning group deliberation and (b) ingredient to every virtue. The former claim (a) distinguishes a rooted virtue ethics from Aristotle's or Confucius's sort. The latter claim (b) is shared, following suitable alterations, with Aristotle. Claim (b) amounts to asserting that the virtues are unified, are "one," insofar as they are reciprocally entailed. We have reason to think this is so and no absurdities immediately follow from that reasoning. This book's arguments rest on these claims, but with the observations presented here and what is covered in Lesson 8, they are defended. Almost nothing in philosophy is definitively settled, but you and I have worked enough now to shift the burden of proof onto the backs of those who would form objections.

APPENDIX III

BLOOD SACRIFICE

Shield Flower's story raises the one Aztec practice that almost any reader is guaranteed to have known about before cracking these pages: human sacrifice. This subject is complex and has been sensationalized for centuries, both for marketing purposes and for political legitimization. The latter has historically proven the most dangerous. If the Indigenous people were truly, as their Christian colonizers saw them, a demonic class of individuals who practiced homosexuality freely, ate human flesh, and engaged in human sacrifice on an unimaginable scale, then the Spaniards might have seemed morally justified in their otherwise indefensible aggression. These portrayals served to legitimize the Spaniards' actions, allowing them to destroy Indigenous culture by eradicating its written works and interrupting the transmission of its lessons. If accurate, perhaps such an epistemicide would have been seen as warranted.

I do not believe these people were the demons that Cortés and others suggested. This book is partly an effort at cultural restoration. For that process to occur, an extensive discussion about the broader practice of blood sacrifice, in which human sacrifice plays a part, while intellectually worthwhile, should be deemphasized in this context. It is too easily distorted and sensationalized. As a philosopher, I find that the practice does not constitute an essential feature of the Aztec ethical framework that this work covers. The book does not address many Aztec practices, such as the use of sweat baths to treat poisonous injury. These baths may have involved sexual intercourse, and so they also raise ethical questions. But they are equally unrelated to the ethical framework as I understand it, and that is why I did not treat them in the book. However, because the practice of blood sacrifice is sensational and widely known, I thought it prudent to address it at least in an appendix.

My aim is to explain why this set of practices, which have ethical dimensions, is distinct from the rooted virtue ethical framework discussed previously. I advance two related claims. The first holds that it is possible to conceptually articulate the ethical framework the Aztecs held in a way that is distinct from what they did. This means that, perhaps, they did not live up to their own best standards of ethical assessment. Philosophers typically treat historical figures in this way, so that contemporary Aristotelians reconstruct a form of his virtue ethics that provides grounds to criticize Aristotle for his sexism, and contemporary Kantians do likewise with his racism. The present work is, principally, a work of ethical philosophy, and I believe that the framework articulated provides ample resources for criticizing repugnant practices. My second claim holds that (at least some) Aztecs were less blameworthy than they might otherwise have been in their actions because they had a faulty understanding of the physical world. Let's begin with an intuitive analogy.

IF YOU'VE checked your phone today or dashed off an email, you have George Boole to thank (or blame if that's your persuasion). He was a nineteenth-century philosopher and mathematician who developed an algebraic logic that is now typically called Boolean algebra. This is the sort of logic that runs your phone's computer; it makes our light switches work and our televisions glow. He wasn't the only one to get us to this point, but his logic has proved indispensable for our modern, technological world. It's for this reason that he's often called the "father of computer science."

In November of 1864, he became ill with pneumonia, which people at the time said he caught after walking home in the rain. His wife, also a rigorous academic and intellectual, sought out the best care available to save his life. Reasoning that because cold and wet conditions led to his illness, she wrapped her husband in damp sheets as he developed severe bronchopneumonia—it was a treatment like therapeutic hypothermia. Of course, his illness was caused by an infection, so rather than help her husband, she worsened his condition. He died shortly after.

The question of philosophical interest for us is this: How much is Boole's wife to blame for his death?

My students typically state that she is not blameworthy at all. She did the best that she could, using the best medicine of her time. Comparatively, it was not that advanced, but it would appear ridiculous to blame someone from an age before penicillin was discovered for not having used it. Given our present understanding, we can say that she was (in part) responsible for his death, but not to blame for it.

In broaching the topic of blood sacrifice among the Aztecs, a similar point holds regarding their blameworthiness. At least some of them acted in accord with the best physical principles available to them. Those principles, like nearly all principles about the natural world before the modern period, were in error. But while responsible for their actions, they are not blameworthy—or at least not in the way that typically troubles people. Let's start with the appropriate context for this Aztec practice.

· · ·

BECAUSE HUMAN sacrifice is often sensationalized, heart sacrifice has largely crowded out the general framework in which it occurred. We need to take a step back, then, and place the practice within the broader role of blood sacrifice.

Blood itself, *eztli* (EZ-tlee), was linked to fertility in most Mesoamerican worldviews and was considered a valuable and vital substance. Most people, at some point in their lives, practiced some sort of ritual that included blood sacrifice. The *Florentine Codex* records four such activities:

- the drawing of straws,
- the offering of thorns,
- the bloodying, and
- the cutting of one's ears.

When drawing straws, a priest would pull a straw or twig through an earlobe to gather blood for an offering. In offering thorns, one would use maguey spines to prick oneself for blood. The "bloodying" is a broad category wherein, generally, a person would use obsidian to cut a part of their body for blood, especially the tongue. And finally, "the cutting of one's ears" obviously entailed cutting one's ears, likely with obsidian, for blood. None of these practices are very different from the ascetic practices that priests in the "West" have performed for centuries.

It is beyond these four activities that one finds what scholars call "heart sacrifice." It's an umbrella term that describes any blood sacrifice involving the death of a human being. The most sensational of these, and probably the one you know about, involves a person, usually a war captive, who walks up the steps of a temple after having been prepared for the ritual sacrifice. This preparation varied widely, and in some cases the captive might have been treated as a deity for a full year's time, serving as a "representative" for a god. Once at the top of the stairs, he would be spread and secured on a stone, and killed, most commonly by slitting the throat, though in some cases by slashing the breast. Then the heart would be removed and its vital force would be presented to the sun. Bodies would then be rolled down the temple's steps to spread their blood along the sacred hill.

In other cases, as in the worship of Xipe Totec (SHEE-pe TO-tek / Flayed Lord), heart sacrifice took on a different form. In one case, an adversary is tied to a frame and shot with arrows. His blood then dripped onto the ground, and so transmitted its vital force in that way.

The scale of heart sacrifice seems to have varied quite widely over existing records. Under the temple of Quetzalcoatl at Teotihuacán, near Mexico City, which enjoyed its apex of power during the 1100s CE, excavation teams found about 400 sacrificial bodies. By the time the Spaniards arrived at Tenochtitlán in 1519, the bodies would have numbered in the thousands. One generally accepted reason for this increase was that the so-called "flowery war" practice required more sacrifices. This practice was a military compromise between the "Aztec empire" (the main cities allied with Tenochtitlán) and the Tlaxcalan people. Since neither side was able to subdue the other militarily, they staged ceremonial battles and sacrificed the victims.

But there weren't only military reasons for heart sacrifice. The most obvious explanation derives from the broader Aztec mythical cosmology. Many texts describe Aztec cosmology in great detail, but let's consider two of the most famous ones, collected in the *Codex Chimalpopoca*.

The first of these stories concerns the recovery of human beings for life under the fifth sun, also called "4 Movement." The story tells us that even though fire had been restored after the demise of the fourth sun, the principal deities are still sad, because no one exists. To fix the situation, Quetzalcoatl travels to the Land of the Dead, *mictlan* (MEEK-tlan), where he can find human bones to restore humanity. The Lord of Mictlan doesn't want to let

Quetzalcoatl have the bones, so he gives him an impossible task: Take a conch shell, blow on it, and circle the realm four times. The conch shell, however, has no holes. Using his wiles, Quetzalcoatl summons worms to hollow it out, and then he calls bees to buzz inside it to produce the desired sound as he circles the realm. Defeated, the Lord of Mictlan must let Quetzalcoatl leave with the bones, but the Lord of Mictlan nevertheless sends his spirits ahead to dig a trap for Quetzalcoatl. Quetzalcoatl falls into the trap, loses consciousness, and birds pick at the bones, deforming them. This is said to be the reason humans are of different sizes.

After Quetzalcoatl regains consciousness, he must still bring humans to life from the bones. He returns to his paradisiacal homeland and conducts a ceremony where it is reported that he "bled his penis on them [the bones]" to provide life sustenance. Afterward, all the other gods involved in the process of restoring humanity "did penance" (*tlamaçehua*). In an announcement concluding the ceremony we read: "Gods, the deserved ones [i.e., humans, *maçehualtin*] have been born."

This story clearly links human existence to the sacrifices of the gods and explains why humans literally are described as the ones deserved or merited into existence (*in maçehualtin*) by the god's penance (*tlamaçehua*). Quetzalcoatl's bleeding of his member, moreover, is an instance of what the *Florentine Codex* calls "the bloodying." So, the story establishes a close link among: (1) human existence, (2) our debt to the gods, and (3) the practice of blood sacrifice. What's missing in this story, however, is the role of heart sacrifice.

Some scholars have suggested that these other forms of bloodletting were only a substitute for heart sacrifice. But reflecting on this story, you'll find little reason for that conclusion. We have other texts, moreover, that chronicle how bloodletting was performed *after* a human sacrifice was made. Bloodletting, then, is better understood as its own sort of ritual, not a substitution. To find support for heart sacrifice, we'll need to look at a second myth.

Not long after the Quetzalcoatl story in the *Codex Chimalpopoca*, a legend recounts the revival of our sun, 4 Movement. Since the sun has yet to be restored, humans and the gods alike appear to be living in the dark. To remedy this, the Lord of Sustenance and the Turquoise Lord ask a humble god, Pimply Face (Nanahuatzin / Nana-WA-tzin), to sustain the sky and earth. Another god, 4 Flint, also volunteers for the task. To prepare himself, Pimply Face first does penance, using spines and needles, and then bathes himself. Afterward, he courageously throws himself into the fire. The god 4 Flint, however, is depicted as proud and lacks courage, so he falls into the ashes. Since Pimply Face is courageous, he rises in the east as the new sun, 4 Movement, and 4 Flint rises later as the moon.

After rising, 4 Movement stays in one place for four days. Concerned, the gods ask him why he does not move (*amo ollin*), and he responds, "because I am asking for their blood and color, from those who did the damage." The gods hold council, not wanting to pay recompense, and so first stage a coup, which fails. In retribution, 4 Movement turns the leader of the coup into frost. Afterward, all the gods decide to sacrifice themselves, and it is only after receiving their life force that 4 Movement moves through the sky.

This myth links both the offering of thorns, and the offering of life to the movement of the sun. The terms used in Nahuatl here matter. The three important forms of movement in Aztec thought: *olin* (also spelled *ollin*), which undulates as the sun rises and sets, *malinalli*, which spins in circles as a vortex does, and *nepanotl*, which is a weaving back and forth motion. The language of the story thus indicates that a heart might have the right sort of vital force to enable the sun to take its special sort of movement: hearts move in an *olin* way. Still, the story uses immolation not heart excision to extract vital force.

Beyond the oddities noted, the myth doesn't explain why humans must continue to sacrifice their hearts to keep the sun in motion. It's tempting to think that all the other gods' sacrifices would be enough. But, again, this is just one myth, even if it is likely the most important one, and it does provide some of the rationale for the Aztec practice of heart sacrifice. For the sake of argument, even though the texts don't support it well, let's just accept that heart sacrifice was taken to be necessary for the ongoing motions of the sun.

SO, IF such accounts accurately characterize blood sacrifice, then why isn't heart sacrifice central to the Aztec ethics? The answer hinges on an ambiguity in what you might mean by "central." You could mean "important to" or "an elemental feature of" their ethical outlook in the way that primitive terms function in mathematical proofs. Heart sacrifice is important to the Aztec ethical outlook, but it is not an elemental feature of it.

An analogy proves helpful here. Suppose that you wanted to write an account of our contemporary world. You could claim that the driving of combustion vehicles is central to our contemporary world, and that you can't really understand contemporary human society without talking about environmental pollution. But none of us, except for maybe oil company executives, hold that we have some moral imperative to burn fossil fuels. Burning fossil fuels is a physical principle that we observe, not a moral aim we hope to achieve.

Similarly, the Aztecs thought that human heart sacrifice was necessary, at a physical level, to maintain the sun in its course through the heavens. Given their understanding of natural principles, their activities make sense. They organized their society quite elaborately around the procuring of human hearts to keep the sun in motion, just as we elaborately rearrange the surface of the earth to extract fossil fuels. The goals that the Aztecs had for this life, however, centered on growing roots and supporting each other in a community. They didn't involve heart sacrifice as an intrinsic aim any more than you and I aim at burning fossil fuels in commuting to work.

Historians and anthropologists sometimes claim that heart sacrifice was more important than this analogy suggests. They sometimes write that heart sacrifice, if not the goal of life itself, is basic to the Aztec ethical outlook because it features as a form of justice with the gods, or as a courageous activity. In both cases, heart sacrifice would be a part of virtue, and so would constitute an elementary feature of their ethical outlook.

The matter, at this point, moves into the philosophically technical domain. But the general confusion at work in those claims is not difficult to understand. Suppose that we have some debt to the gods that requires repayment. Suppose further that such repayment qualifies as a form of justice as the Aztecs conceived of the term. Why must that repayment happen by way of sacrificing human hearts? Justice, the ethical concept, does the work of ensuring equivalency of repayment, but *what* is being repaid isn't specified by justice. That only hearts (*yolli*) have the appropriate (*olin*) motion is a physical belief, not an ethical one.

The same kind of reasoning applies to courage or any other named virtue. The only thing that can explain why courage requires hearts (or blood) is a physical principle, not an ethical one.

There is a philosophical counterargument. A philosopher might say that the means-end distinction used in the argument doesn't hold up. If the only way to act on our ethical beliefs is by some problematic *means*, then the means do matter ethically.

I'd like to highlight how this argument moves too quickly in arriving at its conclusion. First, it concedes that, in principle, the Aztec ethical framework is detachable from those means. Yet, because we are interested in reconstructing Aztec philosophy for our contemporary purposes, this, *in principle*, detachability is all that we require (this is my first claim after all). The present book and the activities of philosophers in league with the aims of this book—including you, the present reader—are thus pursuing a viable project.

Second, the counterargument fails to distinguish two sorts of means. In our world, we drive *by* using fossil fuel burning in our cars. Most of us lack the power to change systemic harms in our world, so that this plight remains a part of our contemporary condition. But collectively, as a society, we do know how to solve this problem, though fossil fuel executives would need to find different jobs. We are forced to use these means because of a lack of power, but not a lack of knowledge. The barrier is capacity based, not knowledge based. A second sort of means is at work in Boole's death. His wife employed the best means she could, given the medical knowledge of her day. She was forced to use those means because no one knew any better (i.e., the barrier is epistemic, and not capacity based). Which case most closely approximates the Aztec position? I think it is the latter epistemic sort.

That is important because in cases of knowledge-based instrumentality, responsibility and blameworthiness diverge. While responsible for their actions, what led the Aztecs to their undertaking was an epistemic failing, not a capacity-based failure, and that makes them less blameworthy (just as Mrs. Boole was less blameworthy).

Aztec ethics are thus still illuminating for our contemporary moment, as we've been discussing throughout this book, despite the fact that we no longer share their notions about cosmological physical processes.

A final existential question emerges from these questions. If the physical universe is such that we must engage in human sacrifice to live, what is the value of our existence? Why not just end it all and prevent that suffering? Is there anything that can redeem us, to speak in a Christian way?

Tragedy can't be justified or redeemed. We recognize this now as much as the Aztecs did, and that is why, after the horrors of the twentieth century, appeals to God's divine providence tend to count against belief in God. How could the Holocaust be part of any benevolent God's plan?

I do not mean to draw any equivalence between the Aztecs,

their conquest, and the Holocaust (there can be no such comparison). I mean only to highlight an important quality of what you and I might want in a reply: A good answer cannot be one that provides rational justifications for tragedies.

Rather, a good answer is one that highlights the value in continuing to face what we know will be a tragic end. And, if a philosopher is permitted to muse and hope a bit, perhaps a rational response can help us to think about what a desirable afterlife might consist of. My hope is that this work has moved your reflections some degree in that direction.

APPENDIX IV

GUADALUPE AS GODDESS, DEMON, MASTERWORK

The Museo Antropológico in Mexico City has among the largest collections of pre-Columbian artifacts in the world. At the center of the main hall rests the image of the Aztec "calendar stone." Most pose by it, pretending to shoulder its weight under their own efforts, and I suppose the resulting image makes for a striking social media post.

To the left of that artwork is another statue that was excavated along with it. Standing some 8 feet, 3 inches (2.53 m), it presents the imposing image of the goddess Coatlicue (koat-LEE-ke), meaning, roughly, Her Skirt and Snakes. A slightly different version of her name sounds quite like the Spanish "Guadalupe," which is an Iberian Madonna. It is this goddess, then, who was identified with the Christian Virgin Mary, and today has millions of adherents. Though the meaning of the statue is uncertain, the story of her recovery crystallizes a pattern in our "Western" reception of challenging Aztec notions—of their art and philosophy alike.

After Cortés's military success, the Indigenous people were instructed to destroy the statue, but instead they buried it below the water table for safe keeping. Some centuries later, on August 13, 1790, while executing municipal ordinances to dig a canal, the statue was rediscovered. Some one hundred meters away, the calendar stone was also unearthed. The viceroy at the time sent the Coatlicue statue to Mexico City's university, where it was placed among various copies of Greco-Roman statues to serve as a monument of ancient America.

Catholic clergymen, however, feared that the statue would revive ancient beliefs; it also stood as an affront to the Greco-Roman aesthetic sensibilities that surrounded it. As a result of these concerns, Antonio de León y Gama, a notable scholar, was given the opportunity to pen a description of the artwork before the locals then reburied it where they had found it.

Some time passed, and in 1804 León y Gama published his description of the statue. As fate would have it, Baron Alexander von Humboldt was journeying through Mexico at the time and read the description. He prevailed on the local Mexican authorities to see the statue for himself, and the locals once again unearthed the former goddess. The erudite German, having thus satisfied his curiosity, signaled that they could yet again rebury the demonic symbol, which they promptly did.

The *Coatlicue Mayor*, as archaeologists now call her, remained beneath the central square until after the Mexican revolution in the early twentieth century. Then, knowing about the statue, several powers arranged to resurface the symbol of their past but were uncertain about where she should ultimately be displayed. Thus, she was placed in a hallway of the university along with other bobbles as a curiosity of pre-Columbian antiquity. Eventually, it was decided that the Coatlicue was indeed a great work of ancient Mexican art and she took her place in the central hall of the National Anthropological Museum, which is where the masterwork, carved by an unknown sculptor, now stands.

These recounted events, which briefly chart the course of the Coatlicue statue from goddess, to demon, to masterwork, illustrates the trajectory of many pre-Columbian works, whether artistic or intellectual. It is also, in rough form, the path that Aztec philosophy has charted, having been preserved through great effort and peril, then destroyed for its supposedly demonic nature, and then haltingly recovered as what I hope will be recognized as a global masterpiece.

Though I am trained as a philosopher in mathematical logic, ethics, and the work of classical antiquity, I never attended a class on Aztec philosophy in graduate school because no one was teaching such classes. Rather, I stumbled upon its existence quite by accident. To explain the circumstances of that accident and why I would care about Aztec philosophy when I did stumble upon it, I need to tell you a bit about my peculiar life story.

MY PARENTS married in secret. My father's mother, who is of British heritage, would never have accepted my mother, who is Mexican and of both Spanish and Nahua heritage, into the family.

As you might imagine, my father and mother met quite by accident. It was the early 1970s, and for his study abroad, my father (Jeffrey, though he uses Jeff) traveled to Mexico. He and his roommate were unusually studious and quiet. As a result, their host family worried that something was wrong. The mother of the host family called her niece over to translate and to discern where the problem lay. That niece was my mother, Nora.

After that meeting, they began dating. Eventually Jeff had to return to the United States, and so they continued their relationship in the old way—by writing letters to each other. It was through these letters that Jeff finally won Nora's heart, and she agreed to fly over and visit him at a small town just outside of Salem, Oregon, to see if things might work out. After staying only two weeks, they married before a justice of the peace and a small number of witnesses—mainly Jeff's hippie friends. When Jeff told his mother about it, she was predictably furious, and demanded that they have a proper marriage before a Protestant minister, which is a religious decision my mother has never forgotten.

It was into this environment that I was born, and as you might imagine, I was not my grandmother's favorite grandchild.

This beginning, however, was complemented by my frequent and extended travels to Mexico, where I would live with my mother's family. From these formative experiences, I not only learned to speak Spanish *como un mexicano* (like a Mexican), but also began my own journey of philosophical reflection.

It was not until I had a chance encounter in a library, however, that I discovered the existence of Aztec philosophy for myself. I was searching for materials on comparative philosophy for a class that I was planning to teach the next semester as part of my final year of graduate study. I happened along a copy of Miguel León-Portilla's *La filosofía nahuatl*, or in English *Nahua Philosophy* (recall that "Nahua" is another name for "Aztec").

I read the book with fascination and disbelief. I learned that León-Portilla's book fell dead off the press in 1956 when it was first published, panned by the anthropological community who believed, at the time, that the Indigenous population of Mexico could not possibly have been so civilized as to undertake philosophical inquiry. The book, when it was translated into English a decade later, was given the title *Aztec Thought and Culture*, since this was thought the only format acceptable for León-Portilla's claims.

Since I was trained in classical languages, I thought that I might do well to take up León-Portilla's cause. And so, I began to learn classical Nahuatl as a dead language, just as I had Greek and Latin, even though my maternal grandmother used to speak to the family using Nahuatl. Eventually, I had in mind that I might write a small number of articles on ideas related to those developed in the book.

Yet, remembering the experiences of my youth, I thought it prudent to wait before focusing seriously on this project. It was only after publishing enough on traditional philosophical problems to receive tenure that I revisited *La filosofía nahuatl*. When I did, I found myself in a centuries-long, halting recovery of Aztec philosophy.

BEFORE THE SPANISH arrived in central Mexico, the Aztecs had a system of writing that specialists call "ideographic," which is similar in form to the Egyptian hieroglyphics. The principal features of this writing combined images and phonetic symbols to communicate ideas in written form. Their books, inscribed in red and black ink, were organized without bindings, which is a modern invention, and instead interlaced pages in a screen-folding way—like an accordion. These were called amoxtli (a-MOSH-tli) and the works featured calendrical events that would have been distributed in every small town throughout the Aztec empire.

Despite their ubiquity, only nine of these books, including some painted in the Indigenous tradition after contact, survived the Spanish bonfires—the numerous conflagrations in which banned books and supposedly "unworthy" cultural artifacts were destroyed. Several copies of these books, painted on European paper, also survived.

Now, as then, they require specialist training to read. Modern scholars have made significant advances in this regard, but the materials are still hard to interpret, and even when interpreted well, they do not often lend themselves to the sorts of formulations philosophers typically seek. Fortunately, they are not the only sources remaining.

Before the Catholic church lost patience with the low rate of conversion of the Indigenous people, members of the clergy thought it prudent to collect the most in-depth information possible on the Indigenous peoples of Mesoamerica. They believed that if they understood the natives better, they could better convince them to become Christians.

That view on conversion, though dubious psychologically, proved a boon to our global canon of philosophical history. The mostly Dominican clergymen who first arrived in Mexico established several schools and devised a way to transcribe Nahuatl as a spoken language into Latin letters—these are the sort you're reading right now. The church fathers went on to train promising Indigenous children to become trilingual interpreters, so that they learned Spanish and Latin to fluency, and how to write Nahuatl in the "Western" style. Of course, the children were trained as Catholics too.

Then, equipped with teams of assistants, these clergymen acted as the principal investigators for what we would now call ethnographic research programs. The teams would travel from city to city asking the reputed wise men and women of those cities what they thought about various topics, what songs and poems they treasured, what their history was. The philosophers and priests responded by reading from their own *amoxtli*, which are now lost in their original form, and whatever they remembered from oral tradition. All these responses were then dutifully recorded by the trilingual assistants in books that scholars now call "codices," though they stand at some distance from their European counterparts.

It is from these efforts that we have amassed thousands of pages of Aztec thought—from poetic song, to history, to religious views, to medical knowledge, and to philosophy. Importantly, the clergymen who first recorded this work were "schoolmen," knowledgeable about St. Thomas of Aquinas and his interlocutors during the medieval period, and they labeled parts of what they recorded as philosophical. Members of the public praised their contents. In 1554, Alonso de Zorita, the judge (*oidor*) for the Royal Court of Mexico, wrote the following about the *Discourses of the Elders* that Andrés de Olmos had recorded:

> Beyond raising their children with the discipline or prudence that their [Indigenous] fathers had taught to them, they [the Aztecs] also gave them a great deal of advice, which was very good advice—that which those Indians presently have in

their painted books [i.e., *amoxtli*] that they use in facilitating their memory.

What this praise shows is that there was no initial attempt to deny that the Aztecs held philosophical views. The Spaniards didn't even deny that those views were worthy of admiration. The work of depreciation and neglect that follows this tradition emerged later. Among the works recorded by the clergymen and their assistants, four prove critical for philosophers. The first is a series of creation myths recorded in the *Codex Chimalpopoca*. The second are two volumes of philosophical poetry that were collected in the *Cantares Mexicanos* (*Mexican Songs*) and the *Romances de los Señores de la Nueva España* (*Ballads of the Lords of New Spain*). These works, though difficult to translate and interpret, make important metaphysical claims. The third concerned the genre called "discourses of the elders." The most important of these is *Discourses of the Elders*, which Andrés de Olmos recorded circa 1535, which I translated for the first time from Nahuatl into English in 2023. Unfortunately for philosophical purposes, Fr. Juan Baptista Viseo recovered the documents and altered them in the later chapters with the goal of more effectively converting the natives, so that it is this product that was published in 1600. Nonetheless, Olmos's *Discourses* are the earliest to have been recorded in Latin letters. Moreover, their earlier portions are relatively uncorrupted by Christian interpolations so that they may be understood to reproduce the ethical views of the Aztecs before European colonialism. The final and perhaps most important group of preserved texts are collected in a work that is now called the *Florentine Codex*.

Fr. Bernardino (Bernie) de Sahagún served as the principal investigator for this massive enterprise, which sought to produce an encyclopedia of the entire Aztec world. Initially transcribed in Nahuatl, the work was later translated into Spanish, while several native painters produced accompanying images for text in a style that blends the native *amoxtli* writing with European forms.

The falling sands of history have claimed the names of the priests and philosophers interviewed. So too have they claimed those of the painters who rendered the accompanying images for the text. Nevertheless, we do know the names of Sahagún's four trilingual assistants. They are Antonio Valeriano of Azcapotzalco, Martín Jacobita of Tlatelolco, Pedro de San Buenaventura, and Alonso Vegerano of Cuauhtitlan.

The twelve volumes of the codex were not originally compiled with this encyclopedic aim. The first matters to be recorded were the discourses of the elders that now make up most of volume 6—and remember "discourses of the elders" is a genre in Aztec philosophy. It is a distinctive ethical genre, a little bit like Plato's dialogues are a distinctive genre in "Western" philosophy. The contents of each discourse thus vary in the same way Platonic dialogues cover different topics. The next subject that Sahagún recorded was the history of the Spanish-Aztec war—a sequence of events often, and misleadingly, called the "conquest" of the Mexican people. Interestingly, he did so largely from the point of view of the natives. Eventually, these recorded statements made up volume 12.

Lost to history is the title that Sahagún selected for this enormous work. When the volumes were given a new binding, apparently, the title was omitted. Using Sahagún's notes as a source, scholars have titled it the *General History of the Things of New Spain*, but because they cannot be certain of its name, it is more commonly identified by the location of its rediscovery in the Florence library. Likely, after completion, the volumes were sent to Spain and then gifted to the Medici family. It was placed in the library and promptly forgotten for some two hundred years.

In 1783, the first mention of the existence of the work appears in the Biblioteca Medicea Laurenziana. It was at this point, you might claim with all the awareness that is typical of definitive dates in historical work, that the *Florentine Codex* was recovered from its apparent neglect.

Scholars did not, however, immediately make much use of the strange cultural artifact. The first serious scholar to do so appears to have been Alexander von Humboldt—the same one who requested that the Coatlicue be unearthed during his 1803–1804 Mexico voyage. He proved quite the polymath, and since his older brother was the famed Prussian philosopher Wilhelm von Humboldt, it did not escape Alexander's notice that the Aztec understanding of god as nature (*teotl*) was quite like the view of the seventeenth-century rationalist philosopher Baruch Spinoza—who is the first widely recognized early modern "Western" philosopher to claim that god is nature, not as a force, but as the being itself. This episode might have been the point at which Aztec philosophy was recovered. But philosophers at that time in Europe did not notice von Humboldt's remarks, and his work's impact remained confined to anthropological circles.

Some decades later, in 1839, the American historian William H. Prescott used von Humboldt's work to write his own *History of the Conquest of Mexico*. His book was massively successful upon publication, and it was well researched for its time. Notably, it was Prescott who popularized the name "Aztec," which has stuck ever since. The name was suggested by anthropological work prior to his own, which dubbed the people "Aztecs" because their myths suggest that they hail from the mythical land of Aztlan. Also notable is that Prescott's work focused primarily on historical and military topics. There is no sense in his exposition that the Aztecs might have a philosophical (as opposed to merely religious) tradition. Interest in Aztec philosophy, as a result, had to wait another century.

In the post-WWII era, Miguel León-Portilla, who was the first anthropologist to argue at length that the Aztecs were a philosophical culture, was trained in philosophy in the United States for both his undergraduate and master's degrees. When he returned to Mexico to undertake his doctoral studies, his director followed the German line of scholarship, which used von

Humboldt's work. It became obvious to León-Portilla that the Aztecs were a deeply philosophical people.

Because León-Portilla's key claims were disregarded, it was not until the late 1990s and early 2000s that two American philosophers, James Maffie and Alejandro Santana, separately stumbled onto León-Portilla's early work. Maffie was also the first to write a book titled *Aztec Philosophy* in English, before retiring. Alejandro Santana, who was trained in the philosophy of classical Greek and Roman antiquity, argued that an idea or set of ideas could count as philosophy even if you couldn't identify a single author, or if the people whose philosophy it was attached to didn't write it down themselves. Though I "discovered" León-Portilla after they did, Jim, Alejandro, and I eventually met, and one day, at a 2020 conference of the American Philosophical Association held in San Diego, we held our first, unofficial meeting of the "Aztec Philosophical Society" in a Mexican food restaurant while eating tacos and drinking horchata. We disagreed, and still do, about many topics in Aztec philosophy, from metaphysical questions about basic entities to means-ends distinctions in ethics, but we do have points of commonality. One, I think, is that the Aztecs did hold that something was metaphysically basic, likely either *teotl* or *ometeotl*. Another, more important for ethics, is that the Aztecs favored a philosophically "pessimistic" world view—one in which our "Sun" world comes to an end, where human actions are fragile, and yet that none of that makes our undertakings less worthy of performing.

ABBREVIATIONS AND EDITIONS

Because there is no standard practice of citation among many of the sources of Aztec philosophy, what follows is a list of abbreviations used.

CC   *Codex Chimalpopoca*
   Codex Chimalpopoca: The Text in Nahuatl with a Glossary and Grammatical Notes. Edited and transcribed by John Bierhorst. Tucson: University of Arizona Press, 1992.

CM   *Cantares Mexicanos*
   Cantares Mexicanos: Songs of the Aztecs. Transcribed and translated by John Bierhorst. Stanford, CA: Stanford University Press, 1985.

D   *Discourses of the Elders*
   Discourses of the Elders: The Aztec Huehuetlatolli: A First English Translation, Collected by Friar Andrés de Olmos circa 1535 with Supplemental Texts. Translated by Sebastian Purcell. New York: W. W. Norton & Co, 2023.

FC   *Florentine Codex*, all 13 volumes
   Sahagún, Bernadino de. *Florentine Codex, General History of the Things of New Spain*, 13 volumes. Edited and translated by Arthur J. O. Anderson and Charles E. Dibble. Santa Fe: School of American Research and the University of Utah, 1953–1982.

NE   *Nicomachean Ethics*
   Aristotelis Ethica Nicomachea. Edited and annotated by I. Bywater. Oxford: Oxford University Press, 1894.

PM Primeros Memoriales
   Sahagún, Bernardino de. *Primeros Memoriales: Paleography of Nahuatl Text and English Translation*. Paleography of Nahuatl text and English translation by Thelma D. Sullivan, et al. Norman: University of Oklahoma Press, 1997.

RS Romances de los Señores de la Nueva España
   Ballads of the Lords of New Spain: The Codex Romances de los Señores de la Nueva España. Transcribed and translated by John Bierhorst. Austin: University of Texas Press, 2009.

In general, I have used a format for citation with the following pattern: abbreviated title, volume number, chapter number, paragraph number, and page number, where these refer to the edition cited in the bibliography. If the work does not have all of these, then as many as possible, and if the citation is from an appendix, one will read an "a" between the chapter and paragraph number. For example, the following citation, *FC* 10.3, 11, indicates volume ten, chapter three, page eleven in the Dibble and Anderson edition of the *Florentine Codex*.

A similar pattern holds for other texts. For the *Discourses of the Elders* a citation such as *D* 37, 23 indicates paragraph 37, page 23. The *Codex Chimalpopoca* numeration follows a slide and line number format, so that *CC* 75, 7–9 means slide 75, lines 7 to 9. Finally, if the text uses folios, then in the place of chapter and paragraph numbers, one will find: folio numbers, recto or verso, and line designation where those exist. For example, the citation *RS* 21r, 9–13 indicates page 21r of the *Romances de los Señores de la Nueva España*, lines 9 to 13.

To elucidate Aztec concepts the present work draws on Aristotle's ethical outlook for comparison. Citations of Aristotle's work have likewise been abbreviated and refer to Bywater's *Ethica Nicomachea* in canonical form as follows: abbreviated title, book number, chapter number, page number, column letter, and line number.

NOTES

For the notes that follow, please see the Abbreviations and Editions section above for a discussion of the textual abbreviations and the format of volume and pagination used when citing works.

Lesson 1

1 **as an inalienable right:** Jefferson, "Declaration of Independence: A Transcription," National Archives.
1 **"Western" philosophy:** The idea of the "West" is contested by intellectuals in Latin America. While it is possible to trace a line of influence from classical Greek antiquity to the present, which influential members and notions are included are often quixotic. Aristotle, for example, was only preserved through the interventions of Arabic speaking regions. Why, then, are these persons typically excluded? Moreover, why do "Western" peoples have a right to name everyone else? These Latin American intellectuals, which include Enrique Dussel and Walter Mignolo, prefer to call the "West" the "North." This is also inaccurate, geographically, but it serves the symbolic purpose of highlighting that the "West" is itself a construction, often a self-serving one. In this text, I shall use "West" in quotations to highlight the self-construction, but retain the term so as not to confuse the reader greatly.
1 **"the good as what everything seeks":** *NE* I.1, 1094a1–2.
2 **"*Odyssey* underscores the Aztec point":** I think it's also pertinent to use an example from the "West" to highlight the point that the tradition is hardly uniform. In some ways, the Aztec point of view might be thought to give further voice to the outlook of Greek tragedians and epic authors—though with some important differences too. The scene that follows may be found in the Homer, *Odyssaea* in *Homeri Opera*,

volume 3, edited and annotated by Thomas W. Allen (Oxford: Oxford University Press, 1922) V, 77–147.

3 **A study found . . . time and money:** See R. Margolis and M. Myrskylä, "Parental Well-Being Surrounding First Birth as a Determinant of Further Parity Progression," *Demography* 52 (2015): 1147–66. See also C. Walker, "Some Variations in Marital Satisfaction," in *Equalities and Inequalities in Family Life*, ed. R. Chester and J. Peel (London: Academic Press, 1997), 127–39 and D. Myer's assessment that quite contrary to the perception that parents experience sadness, or empty nest syndrome, after their children leave the house, they report higher levels of satisfaction in *The Pursuit of Happiness: Discovering the Pathway to Fulfillment, Well-Being and Enduring Personal Joy* (New York: Avon, 1992), 71. See finally A. Roeters, J. Mandemakers, and M. Voorpostel, "Parenthood and Well-Being: The Moderating Role of Leisure and Paid Work," *European Journal of Population* 32 (2016): 381–401 and M. Pollmann-Schutt, "Parenthood and Life Satisfaction: Why Don't Children Make People Happy?," *Journal of Marriage and Family* 76 (2014): 319–36.

4 **(huehuetlatolli / way-weh-tla-TOL-lee):** See the first appendix explaining pronunciation and orthography. The language of the Aztecs, Nahuatl, does not have a standard orthography so that even the same word can be written differently—even by the same author in the same text! These details are outlined in Appendix I and worth a review.

4 **on how best to live:** Scholarship is still evolving, so it may turn out that these are a class of dialogue like the sort that Plato represented in his works. These discussions, however, do not appear to be devoted to eliciting insights from an interlocutor so much as practicing wisdom through a ritualized form.

4 **"Oh my daughter . . . our life and love":** *FC* 6.18, 93.

4 **has at least three terms for "happiness":** The topic of "happiness" in Nahuatl has yet to receive any sustained philosophical attention in its own right. What I present here are but the initial points for a broader discussion.

5 **perhaps indulging a bit:** Frances Karttunen, *An Analytical Dictionary of Nahuatl* (Oklahoma: University of Oklahoma Press, 1983), notes both points in her entry, 8.

5 **Maybe one of those approaches:** I have in mind, for example, Roger Crisp's view articulated in *Reasons and the Good* (Oxford: Oxford University Press, 2006).

6 **"In contemplating . . . unmitigated ferocity":** William Prescott, *History of the Conquest of Mexico* (New York: Random House, 2001), 50.

Notably, his study was missing the accompanying images to the text, some of which offer quite different accounts of the subject matter discussed in Spanish and Nahuatl.

7 **Daniel Russell ... modern concerns:** Daniel Russell, *Practical Intelligence and The Virtues* (Oxford: Oxford University Press, 2009) and Massimo Pigliucci, *How to Be a Stoic: Using Ancient Philosophy to Live a Modern Life* (New York: Basic Books, 2017).

8 **European powers in the early 1800s:** A direct intellectual connection on this score seems unlikely to me. At least, it is not something that Bolívar would have learned through his formal education in Europe. But in his speech to the National Congress of Venezuela at Angostura, February 15, 1819, his statements on the character of political office bear an uncanny resemblance to the Aztec view. See "Address Delivered at the Inauguration of the Second National Congress of Venezuela at Angostura," translated by Lewis Bertrand (New York: Colonial Press, 1951). He repeats, nearly verbatim, the Aztec view that political obligation is an obligation and a heavy burden to be carried one's shoulders, and that one's role is to serve as an "instrument" for another's purpose. One may read about the king's role as an obligation that is a heavy burden to be carried on one's shoulders in *FC* 6.5, 22, and that the king's role is to serve as an instrument or substitute a chapter earlier at *FC* 6.4, 17. At the very least, he held a view on the world that was deeply aligned with a key feature of the rooted life as it is evidenced in Aztec philosophy.

8 **ancient Greek and Roman Stoicism:** With respect to Buddhism, especially Zen Buddhism, I have in mind the works of Alan Watts, especially *The Way of Zen* (New York: Vintage Press, 1999) and D. T. Suzuki, including *An Introduction to Zen Buddhism* (New York: Grove Press, 1994). With respect to Stoicism, I have in mind Massimo Pigliucci's *How to Be a Stoic* (New York: Basic Books, 2018), and especially Ryan Holiday's *The Obstacle Is the Way* (New York: Penguin Press, 2014).

9 **"Some things are up to us ... not our doing":** Epictetus, *The Handbook (The Enchiridion)*, translated by Nicholas P. White (Indianapolis: Hackett, 1983), 11. *The Handbook*, of course, was written by Arrian, since Epictetus wrote nothing.

9 **similarly inward-looking:** Other forms of Buddhism do not follow what I am here calling the inward path. Various forms of Mahayana Buddhism, for example, clearly make use of institutional support to make a person better.

9 **"What was the appearance ... hand clapping":** The formulation of these koans appears in Alan Watt's *The Way of Zen*, 164–66, but the

specific translations at work are taken from Huston Smith's *The World's Religions* (San Francisco: Harper Collins, 1991 [1956]).

10 **"emerge as human"**: *D* 32, 19. Translation modified. For the path of principles and its opposite, that of the deer and rabbit, see *D* 7–10, 5–8. For the father's statements on the first path see his statements at *D* 37, 23 and *D* 33, 20 respectively.

Lesson 2

14 **"Zapata assumes... on the surface"**: Gildaro Magaña and Pérez Guerrero Carlos, *Emiliano Zapata y el agrarismo en México*, vol. II (Mexico City: Editorial Ruta, 1952) 7, quoting Deputy José María Lozano.

14 **Calmly... to bring his arms:** Paul Hart, *Emiliano Zapata: Mexico's Social Revolutionary* (Oxford: Oxford University Press, 2018), 89.

15 **Beyond his heroism... fragile:** This is another feature of "Aztec pessimism." The idea that pursuing what is genuinely good exposes you to physical peril is somewhat controversial, though I wager that philosophers as diverse as Socrates, Aristotle, and Confucius would agree. The Zapata case raises this possibility, but I think it also raises the possibility that you might also be exposed to *moral* peril. If friendship is a moral good in human life, for example, and this is ruined through betrayal, one is harmed in a moral way through this misfortune. This broader view is something that one finds (perhaps) only among the Greek tragedians (not Euripides), Norse mythology, Arthur Schopenhauer, Friedrich Nietzsche, the earl Jean-Paul Sartre, Octavio Paz, and (I think) Bernard Williams.

15 **"and now that you are of age... happiness-pain"**: *FC* 6.18, 93. I can only present some of the textual evidence for this pessimistic world view here. My argument is holistic and maintains that the view presented is coherent, adequate to our standards of natural science, and compelling in a way that most can verify by drawing on their common sense. Further points are developed in Lesson 4, which addresses the inherent reasons why *moral* luck is woven into our human condition. Lesson 5 develops the related points about which goal one could pursue on "earth" (*tlalticpac*), that is, given our human circumstances. In general, the more socially centered paradigm of virtue ethics articulated in this book—one in which the virtues are enacted (paradigmatically) through shared agency—makes the good inherently more fragile, more open to the vicissitudes of luck.

19 **"A curious thing... true"**: W. V. O. Quine, "On What There Is," in *From a Logical Point of View: Nine Logico-Philosophical Essays* (Cambridge, MA: Harvard University Press, 1980), 1.

20 **"pro drop" fallacy:** This is a point Andrews makes in his *Introduction to Classical Nahuatl*, page 5.
20 **the fundamental energy of the universe:** This is James Maffie's approach in *Aztec Philosophy*, and I think it's as fair an approximation as we will find.
21 **Although *teotl* is all of reality:** I am drawing from James Maffie's characterization of *teotl* as a basic energy in *Aztec Philosophy: Understanding a World in Motion* (Colorado: University of Colorado Press, 2014). Perhaps this is a logical step too far—thank you to Alane Mason for pointing this out—as a moving basic reality does not quite imply that it constitutes some form of "energy." For our work, if it helps you to understand the idea better, then use it. If not, think of *teotl* as mere reality. Relatedly, the Aztecs used far more than these merely conceptual doubles. I am focusing only on these to simplify the discussion.
21 **these relational pairs as the basic features of our world:** This is a notion that Alfred López-Austin first articulates in Chapter 2 of *Cuerpo humano e ideología: las concepciones de los antiguos nahuas* (Mexico City: Instituto de investigaciones antropológicas UNAM, 2004 [1980]). The list to follow is from page 59 of Chapter 2.
22 **the surviving humans are turned into turkeys:** See *CC* 75.6–40.
23 **where it begins misses the point:** see Jessica Wilson, "Determinables and Determinates," *Stanford Encyclopedia of Philosophy*, February 7, 2017, rev. January 18, 2023.

Lesson 3

26 **"It's not about being content . . . and it still sucked":** "Trent Reznor—Most Vital Person," interview from the April 1, 1997 issue of *Spin* archived at @NINHOTLINE.
27 **"How's it going? . . . you golden fish":** *FC* 6.41, 228.
27 **"The earth . . . slipped in the mud":** *FC* 6.41, 228.
28 **"My friends . . . will have to go away":** *RS* 3v–4r, 86. It is helpful to recall that these philosophical poems were sung and danced, so that the subject of address is likely an audience member hearing and viewing the performance.
28 **"Let us eat . . . we die":** *The Greek New Testament*, edited by Kurt Aland et al. (Stuttgart: United Bible Societies, 1966).
31 **"Something resembling . . . underworld":** Gonzalo Fernández Ovidedo y Valdés, *Historia general y natural de las Indias, Islas, y Teierra-firme del Mar Océano*, volumen 4 (Madrid: Real Academia de la Historia, 1855), 42. In Spanish, the entire text reads: *"sale por la boca como una*

persona que se diçe yulio, *é vá allá donde está aquel hombre é mujer, allá está como una persona é no muere allá, y el cuerpo se queda acá.*"

32   **"The vaporous . . . the flatus":** Jill Leslie McKeever Furst, *The Natural History of the Soul in Ancient Mexico* (New Haven, CT: Yale University Press, 1995), 169.

33   **one name for *teotl*:** *FC* 6, 206.

33   **"portion of each . . . another":** Alonso de Molina, *Vocabulario en lengua castellana y mexicana y mexicana y castellana*, fascimile of 1571 edition (Mexico City: Editorial Porrúa, 1970), 110v.

33   **thought experiment to illustrate this idea:** This discussion in the *Platonis Repvblicam*, edited and annotated by S. R. Slings (Oxford: Oxford Classical Texts, 2003), occurs at 439a–e.

35   **last word on the topic of classical Greek grammatical particles:** J. D. Denniston, *The Greek Particles*, second edition (Oxford: Oxford University Press, 1950 [1934]).

35   **two dimensions of analysis:** What follows is a schematized presentation of the material López-Austin develops in Chapters 5 and 6 in volume 1 of *Cuerpo humano e ideología: las concepciones de los antiguos nahuas*, volumes 1–2 (Mexico City: Instituto de investigaciones antropológicas UNAM, 2004 [1980]).

36   **"eye" and only in a more extended sense does it mean "face":** This is one of those scholarly disputes where I doubt there will ever be enough evidence to settle it.

36   **our role as ethical agents:** See, for example, *D* 78, 49.

36   **"Your dear face . . . teachings]":** *D* 55, 35. Translation altered.

36   **"Damage not your face . . . clean":** *D* 43, 27. Translation altered.

37   **"My blood and color . . . face":** *D* 57, 37.

38   **paradigm shift in the robotics team's approach:** See, for example: Macs Media, "The Evolution of Asimo," April 25, 2013, YouTube, https://www.youtube.com/watch?v=cqL2ZvZ-q14.

38   **"a kind of rigor mortis":** Quoted in Matthew Crawford, *The World Beyond Your Head: On Becoming an Individual in an Age of Distraction* (New York: Farrar, Straus and Giroux, 2016), 51.

39   **"joint intelligence":** This is Guy Claxton's term, *Intelligence in the Flesh: Why Your Mind Needs Your Body Much More Than It Thinks* (New Haven, CT: Yale University Press, 2016), 42. Note also, by defining your hand's movement in this way, as an equilibrium or set of conditioned possible options, makes the item under discussion objective. These are not subjective projections onto the world, but actually existing conditions "in the world."

39   **so might a mountain:** Arguably, it is this insight that began Aldo

Leopold's career as the "father" of the contemporary environmental conservation movement in the Anglophone world.

40 **your hand is "smart":** To be clear to my fellow historians and anthropologists, I am here offering a philosophical framework by which to make sense of the "ecosystem of minds" that the Aztecs had which is defensible using contemporary science, even if it is not what they held exactly. It is a modern "work up" of the Aztec view, which is what philosophers do with all historical figures.

40 **Lakoff and Johnson's examples . . . are striking:** The following examples are all taken from G. Lakoff and M. Johnson's *Philosophy in the Flesh: The Embodied Mind and Its Challenge to Western Thought* (New York: Basic Books, 1999), 49–54.

41 **This model of thinking, beginning with a seed:** Heinz Werner was among the first to discuss cognition as emerging from seed points in "Microgenesis and Aphasia," *Journal of Abnormal Social Psychology*, volume 52 (1956): 347–53.

41 **"Many of us . . . notice the unfurling":** Claxton, *Intelligence in the Flesh*, 172.

42 **a rider on an elephant:** Jonathan Haidt, *The Happiness Hypothesis: Finding Modern Truth in Ancient Wisdom* (New York: Basic Books, 2006), 1–5.

42 **"the deer and the rabbit:"** *D* 35, 22.

Spiritual Exercise I

43 **"in the chambers of your heart":** *FC* 6.19, 99.

43 **"I'm a convert . . . smart":** Robert Cialdini, *Pre-suasion: A Revolutionary Way to Influence and Persuade* (New York: Simon & Schuster, 2016), 102.

44 **There is scientific support:** For example, see G. R. Semin, "The Linguistic Category Model," in *Handbook of Theories of Social Psychology*, volume 1, edited by P. A. M. Van Lange, A. Kruglanski, and E. T. Higgins (London: Sage 2012), 309–26, and F. Cavicchio, D. Melcher, and M. Poesio, "The Effect of Linguisitic and Visual Salience in Visual Worlds, *Frontiers in Psychology* 5 (2014): 176.

44 **"You are to speak . . . gossip":** *FC* 6.22, 122.

45 **Speak truly:** It is notable that the Aztecs did not condemn falsehood in a blanket fashion, only when it harmed another. For example, the description of the bad philosopher reads "He claims to know divine matters and boasts falsely and vaingloriously. . . . Like a bad soothsayer, he is one who disorients others, misleads them, destroys their judgment." *FC* 10.8, 30.

45 "**If you make fun of people ... human**": *D* 15, 10.
45 "**And do not ... good**": *D* 16, 11.
45 **a strategy that turns kind words into action:** Chriss Voss and Tahl Raz, *Never Split the Difference: Negotiating as if Your Life Depended On It* (New York: Penguin Press, 2016), 35ff.
46 "**We've got a van ... scene]**": Voss, *Never Split the Difference*, 35.

Lesson 4

49 **the schooling system:** It is of course not directly known whether the *calmecac* system in place at the time of Cortés's arrival existed in roughly similar form a century earlier. Something like it looks to have been, though Nezahualcoyotl was himself instrumental in bringing about many such institutions. At the very least, we know that Nezahualcoyotl received training in the matters that make up the education of *calmecac* system.

49 **a famed philosopher in his own right:** I am developing what is recorded in Domingo de San Antón Chimalpahin Cuauhtlehuanitzin's "Seventh Relation" in *Las ocho relaciones y el memorial de Colhuacan*, translated by Rafael Tena (Mexico City: Consejo Nacional para la Cultura y las rates, 1998) and Alva Ixtlilxochitl in his *Obras históricas de Don Fernando de Alva Ixtlilxochitl*, volumes 1–2, edited by Edmundo O'Gorman (Mexico City: Instituto de Investigaciones Históricas, UNAM, 1975). On Nezahualcoyotl's tutelage, see *Obras históricas*, vol. 2, 82. Notably Ixtlilxochitl's account has been questioned for historical accuracy, but the legend is sufficient for philosophical purposes. Recall also that "philosophers" were unlikely to be people exclusively dedicated to this social role as distinct from priests or other wise people.

49 **murder his father:** This point is mentioned in Domingo Chimalpahin, *Las ocho relaciones*, fol. 162v. It also appears as noted in the *Códice Xolotl*, edited by Charles E. Dibble (Mexico City: Instituto de Investigaciones Históricas UNAM, 1980), vii. It is possible, however, that it was Alva Ixtlilxochitl who produced this codex, so that it is not an independent piece of historical evidence. The legend remains instructive.

50 "**I was born in vain! ... born**": *RS* 21r, 9–13.

50 "**I am sad. ... one-exists**": *CM* 25r. The translation is Miguel León-Portilla's from *Fifteen Poets of the Aztec World* (Norman: University of Oklahoma Press, 1992), 93. These texts always require holistic translations, but while it is my favored approach, nothing philosophically deep hinges on my preference. I take those points to be compatible with other possible translations.

Notes • 247

51 **all involve moral luck:** These cases are, of course, inspired by Bernard Williams's reflections on moral luck, especially his account of the lorry driver in *Moral Luck* (Cambridge: Cambridge University Press 1981), 28.

52 **nothing untoward happens:** These are, of course, nothing more than modern developments of the situations suggested in the gloss on the saying "How's it going? Be especially prudent you golden fish," *FC* 6.41, 228.

54 **"The claim ... living being":** Diogenes Laertius, *Lives of Eminent Philosophers* volume 2, translation by R. D. Hicks (Cambridge, MA: Harvard University Press, 1931), 7.142–43. Translation modified.

54 **the entire outlook of Indian philosophy:** The lone exception is, of course, the school of Cārvāka materialism.

54 **inviolable moral order Rta:** Satischandra Chatterjee and Dhirendramohan Datta, *An Introduction to Indian Philosophy* (New Delhi: Rupa Publications, 2012), 14.

55 **"Indeed ... will to power":** Friedrich Nietzsche, *Thus Spoke Zarathustra: A Book for None and All*, translated by Walter Kaumann (New York: Penguin, 1966), 115.

56 **"I judge this indeed ... audacity":** Niccolò Machiavelli, *The Prince*, translated by Harvey C. Mansfield (Chicago: University of Chicago Press, 1998), 101.

57 **with a philosopher king:** for Plato's view see *Republic*, 472c–d. In neither case would this person have had an exclusively philosophically social role.

Spiritual Exercise II

59 **"Like a watchful physician ... content":** *FC* 10.8.29.

60 **one should never lie:** This is Immanuel Kant's view as he explains it in his essay "On a Supposed Right to Lie Because of Philanthropic Concerns," in *Grounding for the Metaphysics of Morals*, translated by James W. Ellington (Indianapolis: Hackett Publishing, 1981).

Lesson 5

62 **born in the twilight of the Aztec empire:** Beyond Chimalpahin's own work, the present section is indebted to Camilla Townsend's historical research and presentation of his situation in the "Introduction" and Chapter 8 of *Fifth Sun: A New History of the Aztecs* (Oxford: Oxford University Press, 2019).

64 **the great ceiba:** I would like to thank Steven Broyles for helping me in

identifying excellent specimens of these trees, and for lending me his knowledge as a dendrobiologist.

64 **magnanimous individual:** See, for example, where Aristotle speaks of magnanimity as the crown of the virtues, *NE* IV.3, 1124a1–2. Notably, and like Aristotle's description, the Aztec description ties the conception to nobility. The difference is that the connection is even more direct for the Aztecs, as the man described is one who wears all the ornaments of a king. For the present ethical reconstruction, I will be careful to develop the framework in a way that does not commit it logically to this aristocratic outlook.

64 **"And he is esteemed . . . refuge":** *FC* 6.14, 73.

64 **"And now . . . ahuehuete":** *D* 100, 61–62.

66 **"It is virtuous . . . live":** *D* 25, 16. Translation altered for context as the phrase "earthly matters" translates *tlalticpa-ca-yotl*. I have used the philosophical translation "virtue" for the more literal "good and straight." See the Postface for an explanation of my reasoning.

68 **"So this is how . . . *tlalticpac*]?":** *CM* 9v, 22–24.

68 **another dimension to this proposal:** Among specialists of the Nahuatl language, the connection between *"nelli"* and *"nelhuatl"* and related terms was for a time unquestioned. Remi Simeon, who put together an earlier dictionary of Nahuatl, puts a (?) after suggesting that the root of *nelhuatl* is *nelli*, but apparently held it was a good guess. Miguel León-Portilla, in Chapter 3 of his *La filosofía náhuatl: Estudiada en sus fuentes* (Mexico City: Instituto de investigaciones antropológicas UNAM, 1993 [1956]), set the tone for most of the second half of the twentieth century, arguing that they were linguistically connected. More recent scholarship, however, has come to wonder whether the connection is an apt one. R. Joe Campbell, at least in email correspondence, had stated that he does not think there is a connection on both morphemic and semantic grounds, though he admits that there may be some connection in Proto-Uto-Aztecan. The broader philosophical point about the aim of the good life does not require a linguistic connection between *nelli* and *nelhuatl*. I have an extended essay on the topic in Sebastian Purcell, "Truth, Rootedness, and the Good Life in Aztec Ethical Philosophy," *APA Newsletter on Native American and Indigenous Philosophy* 21 (2021): 4–11.

69 **"they greeted me *warmly*":** These examples are taken from Lakoff and Johnson's *Philosophy in the Flesh: The Embodied Mind and its Challenge to Western Thought* (New York: Basic Books, 1999), 50–52.

69 **"principle, foundation, base, or root":** I have in mind terms such as *nel-huatl* and *tla-nel-huatl*, which mean "a root," *nel-hua-yotia*, "to take root," and *nel-huayotl*, "a principle, foundation, or root."

69 **or take root:** None of this suggests that *nelli* literally means "a root," any more than "important" literally means "big," or "happy" literally means "up." It suggests, rather, that the primary metaphor behind the idea of calling our top goal *nelli* is one of finding or taking root.

70 **"We are going to lift the headdress":** The characterization of actions like these as "we" or "collective" intentions is John Searle's position in *Making the Social World: The Structure of Human Civilization* (Oxford: Oxford University Press, 2010), 42–60.

70 **"I have in mind that you have in mind... headdress":** This is the approach that Michael Bratman favors. See his "Shared Intentions," *Ethics* 104 (1993): 97–113, and his more recent statement in *Shared Agency: A Planning Theory of Acting Together* (Oxford: Oxford University Press, 2014).

70 **"we're lifting now":** For the professional philosophers, if you do not like this Searlean formulation of shared agency by way of "we" intentions, then please substitute your favored form of individualist reductionism. This point will not matter for the current argument. For a more public audience, the Searlean formulation is certainly the gentler path to take.

70 *Walking with Someone*: Inspiration for this thought experiment is taken from Margaret Gilbert's "Walking Together: A Paradigmatic Social Phenomenon," *Midwest Studies in Philosophy* 15 (1990): 1–14.

71 *The Royal Court Crowns Montezuma*: This is as close to an "emperor" as one finds among the Aztecs. The designation *huey tlatoani* (WAY-ee tla-to-A-nee) indicates a higher station than each city's typical *tlatoani*.

71 **the same stroll as the previous one:** The philosophical point at stake turns on temporality considerations that would distinguish two events of shared agency. I think, intuitively, if two people were strolling, then stop walking altogether and spend several hours doing another activity, then start strolling again, you have two events of strolling.

72 **the ethical evaluation is different:** If it turns out that cases of shared agency by way of groups really is irreducible at an action-theoretic level, then so much the better for our argument.

75 **mental model... area is difficult:** This note is more for the professional philosophers. I suppose that a colloquial understanding of mental models is sufficient for this discussion, provided that one admits that mental models are more than mere collections of knowledge. More completely, I understand them to be notions by which sensory and theoretical data are schematized. I do not mean anything as deep as a Khunian paradigm, but mental models do tilt to a degree in that direction without requiring anyone to give up on realism.

75 **QED:** The abbreviation for *quod erat demonstrandum*, or "that which

was to be demonstrated," and is historically put at the end of mathematical proofs. This is a joke for philosophers, as ethics is not mathematics. A further question turns on the relation between reasons for acting and moral reasons. If they are equivalent, as Roger Crisp in *Reasons and The Good* (Oxford: Oxford University Press, 2008) holds, then QED applies to whatever degree that is possible in philosophy. If they are not, a further argument, which I shall not develop here, would be needed. Even for supporters of a distinctly *sui generis* class of moral reasons, however, most hold that ordinary reasons for acting inform moral reasons—this is what Aristotle appears to have held in arguing that more than virtue was needed for a good life. The Aztecs, at least, would have been among this "mixed view" group.

Lesson 6

77 **"I was excited ... door of the printing house":** Benjamin Franklin, *The Autobiography of Benjamin Franklin* (New York: Dover Publications, 1996), 14.

79 **Mexican-heritage children ... European-heritage peers:** Evidence may be found in L. Alcalá, B. Rogoff, and A. López Fraire, "Sophisticated Collaboration Is Common among Mexican-Heritage US Children" *Proceedings of the National Academy of Sciences* 115 (2018): 11377–84 and R. Mejía-Arauz, B. Rogoff, A. Dayton, and R. Henne-Ochoa, "Collaboration or Negotiation: Two Ways of Interacting Suggest How Shared Thinking Develops," *Current Opinion in Psychology* 23 (2018): 117–23. For the theoretical backdrop to these studies, which are ongoing, see B. Rogoff, M. Callanan, K. D. Gutiérrez, and F. Erickson, "The Organization of Informal Learning," *Review of Research in Education* 40 (2016): 356–401, B. Rogoff, R. Paradise, R. Mejía Arauz, M. Correa-Chávez, C. Angelillo, "Firsthand Learning Through Intent Participation," *Annual Review of Psychology* 54 (2003): 175–203, and A. Dayton and B. Rogoff "Paradigms in Arranging for Children's Learning" in *Amerindian Paths: Guiding Dialogues with Psychology*, edited by Danilo Silva Guimarães (Charlotte: Information Age Publishing, 2016), 113–42.

80 **interested in viewing the videos:** See especially Barbara Rogoff's video "Collaboration as an Ensemble," https://stemforall2019.videohall.com/presentations/1346, last accessed May 30, 2020. You should also take a look at "Learning by Helping," https://stemforall2018.videohall.com/presentations/1318?display_media=video, last accessed May 30, 2020. Finally, see "Learning to Collaborate and Collaborating to Learn,"

https://stemforall2017.videohall.com/presentations/1034?display_media=video, last accessed May 30, 2020.

80 **resisted simplifying important ideas into one word:** For those interested, in my "Introduction" to *Discourses of the Elders*, I cover the aesthetic dimensions at work as part of their broader worldview, xxv–xxxiv.

81 **in the body, the psyche, and society:** It is more natural for us in the "West" to think by way of threes, though the Aztecs might have found a division into four more natural. They might then have grouped these dimensions into body, psyche, society, and natural environment. So long as the range of concerns is grasped, I think that the specific number of levels proves immaterial.

81 **"In vain was I . . . among people":** *RS* 21r–22v, 122–24.

82 **"products" rather than "performances":** A clear example would be Thomas Hurka, *Virtue, Vice, and Value* (Oxford: Oxford University Press, 2003).

82 **only better performances:** At least, this is the general weight of emphasis. They do appear to have held that there are some external reasons that weigh on considerations of right action, so that they defended a "mixed" view in the way that Aristotle appears to have done.

83 **it might count as a vice:** This is assuming the agent has the view of the good in mind, as a prudent person would understand the matter. Aristotle is close on this point, see *NE* II.6, 1106b36–1107a2.

83 **reconstruct your actions:** The articulation of point 1 is precisely worded to achieve this outcome. It articulates how valuational agency—the sort touched on in the discussion of moral psychology—can be expressed through habits. And to be clear, any reconstruction in the ideal case is done in good faith. We are only discussing ideal cases here, since we are addressing standards for assessment from which deviations can be identified as problematic.

84 **"This word . . . earth":** *FC* 6.19, 101–2.

84 **our English "habit" does:** The word "habit" derives from the perfect passive participle *habitum* in Latin, from the verb *habere*, meaning to have or to hold. It was itself a translation of the Greek *hexis*, from the verb *ekhein*, also meaning to have or hold.

85 **deliberation and judgment:** This note is intended for those interested in more philosophic detail. I venture that the term *pixcayotl*, the abstract substantive of *piya*, could serve as a general term for "habit" in the ethical sense we're after. The stem does change, but in the base 2 stem of *piya*, used for the preterit, the "y" is devoiced and becomes "x." I think *pixcayotl* is likely a philosophical term of art, but one does find *pixtinemi* attested, and it means to live with care, to be in control of one's passions.

The proposed sense, then, is in line with a life lived with (good) habits, one that is guarded and watched over more literally. An alternative formation might have been *piyaliztli*, which would be the action noun of *piya*. The difficulty is that the sense would have been closer to habituation, rather than habit. No clear rendering, however, proves entirely accurate and one is to bear in mind that it is our "Western" prejudice to search for a single term and not Nahuas standard practice.

85 **"My son . . . you have guarded":** *D* 73, 46.

85 **"eagle and jaguar":** The most literal translation for *ocelotl*, clearly, is "ocelot," but Nahuatl speakers did not distinguish between the larger jaguar, *Panthera onca*, and the somewhat smaller *Leopardus pardalis*. Dibble and Anderson in *FC* 11.1, 1, in the first footnote, identify the *ocelotl* as the jaguar, following Rafael Martín del Campo's 1941 study of animals in *FC* 11, and consultation with a zoologist at the University of Utah.

85 **at the core of a person:** cf. also *D* 85, 52.

85 **vital parts of his body:** For a passage that closely parallels the father's words to his (noble) son at *FC* 6.17, 87, see *D* 71, 45. For another passage that uses "breast and throat" as a slightly different *difrasismo*, see *D* 60, 39.

86 **the face and the heart:** There are differences between Aristotle's understanding of *ēthos* (character) and the Aztec *ixtli*, *yollotl*, but they serve sufficiently analogous roles for their respective frameworks for our purposes.

Lesson 7

87 **Don Martín:** This section uses the historical work found in Chapter 7 of C. Townsend's *Fifth Sun*, 155–71, especially for dramatic elements. The primary source material is derived from *Noticia histórica de la conjuración del Marqués del Valle, años de 1565–1568*, edited by Manuel Orozco y Berra (Mexico City: R. Rafael, 1853), 228–33.

90 **actions in due measure:** The present study treats actions that are "at the mean," or "aptly expressed," or performed "in due measure" as equivalent terms selected variously for aesthetic purposes.

91 **"Not very tattered . . . clothing":** *FC* 6.41, 231.

91 **not moderation but the mean:** Dibble and Anderson, who translate it as "moderation," of course did not have a philosophical audience in mind.

91 **"Behold . . . on the earth":** *FC* 6.19, 101–2. This discussion is, of course, the mother's version of the parable of the abyss and the mountain peak that the father delivers to his son too at *FC* 6.22, 125. We have seen this

quotation before, but I repeat it here to show that these lines are textually connected to the discussion of the mean.

92 **Let's consider another case:** The approach developed, then, largely agrees with Rosalind Hursthouse's assessment that the parameterized, or central doctrine of the mean as she calls it in *"The Central Doctrine of the Mean"* in *The Blackwell Guide to Aristotle's "Nicomachean Ethics,"* edited by Richard Kraut (Malden, MA: Blackwell Press, 2006), 96–115, is the only defensible form. W. D. Ross, much earlier in *Aristotle* (New York: Routledge, 1995 [1949]), had already criticized the trinitarian scheme, such that a mean is a notion between two vices as inadequate, 205. Hursthouse, for her part, developed many of the difficulties that have informed the contemporary research in her earlier "A False Doctrine of the Mean," *Proceedings of the Aristotelian Society* 81 (1980–81): 57–72. Additional recent support for the parameterized or central view include C. C. W. Taylor's argument in *Aristotle: "Nicomachean Ethics" Books II–IV* (Oxford: Oxford University Press, 2006), 110–11, and Leslie Brown's "Why Is Aristotle's Virtue of Character a Mean? Taking Aristotle at His Word (*NE* ii 6)" in *The Cambridge Companion to Aristotle's "Nicomachean Ethics,"* edited by Ronald Polansky (Cambridge: Cambridge University Press, 2014), 64–80.

93 **poem about the Eucharist:** See "Cruz, Juana Inés de la" in *Appleton's Cyclopaedia of American Biography*, edited by J. G. Wilson and J. Fiske (New York: Appleton, 1900).

94 **"I beg you . . . silence":** Sor Juana Inés de la Cruz, *Poems, Protest, and a Dream*, translated and edited by Margaret Sayers Penden (New York: Penguin Books, 1995), 5.

94 **the (perhaps mandated) divestment:** At least this is a predominant interpretation. The historical evidence one would like to see in favor of this view is not undeniably strong. The other view was that, for whatever reason, Sor Juana was at this point convinced that persisting in the life of the mind was an affront to God and so, by her own will, she abandoned all her talents.

95 **"go along . . . sheer cliffs.":** *FC* 6.19, 101.

95 **sheer drop-offs:** The approach follows Dibble and Anderson's poetical but insightful translation.

96 **You might have the wrong intention:** Two metaphors are thus at work in the Nahua texts, but since the parameters account could include the previous arithmetic account, and since it is a more defensible idea, I take it to be the more complete articulation. One should note that in the father's parable of the mountain peak the same expression is used, so that the notion at work is a deliberate one. See his rendering at *FC* 6.22, 125.

96 **"With respect . . . dress extraordinarily":** *FC* 6.22, 123.

96 **"strong, forceful . . . others":** *FC* 10.3, 11. This translation accepts Dibble and Anderson's reasoning in footnote 5.
97 **found throughout the tenth volume:** For additional developments of the way in which gender informed Nahua social roles, see Cecelia Klein, "None of the Above: Gender Ambiguity in Nahua Ideology," in *Gender in Pre-Hispanic America: A Symposium at Dumbarton Oaks*, edited by Cecelia Klein (Washington, DC: Dumbarton Oaks, 2001), 183–253; Louise M. Burkhart, "Gender in Nahuatl Texts of the Early Colonial Period: Native "Tradition" and the Dialogue with Christianity," in *Gender in Pre-Hispanic America*, edited by Cecelia Klein (Washington, DC: Dumbarton Oaks, 2001), 87–107, and the entirety of Caroline Dodds Pennock's *Bonds of Blood: Gender, Lifecycle and Sacrifice in Aztec Culture* (New York: Palgrave MacMillan, 2011).
97 **the broader neighborhood, or *calpolli*:** For more on the political organization of the city, see James Lockhart's *The Nahuas After the Conquest*, 14–28.
97 **"ordering and arranging":** *FC* 6.4 19.
97 **"Old God":** *FC* 6.4, 19.
97 **even if they were fleeing:** One may read an account of just this sort of obligation in Domingo Francisco de San Antón Muñón Chimalpahin Cuauhtlehuanitzin's *Codex Chimalpahin: Society and Politics in Mexico Tenochtitlán, Tlatelolco, Texcoco, Culhuacan, and Other Nahua Alteptl in Central Mexico*, volume 2, edited and translated by Arthur J. O. Anderson and Susan Schroeder (Norman: University of Oklahoma Press, 1997), 184.
99 **I think it appropriate:** Notably, in my other public writing I have been working at developing the intersection of Aztec and Stoic philosophy because, while different on several points, they often prove to be complementary.
99 **torture without breaking:** James Stockdale, "Courage Under Fire: Testing Epictetus's Doctrines in a Laboratory of Human Behavior," (Stanford, CA: Hoover Institution on War, Resolution and Peace, 1993), 13.
100 **"the character . . . has grown well in me":** *D* 27, 17.
100 **"Will you burnish . . . like an eagle and jaguar":** *D* 64, 41. Translation altered to highlight the philosophical substantives at work. Another translation, as I took in the free-standing book, was to render "*in pillotl*" as "the nobility." The philosophical point does not change, as bravery in both cases is connected to nobility.
101 **"A [Brave] man . . . difficulty by deception":** *FC* 10.6, 23.
102 **"A Lady . . . resolute":** *FC* 10.13, 46. For the scholars, compare also the

discussion of what is closest to the Nahua's magnanimous person, the leader, the mother, the father who is the cypress tree, under whom others take refuge at *FC* 6.14, 73.

103 **An action is right if and only if:** This is my contemporary workup of the formulation, just as Hursthouse works up her formulation from Aristotle in *Virtue Ethics* (Oxford: Oxford University Press, 1999).

Spiritual Exercise III

105 **"because in the market . . . grown well in me":** *D* 27, 17.

Lesson 8

108 **"sending invitations. . . . Mechoacan and Metztitlan":** Diego Durán, *History of the Indies of New Spain*, translated by Doris Heyden (Norman: University of Oklahoma Press, 1994), LIV, 402.

109 **awed by Montezuma's presence:** Durán appears to include the additional historical liberty that many of the kings took their own lives, which would have undermined Montezuma's purpose. I consider it an embellishment.

110 **"The Philosopher . . . better off":** *FC* 10.8, 29–30.

110 **"what is above and below the earth":** The phrase literally reads: "He knows what is above and below." It is implied that what they are above and below is the earth. This is, of course, philosophically interesting since one charge against Socrates as recorded in Plato's *Apology of Socrates*, and for which he was put to death, namely that he claimed to know what was above and below the earth. See *Apologia Socratis* in *Platonis Opera*, volume 1, edited by E. A. Duke, et al. (Oxford: Oxford University Press, 1995), 19b.

111 **"and is disgraced":** Literally, *atoiatl, tepexitl* means a river, a rocky place, but functions as a *difrasismo* for disgrace. Cf. Miguel León-Portilla's explanation in *La filosofía náhuatl*, footnote 27 of chapter 1.

111 **"mysteriously ends up better off":** These last lines are difficult to translate without holistic interpretation. Dibble and Anderson take the description to suffer Christian interpolations, so that *nahualli, tlapouhqui*, and the like are taken as paradigm examples of bad people. On this line of reasoning, the bad philosopher is likened to them because of an association with powers Sahagún and his (Christianized?) informants thought to be from the devil. The approach represented in the present translation does not take this view, but rather, following León-Portilla, seeks to make sense of the terms in a way that is consistent with the

Nahua outlook. The principle of charity suggests that the text might be more profitably read in this way.

112 **"a counselor... a face":** The terms are *teixcuitiani, teixtomani*. A deflationary interpretation of this passage might argue that the philosopher merely serves as a good example for others. But even this is enough for the point under discussion. If the other person comes to form better *judgments*, then there is no material philosophic disagreement.

113 **tempted to call the sophist:** Miguel León-Portilla makes this argument in *La filosofía náhuatl*, 63–74.

113 **personality and property:** One may wonder how this imprudent person ends up mysteriously doing well. The implication seems to be that some of these bad philosophers deceive others deliberately with the aim of gaining an advantage over them.

113 **"wisdom and practical wisdom":** To be clear, I do not think that the Aztecs held to a strong difference between these forms of wisdom. Even among contemporary philosophers the difference is often elusive. I only mean to highlight that the Aztecs did have a sense that some forms of knowledge were different from craftsman-like knowledge, because it was less constrained in scope, and that it enabled them to live well.

115 **"And when he... the youths":** *FC* 9.3, 12–13.

116 **behave in foreign lands:** Though more on this point is developed in Lesson 6, which is specifically devoted the virtue of practical reasoning, please bear in mind that the recorded text is elliptical. It, at one point, states that "all [of the *calpolli* leaders] responded to his [the principle merchant's] words" (*FC* 9.3, 12), but the recorded text only retains the discourse of the leader positioned in the leading position. He warns generally of weather conditions but details moral conduct in cities abroad.

116 **and some at the ends:** The children, including those even who are not able to carry heavy materials, are set to go traveling to gain experience (*FC* 9.3, 12).

116 **ingredient in any virtue:** This topic is important yet somewhat technical. I have thus moved the discussion to Appendix II.

117 **humans are impaired:** In what follows, the arguments developed were helped considerably by John Doris's *Talking to Our Selves: Reflection, Ignorance, and Agency* (Oxford: Oxford University Press, 2017), 103–26, and Scott Page's *The Diversity Bonus* (Princeton, NJ: Princeton University Press, 2019), 162–S83. The argument reviews, joins, develops, and expands them. Evidence for these initial claims is drawn from these sources: Michael Newton, *Savage Girls and Wild Boys: A History of Feral Children* (London: Picador Press 2004), 208–29; Harry Harlow, Robert Dodsworth, Margaret Kuenne Harlow, "Total Social Isolation in

Monkeys," *Proceedings of the National Academy of Sciences* 54 (1965): 90–97; and Harlow, *From Learning to Love: The Select Papers of H. F. Harlow* (Westport: Praeger Publishing, 1986).

117 **You can find data... for developed adults:** Evidence for this paragraph is drawn from these sources: Laura Sullivan's documentary, "At Pelican Bay Prison, a Life in Solitary Confinement," film (NPR 2012); Stuart Grassian, "Psychopathological Effects of Solitary Confinement," *American Journal of Psychiatry* 140 (1983): 1450–54, and Dorte Sestoft, Henrik Andersen, Tommy Lillebaek, and Gorm Gabrielsen, "Impact of Solitary Confinement on Hospitalization Among Danish Prisoners in Custody," *International Journal of Law and Psychiatry* 21 (1988): 103.

118 **Similar negative evidence... psychopathy:** Evidence for this paragraph derived from these sources: Otto Kernberg "The Psychotherapeutic Management of Psychopathic, Narcissistic, and Paranoid Transferences" in *Psychopathy: Antisocial, Criminal, and Violent Behavior*, edited by T. Millon, E. Simonsen, M. Birket-Smith, and R. D. Davis (New York: Guilford, 1998), 372–92; and Linda Mealey, "The Sociobiology of Sociopathy: An Integrated Evolutionary Model," *Behavioral and Brain Sciences* 18 (1995): 523–99; and James Blair, Derek Mitchell, and Karina Blair, *The Psychopath: Emotion and the Brain* (New York: Blackwell Press, 2006), 1–17.

119 **Three features characterize... ethical reasoning:** Much of the subject matter in this paragraph is taken from the American Psychiatric Association, *Diagnostic and Statistical Manual of Mental Disorders* (Washington, DC: American Psychiatric Publishing, 2013), 715. In the fifth edition of the manual, controversy followed the inclusion of narcissism as a clinical condition. Yet narcissistic tendencies have been found clinically significant. See, for example, Joshua D. Miller, Thomas Widiger, and W. Keith Campbell, "Narcissistic Personality Disorder and the DSM-V," *Journal of Abnormal Psychology* 119 (2010): 640–49; Elsa Ronningstam's work in "Narcissistic Personality Disorder: A Current Review," *Current Psychiatry Reports* 12 (2010): 68–75, and Ronningstam's "Narcissistic Personality Disorder in DSM V—In Support of Retaining a Significant Diagnosis," *Journal of Personality Disorders* 25 (2011): 248–59. Even subclinical cases suffice for the present point: narcissism results in difficulties in practical and ethical reasoning. For empirical support on this point see Erika Carlson, Simine Vazire, and Thomas Oltmanns, "You Probably Think This Paper's About You: Narcissists' Perceptions of Their Personality and Reputation," *Journal of Personality and Social Psychology* 101 (2011): 185–201 and Simine Vazire, Laura Naumann, Peter Rentfrow, and Samuel Gosling, "Portrait of a

Narcissist: Manifestations of Narcissism in Physical Appearance," *Journal of Research in Personality* 42 (2008): 1439–47. Although sophisticated tests have been developed to determine whether a person qualifies as a narcissist, Sara Konrath, Brian Meier, and Brad Bushman, in "Development and Validation of the Single Item Narcissism Scale (SINS)," *PLoS One* 9 (2014), found that it was possible to administer a one-question test to determine whether a person is a narcissist. It reads: "To what extent do you agree with this statement: "I am a narcissist." Note: The word "narcissist" means "egotistical, self-focused, and vain." Participants are to score their agreement on a scale from 1 (least) to 7 (most). Apparently, the exam functions as effectively as much longer instruments because narcissists are aware of their extraordinary self-love and proud of it. Finally, the claims in this paragraph make use of Steven Schwartzberg's *Casebook of Psychological Disorders: The Human Face of Emotional Distress* (New York: Pearson, 1999), 106–88.

120 **Early studies of group reasoning:** See, for example, Frand Restle and James H. Davis, "Success and Speed of Problem Solving by Individuals and Groups," *Psychological Review* 69 (1962): 520–36, and James H. Davis's later development in "Group Decision and Social Interaction," *Psychological Review* 80 (1973): 97–125. For a review of related studies see Helmut Lamm and Gisela Trommsdorff, "Group versus Individual Performance on Tasks Requiring Ideational Proficiency (Brainstorming)," *European Journal of Social Psychology* 3 (1973): 361–88.

120 **Later studies:** Gayle Hill, "Group versus Individual Performance: Are N + 1 Heads Better Than One?," *Psychological Bulletin* 91 (1982): 517–39. See also Paul Paulus, Timothy Larey, and Anita Ortega, "Performance and Perceptions of Brainstormers in an Organization Setting," *Basic and Applied Social Psychology* 17 (1995): 249–65.

120 **bonuses for complex problems:** Evidence for these claims may be found in Hill, "Group versus Individual Performance," 524 and Daniel Schwarz, "The Emergence of Abstract Representations in Dyad Problem Solving," *Journal of the Learning Sciences* 4 (1995): 321–54.

120 **Evidence for superior performance ... categories:** Data for Billboard 100 hits are taken from Dan Kopf, "How Many People Take Credit?," *Priceonomics*, October 30, 2015. https://priceonomics.com/how-many-people-take-credit-for-writing-a-hit-song/. Last accessed August 26, 2019. Mutual fund performance data is found in Saurin Patel and Sergei Sarkissian, "To Group or Not to Group? Evidence from Mutual Fund Databases," *Journal of Financial and Quantitative Analysis* 52 (2017): 1989–2021. To be clear, a basis point is one-hundredth of a percent, so the 60 basis points under discussion is a 0.6 percent increase in risk-adjusted

returns. This is significant. Compounded, over one's working life, say fifty years, the difference is more than a 30 percent increase in one's overall equity. Patent data are studied in Stephan Wuchty, Benjamin F. Jones, and Brian Uzzi, "Increasing Dominance of Teams in Production of Knowledge," *Science* 316 (2007): 1036–39. See also Jasjit Singh and Lee Fleming, "Lone Inventors as Sources of Breakthroughs: Myth or Reality?," *Management Science* 56 (2010): 41–56. And coauthored research data is supported by Benjamin F. Jones, Brian Uzzi, and Stephan Wuchty, "Multi-university Research Teams: Shifting Impact, Geography and Social Stratification in Science," *Science* 322 (2008): 1259–62.

121 **Perhaps the most compelling and most direct evidence ... period:** Data for cooperation in social scientific research is found in National Research Council, *Enhancing the Effectiveness of Team Science*, edited by Nancy J. Cooke and Margaret L. Hilton (Washington DC: National Academies Press, 2015),1. Data for outperformance in scientific and engineering work may be found in Wuchty, Jones, and Uzzi, "Increasing Dominance of Teams," 1036 and National Research Council, *Enhancing the Effectiveness of Team Science*, 20.

122 **surpass one thousand citations in science and engineering:** Wuchty, Jones, and Uzzi, "Increasing Dominance of Teams," 1037.

122 **that ethical reasons are practical reasons:** I have in mind the view that Roger Crisp advances in *Reasons and the Good*, see especially the Introduction and chapter 1.

123 **value of future environmental harm:** See Nicolas Stern's initial *The Economics of Climate Change: The Stern Review* (Cambridge: University of Cambridge Press, 2007) and his later reply to Nordhaus, "The Structure of Economic Modeling of the Potential Impacts of Climate Change," *Journal of Economic Literature* 51 (2013): 838–59. With respect to William Nordhaus's views see "A Review of the Stern Review on the Economics of Climate Change," *Journal of Economic Literature* 45 (2007): 686–702 and his book *A Question of Balance: Weighing the Options of Global Warming Policies* (New Haven, CT: Yale University Press, 2008).

124 **facilitates ethical reasoning:** One may be bothered that the argument at points shifts between "deliberation" and "reasoning." The switch in terminology is largely stylistic. Where it is not, I intend "reasoning" to serve as a broader class than "deliberation." Support for reasoning, then, should at worst be taken as indirect support for deliberation.

124 **experiments illustrate this concept's dark side:** Stanley Milgram, *Obedience to Authority* (New York: Harper and Row, 1974), 55–57.

124 **continue the shocks:** Milgram, *Obedience to Authority*, 119.

124 **The agreement that "the biggest problem":** Doris, *Talking to Our Selves*,

121. For a more extended discussion of such data, see Bruce Ackerman and James Fishkin, *Deliberation Day* (New Haven, CT: Yale University Press, 2004), 52–59.
125 **better overall judgments:** Robert Luskin, David Crow, James Fishkin, Will Guild, and Dennis Thomas, "Final Report on the Deliberative Polling® on 'Vermont's Energy Future,'" (Austin, TX: Center for Deliberative Opinion Research, University of Texas at Austin, 2008), 23.
126 **"I was dead wrong ... me":** Ray Dalio, *Principles* (New York: Simon & Schuster, 2017), 33–34.
126 **"In retrospect ... how arrogant I was:** Dalio, *Principles*, 35.
127 **"And lower your head ... with them":** *D* 42, 26. The mother's imperatives include "lower your head" / *xi-tolo* and "humble yourself" / *xi-mopechteca*. The term *pechteca* (pech-TE-ka) means to bow down, and in a more extended sense to humble oneself. Since the abstract noun for bowing one's head, *toloa*, is attested as *tololiztli* in historical sources, this is probably the best we'll find for a single Nahuatl word to express the philosophical notion of "humility." For a different context, but a similar expression, see *D* 115, 72 and in the *Florentine Codex* 6.20, 106.
127 **three further crucial dimensions:** To be clear, then, the analysis proposes that there are at least four dimensions to humility: respect, social role, accurate self-estimation, and the ability to heed council well.
127 **"that [he] should ... on the earth":** *FC* 6.20, 105.
127 **"Oh my son ... presumptuous":** *FC* 6.20, 110.
128 **"he esteems himself ... exceedingly":** *FC* 6.43, 248.
128 **I heed no mother ... own accord":** *FC* 6.43, 247.
129 **"I make the ash heap ... there":** *FC* 6.43, 247.
129 **place in society:** In *D* this path of the fallen is described as the path of the rabbit and the deer (*D* 35–36, 21–23). It is opposed in the very next paragraph, to the way which enables one to stand up on one's own feet.

Spiritual Exercise IV

131 **"In vain was I born ... earth":** *RS*, fol. 21r. Originally translated by Miguel León-Portilla and altered for readability.

Lesson 9

134 **Quecholcohuatl:** My guide in this historical reconstruction is again Camilla Townsend, *Fifth Sun*, 60–65, but the original material derives from Domingo Chimalpahin's *Las Ocho Relaciones y el memorial de Colhuacán*, fol. 175–76.

135 **song of great beauty:** Alva Ixtlilxochitl, *Obras históricas de Don Fernando de Alva Ixtlilxochitl*, vol. 2, 268. While Ixtlilxochitl often embellished his works, the central incident is plausible and coheres with Chimalpahin's story, so there is no prima facie reason to doubt it.

135 **for specific festivals:** *FC* 6. 23, 132.

136 **not one thing but three:** The tripartitioning of willpower is phenomenological and intended to follow the insights found in Aztec texts. It is somewhat like the division Kelly McGonigal outlines in the first part of *The Willpower Instinct: How Self-Control Works, Why it Matters, and What You Can Do To Get More of It* (New York: Penguin 2010). Neither drive (for intense situations and for consistency over time), nor durability (the ability to resist temptation), nor discipline (the ability to resist temptation), map neatly onto one area of the brain. The frontal cortex's job is largely to enable us to do the "harder" thing as R. M. Sapolsky explains in "The Frontal Cortex and the Criminal Justice System," *Philosophical Transactions of the Royal Society of London. Series B, Biological Sciences* 359 (2004): 1787–96. This gives us drive and discipline, but the consistency of durability additionally requires access to our semantic memories. Phineas Gage's brain trauma, in 1848, provides one of the earliest cases in support of the role of the prefrontal cortex in resisting temptation. The loss of his prefrontal cortex made it impossible for him to exhibit impulse control. See M. Macmillan, "Restoring Phineas Gage: A 150th Retrospective," *Journal of the History of the Neurosciences: Basic and Clinical Perspectives* 9 (2000): 46–66. Resisting temptation, however, is also made possible by midbrain activity, as prompted by feelings of fear or disgust. The two minds thus may work toward the same goal in resisting temptation. From J. D. Cohen, "Neural Perspectives on Cognitive Control and the Multiplicity of Selves" (invited address at the annual meeting of the American Psychological Association, San Diego, California, August 13, 2020) and J. A. Anson and D. T. Kuhlman, "Post-Ictal Klüver-Bucy Syndrome After Temporal Lobectomy," *Journal of Neurology, Neurosurgery & Psychiatry* 56 (1993): 311–13.

136 **points turned out to be true:** Though the original studies were conducted in the 1960s, the central essay in the field is W. Mischel, Y. Shoda, and M. L. Rodriguez, "Delay of Gratification in Children," *Science* 244 (1989): 933–37. For follow-up studies see D. C. Funder, J. H. Block, and J. Block, "Delay of Gratification: Some Longitudinal Personality Correlates," *Journal of Personality and Social Psychology* 44 (1983): 1198–1213 and A. W. Logue and A. Chavarro, "Self-Control and Impulsiveness in Preschool Children," *The Psychological Record* 42 (1992): 189–203. For an example of more recent work developing possible interventions see Nadine Joseph,

"Delayed Gratification Behavior Among Elementary School Children: An Intervention Model," *Journal of Research Initiatives* 1 (2015): 1–13.

137 **rolls right off the tongue:** This is sarcasm.

138 **skin in its own way:** See Alfredo López-Austin's detailed account of these forms of cognizing in chapters four through six in his *Cuerpo humano e ideologia*.

138 **Additional prudence:** The phrase used is "*in nematcaiotl, in nematiliztli*," which is a common *difrasismo* for prudence, in addition to the term *ixtlamatiliztli* discussed in Lesson 8.

138 **"Listen!... a ridiculous spectacle":** FC 6.22, 124. The father's discussion is centered on the narrower vice of gluttony. The word in Nahuatl is *tequitlaqualiztli* (te-qui-tla-kwa-LEEZ-tlee). But since this is one dimension of temperance's broader umbrella, it illuminates this broader domain.

138 **"Go on living.... is necessary":** FC 6.31, 126. The term for "mean" is *tlanepantlacaiotl*.

138 **leading a life on earth:** I do not think there is a single term for the virtue, or not one that is used consistently among multiple texts. Note that *dikē* was used as both "just" and "teratogenic path" in classic Greek. It is enough for us that there is evidence that *mimatiliztli* is used here in this way, and so can fruitfully guide philosophical reflection.

138 **virtue to the mean:** The term is quite general here, meaning literally middle-way-ness. It thus aptly covers both the inner and outer mean, even if the Nahuas did not rigorously distinguish these using the terms *tlacoqualli* from *tlanepantla*.

139 **expression for practical wisdom:** The *difrasismo* is *nematcaiotl, nematiliztli*. It appears to be the more poetic formulation for practical wisdom than *ixtlamatiliztli*.

139 **"Be temperate.... to go":** FC 6.22, 121.

139 **"Although she... do not simply give in":** FC 6.21, 117.

139 **"old and wrinkled":** FC 6.21, 117. There may be some sense of connection with *ihiyotl* as a life force on this matter.

140 **"the origin... perdition":** FC 6.14, 68.

140 **"becoming drunk":** FC 6. 23, 132.

140 **"Fifth chapter... not belittle his spirit":** FC 4.5, 15.

140 **Four Hundred Rabbits:** The appearance of rabbits in this context appears to be different from the discussion of the way of the deer and rabbit discussed in Lesson 1. I am unaware of any study that has systematically organized the meaning, or symbolism, of rabbits in Aztec literature—especially with an eye to their ethical dimensions. They do appear to connote excess in this circumstance.

140 **the passage details various games:** *FC* 4.12, 47.
140 **"wine" (*octli*):** *FC* 4.36, 118.

Spiritual Exercise V

142 **"it was . . . yet dark:** *FC* 3.a.8, 65.
142 **attributed to Admiral William McRaven:** University of Texas at Austin, "Admiral McRaven Addresses the University of Texas at Austin Class of 2014," May 23, 2014, YouTube, https://www.youtube.com/watch?v=yaQZFhrWofU.

Lesson 10

144 **Tenochtitlán to outside powers:** I am drawing on Camilla Townsend's historical work in piecing together Malintzin's life in *Malintzin's Choices: An Indian Woman in the Conquest of Mexico* (Albuquerque: University of New Mexico Press, 2006) and her *Fifth Sun*, 85–106. It is James Lockhart who catalogued the many names for women in his *The Nahuas After the Conquest* (Stanford, CA: Stanford University Press, 1992): 118–22.
145 **some nobleman in his bed:** To be clear, I am writing in euphemisms. This would not have been voluntary, and she would have been raped. We cannot know for sure whether this happened, but it is likely.
147 **"Soc.: But before . . . speaking the truth?":** Plato, "Alcibiades," in *The Roots of Political Philosophy: Ten Forgotten Socratic Dialogues*, translated by Carnes Lord (Ithaca, NY: Cornell University Press, 1987), 110a–b. Translation altered.
148 **"became wealthy . . . pity for others":** *FC* 4.35, 114–15. The translation is an altered form of Dibble and Anderson's.
148 **"A woman . . . Why or why not?":** Lawrence Kohlberg, *Essays on Moral Development, Volume I: The Philosophy of Moral Development* (San Francisco: Harper & Row, 1981).
149 **recorded in the *Primeros Memoriales*:** This may not be a notion shared with Tenochtitlán, then. But perhaps Sahagún thought it otherwise objectionable or unnecessary, so we are only left to speculate.
149 **"These are . . . duties":** *PM* fol. 62v col. B, 234.
150 **"He [i.e., the vicious man] . . . into wickedness":** *D* 9–10, 7. Translation slightly altered.
151 **the virtuous path:** The Nahuatl reads *in ah-qualli, in ah-yectli* for vice, while virtue is *in qualli, in yectli*.
151 **constitute the path, *in ohtli*:** Recall also the mother's parable of the

abyss and the mountain peak analyzed previously; section 51, at *FC* 6.19, 101. He also begins by recalling the path, *in otli*, and connects it explicitly to the wisdom of tradition, to those who came before and had heads of white hair.

151 **those that fostered temperance:** As a point of clarification, the terms "temperance" and "moderation" are two names in English for the same virtue.

151 **such as collecting firewood:** *FC* 3.a.8, 65–66.

152 **probably shouldn't refrain:** The quoted sections from the *FC* 6.23 appear to suggest that the Nahuas had something like our sense of alcoholism, but it is not shared in the sources from *FC* 4.5. The historical point deserves more attention, but for our philosophical retrieval of Aztec philosophy a rough and ready sense of the topic is sufficient.

152 **call this the "enumeration problem":** Daniel Russell raises this problem specifically in chapter five of *Practical Intelligence and the Virtues*. It is not clear that the Stoics developed their cardinal virtues framework for the purpose of resolving the enumeration problem, but at least a desire for logical simplicity appears to have motivated their move.

153 **specific class of virtues:** The conceptual framework for "virtues of relationships" as opposed to virtues of character is something that I have developed from Elyse Purcell's work on virtue ethics as presented in several conference talks. I found her discussion illuminating for a range of passages in Aztec work that were otherwise opaque. See her forthcoming article "Virtues of Relationship."

Spiritual Exercise VI

154 **rising early in the morning:** *FC* 3.a.8, 65. The appendix details several such activities.

154 **"At daybreak . . . rising to act as a human":** Marcus Aurelius, *Meditations*, in *Marcus Aurelius*, edited and translated by C. R. Haines (Cambridge, MA: Harvard University Press, 1916), vol. 1, 98. Translation modified.

Lesson 11

157 **"covered him . . . lord vassals":** Alva Ixtlilxochitl, *Obras históricas de Don Fernando de Alva Ixtlilxochitl*, vol. 2, 241–42. These episodes clearly make up part of Nezahualpilli's legend. Their historical accuracy is immaterial to the philosophical point they illustrate.

158 **proved difficult:** These stories are to be found in Alva Ixtlilxochitl's

histories. Because they are so astonishing, some historians do not take them to be true. On the other hand, these stories do little to paint Nezahualpilli in a good light, and given that Alva Ixtlilxochitl is generally only questioned for his promotion of the Tezcocan line, the reasons for doubt are murky.

158 **"she began... they were her gods"**: Ixtlilxochitl, *Obras históricas*, vol. 2, 285–86.

159 **heightened romantic attraction:** This is, roughly, the way that Alain de Botton characterizes the Romantic conception of love in the first chapter of his *Essays in Love* (London: Picador, 2015), and I am inclined to agree with this broad-strokes characterization.

159 **along ethical lines: daily rituals, romance rituals, and intimacy rituals:** In some ways, you could understand this part of the book as an expansion on contemporary empirical work, which examines love cross-culturally. For example, Susan Sprecher, Arthur Aron, et al., "Love: American Style, Russian Style, and Japanese Style," *Journal of the International Association for Personal Relationships* 1 (1994): 349–69 found significant differences in expected gender norms among these nations.

159 **virtues of relationships:** Perhaps especially fitting for this chapter, this is a concept that my wife, Elizabeth (Elyse) Purcell, developed in a forthcoming essay (see the note to p. 153, above).

160 **learned from Philoctetes's tragedy:** Likely drawing on inspiration from Hegel's argument, ethical philosophers tend to regard an ethical tragedy as one in which two real goods are put into conflict and there is no rational trade-off that can be considered a good outcome. It is in this narrow sense that *Philoctetes* qualifies as a tragedy.

160 **we might have with people:** To clarify the argument that follows, I'm here using the episode in the Philoctetes to highlight two important philosophical concepts: relational agency and the virtues that sustain them. We thus have three forms of shared agency at work: plural groups, corporate groups, and relational groups. These notions form core features of the Aztec view, but it's easier to identify in a play like this one.

161 **loyal to an object:** Notably, you can be "loyal" to a cause, but there is no relational agency at work so that this is a different sense of "loyalty" than the one under discussion. Causes are not agents in the sense we've used in this book—as developed in Lessons 5–8.

163 **"When the ruler... as his wife":** *CC* 13.54–14.11. The translation is John Bierhorst's from *History and Mythology of the Aztecs: The Codex Chimalpopoca* (Tuscon: University of Arizona Press, 1992).

164 **"[s]eize the... sweeping":** *FC* 6.18, 95.

164 **courtyards and homes before dawn:** *FC* 2.a, 199.

164 **"true woman" holds vigil and sweeps:** *FC* 6.14, 73.
164 **both recording similar accounts:** Diego Durán, *Historia de las Indias de Nueva España y islas de la tierra firme*, volumen 1, edited by Ángel María Garibay K. (Mexico City: Editorial Porrúa, 1967), 65, Gerónimo de Mendieta, *Historia eclesiástica indiana, obra escrita á fines del siglo XVI* (Mexico City: Editorial Porrúa, 1980), 419, 429. In general, Louise Burkhart's catalog of sweeping activities in and their survival into the early colonial period *The Slippery Earth: Nahua-Christian Moral Dialogue in Sixteenth-Century Mexico* (Tucson: The University of Arizona Press, 1989), 117–24 is instructive.
164 **avoid contamination within:** Burkhart, *The Slippery Earth*, 98.
164 **should have been swept up:** Mendieta, *Historia*, 82–83.
164 **preparation of food for banquets:** *FC* 9.9, 41.
165 **"Exert yourself . . . city to city":** *FC* 6.23, 133.
165 **by regular, mutual support:** The evidence does not center on the role of daily rituals, only constant, likely daily, activities. Given the cultural differences between our "Western" culture and the Aztecs' culture, such support is likely the best available.
165 **maintain a positive environment:** Stephen R. Flora, "Praise's Magic Reinforcement Ratio: Five to One Gets the Job Done," *The Behavior Analyst Today*, vol. 1, (2000): 64–69. See also J. M.Gottman, J. Coan, S. Carrere, and C. Swanson, "Predicting Marital Happiness and Stability from Newlywed Interactions," *Journal of Marriage and the Family*, vol. 60 (1998): 2–22.
165 **latter may prove corrosive:** See K. S. Sutherland, J. H. Wehby, S. R. Copeland, "Effect of Varying Rates of Behavior-Specific Praise on the On-Task Behavior of Students with EBD," *Journal of Emotional and Behavioral Disorders*, vol. 8, (2000): 2–8.
166 **its exclusive outlet in marriage:** Dodds Pennock provides a helpful summary of these condoned extramarital and multi-marital relationships among the nobles in *Bonds of Blood: Gender, Lifecycle and Sacrifice in Aztec Culture* (New York: Palgrave MacMillan, 2008), 100–1.
166 **"Ye men . . . sluggish ones":** *FC* 6.21, 118–19.
166 **at least for commoners:** It also suggests that the Aztecs may not have a notion of sexual or marital monogamy as we have in the post-Christian, secularized "West." In the present discussion, I prescind from the topic.
167 **"If a boy became . . . noble feat":** Diego Dúran, *Book of the Gods and Rites and The Ancient Calendar*, translated and edited by Fernando Horcasitas and Doris Heyden (Norman: University of Oklahoma Press, 1971), 292. Translation slightly modified for clarity.
168 **singing improves lung function:** Leanne M. Wade, "A Comparison of

the Effects of Vocal Exercises/Singing Versus Music-Assisted Relaxation on Peak Expiratory Flow Rates of Children with Asthma," *Music Therapy Perspectives* 20 (2002): 31–37.

168 **the need for medication:** Daniel Weinstein et al., "Singing and Social Bonding: Changes in Connectivity and Pain Threshold as a Function of Group Size," *Evolution and Human Behavior* 37 (2016): 152–58.

168 **alleviates irritable bowel syndrome:** R N Christina Grape, Töres Theorell, Britt-Maj Wikström, Rolf Ekman, "Choir Singing and Fibrinogen: VEGF, Cholecystokinin and Motilin in IBS Patients," *Medical Hypotheses* 72 (2009): 223–25.

168 **boosting endorphin levels:** Bronwyn Tarr, Jacques Launey, and Robin I. M. Dunbar, "Music and Social Bonding: 'Self-Other' Merging and Neurohormonal Mechanisms," *Frontiers in Psychology* 5 (2014): 1–10; Björn Vickoff et al., "Music Structure Determines Heart Rate Variability of Singers," *Frontiers in Psychology* 4 (2013): 1–16.

168 **Parkinson's or strokes:** Penelope Monroe, Mark Halaki, Fiona Kumfor, Kirrie Ballard, "The Effects of Choral Singing on Communication Impairments in Acquired Brain Injury: A Systematic Review," *International Journal of Language & Communication Disorders*, vol. 55 (2020): 303–19.

168 **mood for a significant period:** Margaret M. Unwin, Dianna T. Kenny, Pamela J. Davis, "The Effects of Group Singing on Mood," *Psychology of Music* 30 (2002): 175–85.

168 **sense of purpose and meaning:** Jane E. Southcott, "And As I Go, I Love to Sing: The Happy Wanderers, Music and Positive Aging," *International Journal of Community Music* 2 (2005): 143–56.

168 **members of the choir:** Anat Anshel and David A. Kipper, "The Influence of Group Singing on Trust and Cooperation," *Journal of Music Therapy* 25 (1988): 15–155.

168 **result of singing in *groups*:** An initial study found little difference between solo singing and group singing, but this has later been reversed. See Elizabeth Valentine and Claire Evans, "The Effects of Solo Singing, Choral Singing and Swimming on Mood and Physiological Indices," *British Journal of Medical Psychology* 74 (2001): 15–120; Nick Alan Joseph Stewart and Adam Jonathan Lonsdale, "It's Better Together: The Psychological Benefits of Singing in a Choir," *Psychology of Music* 44 (2016): 1240–54.

168 **singing naturally extend to gesture:** Carlton E. Kilpatrick, III, "Movement, Gesture, and Singing: A Review of Literature," *National Association for Music Education* 38 (2020): 29–37.

168 **dancing elevates mood and self-esteem:** Cynthia Quiroga Murcia, et al., "Shall We Dance? An Exploration of the Perceived Benefits of

Dancing on Well-Being," *Arts and Health: An International Journal for Research, Policy and Practice* (2009): 149–63.

168 **participants who did not dance:** Matthew Woolhouse and Dan Tidhar, "Group Dancing Leads to Increases Person-Perception," *Proceedings of the 11th International Conference on Music Perception and Cognition* (2010): 605–8.

168 **submersion of a hand:** Pavel Goldstein, Irit Weissman-Fogel, Guillaume Dumas, "Brain-to-Brain Coupling during Handholding Is Associated with Pain Reduction," *PANAS* 115 (2018): 2528–37.

168 **improved conflict resolution in couples:** H. J. Conradi, et al., "Improvement of Conflict Handling: Hand-Holding During and After Conflict Discussions Affects Heart Rate, Mood, and Observed Communication Behavior in Romantic Partners," *Journal of Sex and Marital Therapy* 46 (2020): 419–34.

168 **mood to regulating emotions:** Tiffany Field, "Touch for Socioemotional and Physical Well-Being: A Review," *Developmental Review* 30 (2010): 367–83; Anik Debrot, Dominik Schoebi, Meinrad Perrez, et al., "Touch as an Interpersonal Emotion Regulation Process in Couples' Daily Lives: The Mediating Role of Psychological Intimacy," *Personality and Social Psychology Bulletin* 39 (2013): 1371–85.

169 **"To Fall in Love with Anyone, Do This":** see Mandy Le Cantron's article available at: https://www.nytimes.com/2015/01/11/style/modern-love-to-fall-in-love-with-anyone-do-this.html. Last Accessed January 12, 2025.

169 **deeper sense of intimacy:** Arthur Aron et al., "The Experimental Generation of Interpersonal Closeness: A Procedure and Some Preliminary Findings," *Personality and Social Psychology Bulletin*, vol. 23 (1997): 363–77.

169 **questions from each stage:** These are taken from "The 36 Questions That Lead to Love," by Daniel Jones, who uses Len Catron's essay and Arthur Aron's research. The article is available at: https://www.nytimes.com/2015/01/09/style/no-37-big-wedding-or-small.html. Last accessed January 12, 2025.

170 **records the arrangement vividly:** *Codex Mendoza*, edited and translated by John Cooper Clark (London: Waterlow & Sons, 1938), fol. 61r.

171 **"do penance . . . cohabitating":** Alonzo de Zorita, *Relación de los señores de la Nueva España*, ed. G. Vázquez (Madrid, 1992), 94.

171 **it was not a sexual one:** Durán's account, in *Book of the Gods*, 123–24, seems to conflict with this view, but that account is anomalous, inconsistent with broader Aztec practices, and only corroborated by a later historical source that drew on his materials.

172 "Our chronicle ... satisfaction": Durán, *History of the Indies*, 254–55.
173 **individualist or collectivist spectrum:** Suzanne Riela, Geraldine Rodriguez, et al., "Experiences of Falling in Love: Investigating Culture, Ethnicity, Gender, and Speed," *Journal of Social and Personal Relationships* 27 (2010): 473–93.
173 "they are all ... abominable sin": Hernando Cortés, *Letters from Mexico*, edited and translated by A. Pagden (New Haven, CT: Yale University Press, 1986), 37.
173 "Some say that ... against it": Antonio de Herrera, *Historia general de los hechos de los castellanos en las Islas i Tierra Firme del Mar Océano* (Madrid, 1934–1957), vol. 6, 444.
174 **understood role of sex worker:** The idea of a "sex worker" probably still stands at considerable distance from the *ahuianime*.
174 **the following image:** *Codex Mendoza*, fol. 60r.

Spiritual Exercise VII

176 "But when ... noon to eat": *FC* 3.a.8, 66.
177 **you might not consume otherwise:** These points are developed at length in Michael Mosley's *The Fast 800: How to Combine Rapid Weight Loss and Intermittent Fasting for Long-Term Health* (New York: Short Books, 2018).
178 **I feel no cravings at all:** The Aztecs do seem to have discussed states resembling what we call flow in artisanal activities, in dancing, and in singing, though the topic is complex enough to deserve its own careful treatment.

Lesson 12

179 **best lands claimed by others:** The story is found in very many of the Mexica annals of the sixteenth century, though they often disagree on the details of the events. The present story is developed from the *Anales de Tlatelolco: unos annales históricos de la nación mexicana y Códice de Tlatelolco*, edited by Heinrich Berlin (Mexico City: Editorial Porrua, 1948), fol. 8r and 8v, *Códice Aubin: manuscrito azteca de la Biblioteca Real de Berlin; anales en mexicano y geroglíficos desde la salida de las tribus de Aztlán hasta la muerte de Cuauhtemoc* (Mexico: Editorial Innovación, 1980), 32, and *Codex Chimalpahin*, vol. 2, 76. The selection of narrative follows Camilla Townsend's reconstruction in *Fifth Sun*, 13–16.
179 **deceived and defeated in battle:** This is the point repeatedly emphasized in Chimalpahin's account, *Codex Chimalpahin*, vol. 2, 72–74.

180 **they were great warriors:** In writing of the "Aztecs," I mean the Mexica who came to rule in Tenochtitlán as an independent people. These same people clearly had a continuous history for generations prior; and according to their myths, they and related peoples of the central basin of Mexico all emerged from seven caves, though at different times. What is recounted here are the first events that can definitively be distinguished from mythical history for the independent Mexica people. This episode also marks the beginning of the Mexica people's existence as a settled and not nomadic group. A "beginning" is intended in these limited respects.

180 **sacrifice it might involve:** It's worth recalling that "tragedy," in the philosophic tradition following Hegel, holds that it is a circumstance in which a person is forced to choose between two ultimate goods. Sacrifice in these circumstances cannot be made—or at least not cleanly—for a higher good. There may be a better path forward, but it will involve real moral wrong.

181 **"In the days ... Second Inaugural":** Ronald C. White Jr., *A. Lincoln: A Biography* (New York: Random House, 2009), 676.

182 **now standard practice:** For a history of embalming techniques, see Erich Brenner's "Human Body Preservation—Old and New Techniques," *Journal of Anatomy* 224 (2014): 316.44. Notably, these techniques had been used with increased frequency throughout the Civil War to permit burial without excessive haste.

182 **"The city ... appeared in it":** Diego Durán, *History of the Indies of New Spain*, 383–84.

183 **"with all these ceremonies ... tears":** Durán, *History of the Indies*, 286.

183 **body burnt on a pyre:** This was not the only way that the Aztecs disposed of bodies, but it was the most common. In each case, nonetheless, there was a similar mechanism at work for releasing the *yolia*.

184 **one with the divine energy:** FC 3.a., 44.

186 **"Odysseus ... delighted to choose it":** Plato, *Republic*, 620c. Translation by Allen Bloom.

Postface

187 **Set Theory and Its Logic:** W. V. O. Quine, *Set Theory and Its Logic* (Cambridge, MA: Harvard University Press, 1965).

188 **"An Aristotelian ... all but interpret themselves":** C. D. C. Reeve, *Action, Contemplation, and Happiness: An Essay On Aristotle* (Cambridge, MA: Harvard University Press, 2012), ix.

189 **tradition of Mesoamerican Humanism:** This is a term that I take

from Miguel León-Portilla's *Humanistas de Mesoamérica* (Mexico City: Fondo de Cultura Económica, 1997). While I do not take this school to be a self-conscious one, I do think that León-Portilla does identify many of the animating strands for its approach. And I agree that newer historical work calls for a continuous updating of views, but I do not think that the "hard core" of this school has in any way been disqualified by recent findings.

192 **select historical purposes:** For a more recent review of the scholarly discussion about Ixtlilxochitl, see *Fernando de Alva Ixtlilxochitl and his Legacy*, edited by Galen Brokaw and Jongsoo Lee (Tuscon: University of Arizona Press, 2016).

199 **"Take care . . . for you to live":** *D* 25, 16.

200 **"he made himself . . . a deer":** *D* 10, 8.

200 **avoid character discussion altogether:** Christine Swanton, *Virtue Ethics: A Pluralistic View* (Oxford: Oxford University Press, 2003).

Appendix II

211 **from similar "Western" theses:** The scholarly discussion on this topic often rather confusingly uses the same name for both positions. The present analysis follows Daniel Russell's use in "Phronesis and the Virtues (*NE* VI 12–13)" in *The Cambridge Companion to Aristotle's "Nicomachean Ethics,"* edited by Ronald Polansky (Cambridge: Cambridge University Press, 2014), 203–20. The present analysis is helped much by that article and John Cooper's "The Unity of Virtue," *Social Philosophy and Policy* 15 (1988): 233–74.

211 **facets of it:** See Plato's *Protagoras*, in *Platonis Opera*, volume III, edited and annotated by Ioannes Burnet (Oxford: Oxford Classical Texts, 1903), 329C–344C, 349B–360E.

211 **from his understanding of the virtues:** *NE* VI.13, 1144b17–30.

212 **"And so . . . present":** *NE* VI.13, 144b30–1145a25.

212 **goal for your life:** *NE* VI.12, 1144a7–9.

212 **more specific end:** Fortunately, the present analysis is able to prescind from the topic of whether the end at which *phronēsis* aims is a "grand end" or blueprint of one's good life within which all actions are chosen as components or not. The grand end view is advanced by William F. R. Hardie, *Aristotle Ethical Theory* (Oxford: Oxford University Press, 1968), 233; John Cooper, *Reason and Human Good in Aristotle* (Cambridge, MA: Harvard University Press, 1975), 96–97; Terence Irwin, "Aristotle on Reason, Desire and Virtue," *Journal of Philosophy* 72 (1975): 567–78; Richard Sorabji, "Aristotle on the Role of Intellect in Virtue," in *Essays*

on *Aristotle's Ethics*, edited by Amélie O. Rorty (Berkeley: University of California Press, 1980), 206–07; David Wiggins, "Weakness of Will, Commensurability, and the Objects of Deliberation and Desire," in *Essays on Aristotle's Ethics*, edited by Amélie O. Rorty (Berkeley: University of California Press, 1980) 223–25; Alasdair MacIntyre, *Whose Justice? Which Rationality?* (Notre Dame: University of Notre Dame Press, 1988), 131–33; C. D. C. Reeve, *Practices of Reason: Aristotle's "Nicomachean Ethics"* (Oxford: Oxford University Press, 1992), 69; Kristin Inglis, "Philosophical Virtue: In Defense of the Grand End" in *The Cambridge Companion to Aristotle's "Nicomachean Ethics,"* edited by Ronald Polansky (Cambridge: Cambridge University Press, 2014), 263–87. Sarah Broadie, "Aristotle and Contemporary Ethics," in *The Blackwell Guide to Aristotle's "Nicomachean Ethics,"* edited by Richard Kraut (Malden: Blackwell, 2006), 350–53 and Daniel Russell, *Practical Intelligence and The Virtues* (Oxford: Oxford University Press, 2009), 27–30 defend the local end view. In some ways, the analysis of *bioi*, ways of life, in Aristotle's reasoning fits more naturally with the local view, and I think this view more sensible. Nevertheless, the theses advanced in this book are compatible with either side of the controversy.

213 **more specific contexts:** *NE* VI.12, 1144a29–b1.

213 **brought up well:** *FC* 3.a.7, 61.

213 **pursuit of the good life:** In both the father's discourse to his son and the mother's discourse to her daughter, the globality of practical wisdom is explicitly invoked. To recall this analysis, the father speaks of his intention as follows: *"vel timimatiz in jpan muchi, in jpan ixqujch"* (*FC* 6.22, 121). Similarly, the mother speaks of her intention stating *"Injc timonemjtiz, çan nematqui"* (*FC* 6.19, 100).

213 **natural and "real" virtues:** *NE* VI.13, 1144b1–4, b14–17.

213 **appear only intermittently:** *NE* VI.13, 1144b12–14.

214 **feeling in action:** *NE* II.6–9.

214 **that makes the reasons right:** *NE* II.2, 1103b31–34; VI.I, 1138b18–25, b32–34.

214 **gifts to be used well:** In the mother's discourse to her daughter, for example, she tells her to be aware of her nobility and to act appropriately: *"Auh njman ie izcatqui ca nel titecpiltzintli"* (*FC* 6.19, 101).

214 **avoid falling into an abyss:** *FC* 6.19, 101; 6.22, 125.

214 **what is right to wear:** *FC* 6.19, 100; 6.22, 123.

214 **moderate drinking at a fiesta:** *FC* 6.22, 124.

214 **achievement of the virtues impossible:** It is this worry that has motivated Robert Adams in chapter ten of *A Theory of Virtue: Excellence in*

Being for the Good (Oxford: Oxford University Press, 2009) to reject the thesis.
214 **scalar in character:** *NE* II.4.

Appendix III

216 **practiced homosexuality freely:** Recall that in sixteenth-century Europe and Spain in particular, homosexuality was itself thought to be an obvious sin.
217 **faulty understanding of the physical world:** The way that the native historian Ixtlilxochitl (1568–1650) portrays Tlacaelel I (1397–1478), namely a supposedly shadowy secondary figure behind the rulers in Tenochtitlán, present a different case. If Tlacaelel had alternative reasons for accelerating the practice of heart sacrifice for the purposes of political ambition and not an obligation to preserve the natural world, then this is another matter entirely. This argument does not diminish Tlacaelel purported blameworthiness, nor should it.
218 **"father of computer science":** Alan Turing is the father of *theoretical* computer science.
218 **He died shortly after:** Tommy Barker, "Have a Look Inside the Home of UCC Maths Professor George Boole," *The Irish Examiner*, Saturday, June 13, 2015.
219 **the cutting of one's ears:** *FC* 2.a, 197–98.
219 **what scholars call "heart sacrifice":** This is how Michael E. Smith characterizes these practices in *The Aztecs* (Malden: Blackwell, 2011), 221–22.
219 **"representative" for a god:** The translation of *ixiptla* into English is unnatural. The human was thought to be divinized through ritual process, so that he or she became the god after a fashion. There is no representative process involved, then, only a presentative one.
220 **slashing the breast:** For the commoner description see *FC* 2.26, 94 and 2.27, 105.
220 **presented to the sun:** See *FC* 2.29, 115 and 2.36, 156.
220 **the Tlaxcalan people:** See Manuel Aguilar-Moreno's account in *Handbook to Life in the Aztec World* (Oxford: Oxford University Press, 2006), 133–34.
221 **humans are of different sizes:** *CC* 76.18–76.50.
221 **provide life sustenance:** *CC* 76.53–54.
221 **"did penance" (*tlamaçehua*):** *CC* 76.54.
221 **"Gods . . . have been born":** *CC* 77.2. Note, I think it might be something of an over-interpretation to translate the passage this way.

Nevertheless, because I am trying to give the other side the benefit of the doubt, I have given them the most generous interpretation I could.

221 **substitute for heart sacrifice:** Cecilia Klein, for example, writes "auto-sacrifice from the beginning was viewed as a symbolic death substituted for the real thing and, as such, a debt payment made in return for continued life," in "The Ideology of Autosacrifice at the Templo Mayor," *Dumbarton Oaks Pre-Columbian Conference Proceedings* 7 (1987): 297.

221 **human sacrifice was made:** *FC* 2.37, 165; 2.38, 170.

222 **Pimply Face:** *CC* 77.36–37. I'm translating Nanahuatzin's name on its relation to *nanahuatl*, which are pustules or pimples.

222 **falls into the ashes:** He is unable to grasp both the eagle and the jaguar, which is a *difrasismo* for courage.

222 **"because I am. . . . the damage":** Reading *inin tlacoca* for *in intlacoca*, and not as *intlaçoca[uh]*. I have also retained "blood and color" as a typical *difrasismo*.

222 **Movement moves through the sky:** Interestingly, the text does not mention Quetzalcoatl at this point, who plays no active role in this myth. Rather, at the beginning, he is identified with 4 Movement (*CC* 77.30).

222 **back and forth motion:** This is a core argument of James Maffie's *Aztec Philosophy*, which I take to be settled among scholars.

223 **an elemental feature of it:** In making this claim I take a strong position against Inga Clendinnen's *Aztecs: An Interpretation* (Cambridge: Cambridge University Press 2014). At a minimum, my argument advances on hers by drawing on original language sources and through conversances with the relevant ethical scholarship.

225 **find different jobs:** I am cognizant of the scaling difficulties posed by moving onto renewable energy sources. As there is not enough of various rare earth metals in the world to build the batteries necessary—using current battery technology—transitioning immediately onto renewable resources will be difficult. But the difficulties are in principle surmountable.

Appendix IV

227 **"Guadalupe," which is an Iberian Madonna:** Some have proposed, but it is not certain, that it is this phonetic confusion among the Spaniards that led to the identification of the goddess with the Virgin Mary. The matter is contested historically and I'm not certain that we'll ever have definitive evidence.

227 **water table for safe keeping:** What follows is inspired by the retelling of Coatlicue's fate that Octavio Paz gives in his *Los privilegios de la vista:*

Arte Moderno universal, Arte de México, Obras Completas IV (Fondo de Cultura Económica: 2014), 453–57.

230 **family using Nahuatl:** In approaching the language as one learns Latin or Greek, I focused on my ability to read and translate, not to converse, since there is no one now who speaks Classical Nahuatl. Contemporary speakers divide into many forms and I do not mean here to privilege Classical Nahuatl. My goals are historical and philosophical, which has focused my study of the language.

231 **European paper, also survived:** For these points I am relying on the scholarship of Elizabeth Hill Boone's *Cycles of Time and Meaning in the Mexican Books of Fate* (Austin: University of Texas Press, 2007), 5.

232 **"Beyond raising . . . facilitating their memory":** Alonso de Zorita, *Breve y sumaria relación de los señores de la Nueva España* (Mexico City: UNAM, Biblioteca del Estudiante Universitario 32, 1554), 112.

233 **this tradition emerged later:** It is worth remarking that I am uncertain how the work of cultural depreciation evolved after this early period. I do not even know of a single historical investigation that has covered the topic. The matter is, undoubtedly, complex. But I think it crucial to note that the Indigenous peoples of Mesoamerica were not immediately demonized by all the Spaniards and that their cultural achievements were understood, at least by some, to be worthy of admiration.

233 **that is now called the *Florentine Codex*:** Most of the information that follows is to be found in Kevin Terranciano's "Introduction: An Encyclopedia of Nahua Culture: Context and Content" in *The Florentine Codex: An Encyclopedia of the Nahua World in Sixteenth-Century Mexico*, edited by Jeanette Favrot Peterson and Kevin Terraciano (Austin: University of Texas Press, 2019), 1–20.

235 **sense in his exposition:** To my colleagues in Religious Studies departments, I am fully cognizant of how outdated it is to distinguish philosophy from religion so perfunctorily. I ask your indulgence and patience. For this work, I have in mind, because I am speaking to a group of philosophers who are averse to anything religious, that a proposition may be classed as "religious" if and only if it relies on evidence that cannot *in principle* be corroborated *and* that is thought to follow from some sacred work or experience. By "corroboration" I have in mind an evidentiary process as wide as that which the sciences use, noting that "corroboration" is a theory-laden notion. In fact, I agree that there is no "bright line" that distinguishes philosophy from religion even if there are more paradigmatically philosophical or religious forms of reasoning.

236 **eating tacos and drinking horchata:** The "society" is still unofficial.

INDEX

Page numbers in *italics* refer to illustrations.
Page numbers after 238 refer to notes.

absolute good, 197
abyss and the mountain peak, parable of, 91–92, 95–96, 138, 253
accommodation, 190
action theory, 70–72
active conditions, habits vs., 83, 84
Adam (Biblical figure), 2
Adams, Robert, 273
adultery, 166
affection, 166–67, 173
affective cognition, 107
afterlife, 30, 185–86
Agamemnon, 185
agency
  corporate, 72, 162
  individual, 70–72
  plural group, 162
  relational, 162
  shared, *See* shared agency
  valuational, 251
Aguilar, Jerónimo de, 145, 146
ahuehuete tree (Montezuma cypress), 63–68, *65*, 255

ahuianime (pleasure-women), 174, 269
Ahuitzol, 182
ahuiya (happiness), 4, 5
Ajax, 185
Alcibiades, 147–48
Alcibiades (Plato), 147–48
alcohol consumption, 135, 140–41, 152
alcoholism, 264
altepetl (city-state), 97, 150
Alva Ixtlilxochitl, Fernando de, 191–92, 246, 261, 265, 271, 273
amor fati, 54, 55
amoxtli (books), 231
Anderson, Arthur J. O., 252, 255
andreia (courage), 101
Andrews, Richard, 6, 19, 193
Angry Lord, *See* Montezuma (Motecuhzoma)
animating forces, 30–33, 35–36, 41
Apollodorus, 54

Apology of Socrates (Plato), 255
Aquinas, Thomas, 189, 192, 232
aretē, 80, 198
Aristotle and Aristotelian ethics, 198, 242
  on animating forces, 31
  Aztec virtue ethics vs., 130, 200, 202, 210–15
  beingness for, 194
  cardinal virtues for, 152
  on character, 252
  contemporary reconstruction of, 7
  Eudemian Ethics, 191
  on happiness, 1
  holistic coherence for, 188–89
  on justice, 151
  on magnanimity, 248
  metaphysics for, 189
  Nicomachean Ethics, 1, 191
  path to enlightenment for, 10
  on prudence, 251
  sexist criticism of, 217

Aristotle and Aristotelian ethics (*continued*)
  syncretic materials of, 191
  temperance for, 137–39
  in "Western" philosophy, 239
  on wisdom, 109, 117, 125, 126
Aron, Arthur, 169
artificial intelligence, 39
Asbaje y Ramírez de Santillana, Inés de, *See* Juana, Sor
Asimo, 38
Atamalqualo festival, 176
atoiatl, tepexitl (disgrace), 255
attraction, 162, 163
Augustine, St., 192
autopilot, 196
autosacrifice, 274
Axayacatl (Face of Water), 134–35
Ayocuan (Life Giver), 68
Azcapotzalco, 49, 57
Aztec philosophy; *See also* specific topics and texts
  cognitive values guiding discussions of, 188–90
  as complementary to Stoicism, 254
  contemporary reconstruction of, 7
  cosmology, 18, 22
  ethical framework of, 198–201
  ethics, 189, 196–97
  logical doubles in, 21–23
  metaphysics, 18–21, 189
  path to enlightenment in, 10–11
  pessimism of, 15, 18–19, 194–97, 242
  right action in, 197–98
  three truths of, 29–30
  virtue ethics in, 130, 189, 198–99, 201–3, 210, 214–15
Aztec Philosophy (Maffie), 236
Aztec society (Nahua society)
  children's names in, 144
  "conquest" of, *See* Spanish-Aztec war
  method of studying, 190–91
  rank in, 115–16
  Shield Flower's story of origin of, 179–80
  "Western" views of, 6–7, 275

balance, 135, 137, 141, 152, 176, 178; *See also* willpower (temperance)
Baptista Viseo, Juan, 233
basis point, 259
being, *teotl* vs., 19, 192–94
Bible, Christian, 2, 29
bioi, 272
blameworthiness, 51–52, 73–74, 217–18, 225, 273
bloodletting, 35, 221
blood sacrifice, 216–26
  blameworthiness for, 217–18, 225
  context for, 219–23
  and heart sacrifice in Aztec ethics, 223–26
  sensationalism of, 216–17
body; *See also* embodied cognition; embodied mind
  animating forces in, 35–36, 51
  linking of mind, soul, and, 34–36, 251

Boleyn, Anne, 159
Bolívar, Simón, 8, 241
Boole, George, 217–18, 225
Boolean algebra, 217–18
Botton, Alain de, 265
brain structures, mapping willpower to, 261
Bratman, Michael, 249
bravery, 101, 213; *See also* courage
Bridgewater Associates, 125–26
Broyles, Steven, 248
Buddhism
  eightfold path of, 18
  Four Noble Truths of, 18
  on invulnerability, 16
  inward path of, 8–11
  on life without redemption, 24
  Mahayana, 241
  organization of cosmos in, 54, 57
  Zen, 8–11
Bushman, Brad, 258

Cacama, 72–75
calendar stone, 227, 228
calmecac (school for royal court preparation), 49, 142, 167, 246
calpolli (neighborhood), 97, 115
Campbell, R. Joe, 248
Cantares Mexicanos, 233
Cantron, Mandy Le, 169
cardinal virtues, 152–53, 264
Cārvāka materialism, 247
Cassio, 161
Catholic church
  on faith and reason, 23–24
  reburial of *Coatlicue Mayor* by, 228

Index • 279

rituals in, 114
and Sor Juana's scholarship, 93–95
translation of Nahuatl to Latin by, 231–36
Ceiba pentandra, See great silk cotton tree (great ceiba)
ceiba tree, See great silk cotton tree (great ceiba)
celebrating special occasions, 134–36, 140–41, 152, 162, 167–68
"Chalca Woman's Song, The," 134–35
Chalchiuhnenetzin, See Jade Doll (Nezahualpilli's love)
Chalco and Chalcans, 62–63, 134–36
character
  Aristotle on, 252
  as face and heart, 36, 59, 86, 112, 252
  Nietzsche on, 201
character justice, 148
  for Aztecs, 150
  fairness and, 148–49
  general, 148, 151, 262
  the path and, 149–51
Chatterjee, Satischandra, 54
children
  collaboration by, 78–80
  cultivation of habits by, 89, 103, 142
  daily rituals for, 164
  feral, 117
  happiness for parents of, 2–4, 240
  justice for, 147–48
  naming of, 144
  traveling for, 256
Chimalaxoch, 163–64
Chimalpahin (Domingo de San Antón

Muñón Chimalpahin Cuauhtlehuanitzin), 62–63, 147, 186, 261
Chimalxochitl, See Shield Flower
Cholultecas, 108
Chontal Maya, 145, 146
Chortí Maya, 32
Christianity; See also Catholic church
  Coatlicue and Virgin Mary in, 227
  loving actions of Jesus Christ, 93–94
  Nahuatl translations influenced by, 255–56
  on slippery earth, 29
  Spaniards as *cristianos*, 145, 147
  teotl vs. God of, 20
Chrysippus, 54
Cialdini, Robert, 43–44
Claxton, Guy, 41–42
cleaning rituals, 142, 164
Clendinnen, Inga, 274
Coatlicue Mayor (statue), 227–29
Coatzacoalcos, 144
Codex Chimalpopoca
  on daily rituals, 163
  on heart sacrifice and cosmology, 220–23
  translation of, 233
Codex Mendoza, 170, 174
cognition, 36
  affective, 107
  ego as seat of, 37
  embodied, 40–42, 44
  unconscious origins of, 41–42
cohesion, 120
collaboration, 78–80, 82, 117, 121–25
collectivist experiences of love, 173

Columbus, Christopher, 180
complex problems, solving, 120–22
Confucius and Confucian ethics, 242
  Aztec virtue ethics vs., 130, 200, 201, 210, 215
  on organization of cosmos, 56
consciousness, of habits, 83, 85
consequentialism, 199–200
consistency, 61, 83, 136, 142–43
control, right action and, 96
Cooper, John, 271
copula, linguistic, 19, 193
corporate agency, 72, 162
correct (*yectli*), 80, 200–201
correct, expression for good and, 80
Cortés, Hernán, 62
  burial of *Coatlicue Mayor* after success of, 227
  calmecac system and arrival of, 246
  depictions of Aztecs by, 173, 216
  first contact with Aztecs for, 6
  Doña Marina and, 145–46
  Don Martín and, 87
  misconceptions about, 6–7
  in Tlaxcala, 50
Cortés, Martín, See Martín, Don
cosmological organization, 53–58
  in Aztec philosophy, 56–58

Index

cosmological organization (*continued*)
  in Indian philosophy, 54–55
  Machiavelli on, 56
  Nietzsche on, 55
  social role related to, 97
  Stoics on, 53–54
cosmology, 18, 22, 195
council, heeding, 127–29
courage, 87–104, 203
  as "cardinal" virtue, 152
  eagle and jaguar as expression of, 85, 100–101, 252, 274
  formula for right action, 103–4
  as habit, 83, 89, 103
  heart sacrifice for, 224
  for Sor Juana, 93–95
  for Don Martín, 87–89
  and the mean, 89–95
  for men vs. women, 101–2
  and parameters of right actions, 95–99
  and personal vulnerability, 132
  practices to foster, 151
  and social vulnerability, 105–7
  as valor on the battlefield, 99–103
"Courage Under Fire" (Stockdale), 99
cowardice, 101, 102
Coxcox, 179–80
cravings, resisting, 176–78
Crisp, Roger, 250, 259
criticism, openness to, 173
cualli (good), 207
Cuauhtemoc, 75
Cuauhtlehuanitzin, *See* Chimalpahin
Cuerpo humano e ideología (López-Austin), 34

cuicalli (singing house), 167, 170
Culhuacans, 179–80

daily rituals, 162–66, 175
Dalio, Ray, 125–26
dancing, 167–68
Darwinian evolution, 55
Datta, Dhirendramohan, 54
Daughter Child, *See* Marina, Doña (Malintzin)
Day of the Dead, 30, 184
de (power), 80, 200
death; *See also* tragedy
  courage and risk of, 98–100
  meditation on your own, 180–81
  mourning rituals, 182–84
  philosophy and strength to face, 184–86
Declaration of Independence, 1
decolonial movement, 188
deliberative democracy, 124–25
Denniston, J. D., 34–35
deontological ethics, 199
dependence, 160
Descartes, René, 39
Desdemona, 161
Díaz, Porfirio, 13, 14
Dibble, Charles E., 252, 255
difrasismo patterns
  breast and throat, 252
  for core of person, 85
  for disgrace, 255
  eagle and jaguar, 85, 100–101, 252, 274
  face and heart, 36, 86, 112
  good and correct, 80

  one's father, one's mother, 129
  for practical wisdom, 139, 262
  for prudence, 262
  tail and wing, 85
dikē, 151, 262
Diogenes Laertius, 54
discipline, 103, 136–37, 139, 141, 152, 176–78, 261
discount rate, 123
discourses of the elders (in general), 4, 36, 84
Discourses of the Elders (Olmos)
  on character justice and the right path, 150–51
  on courage, 100–102, 105–6
  on ethical significance of trees, 64, 66–68
  on face, heart, and body, 36
  habituation in, 85
  on humility, 127
  Latin translation of, 232–33
  on outward path, 10
  on thoughtful speech, 45
disgrace, 255
disillusionment, 26
doctrine of the mean, 92–93
Domínguez, Robles, 14
dress, the mean for, 91
drive, 136, 137, 154–56, 261
durability, of willpower, 136, 137, 142–43, 151, 261
Durán, Diego
  on affection between youths, 167
  on bonds between married couples, 172–73

on intimacy rituals, 269
on Montezuma's coronation, 108–9, 255
on mourning rituals, 182, 183
on sweeping practice, 164
Dussel, Enrique, 239

eagle, courage expressed as jaguar and, 85, 100–101, 252, 274
Eagle Feast, 140
early rising, 151, 154–55
"Eastern" philosophy, 10; *See also* Buddhism; Confucius and Confucian ethics
ecosystem of minds, 245
ehecatl (wind), 32
embalming, 181–82, 270
embodied cognition, 40–42, 44
embodied mind, 30, 35–40, 137, 138
embodiment, in robotics, 37–38
empathy, 119
empty nest syndrome, 240
endorphins, 168
enlightenment, 9; *See also* path to enlightenment
entitlement, 119
enumeration problem, 152–53, 264
Epictetus, 8–9
epistemology, defined, 188
equity management, 121
Er, 185
esse (to be), 189
ethical assessment, failing to live up to, 217
ethical dimensions of group actions, 72–76
ethical reasoning, 118–19, 122–25

ethical tragedy, 265
Eudemian Ethics (Aristotle), 191
European heritage, collaboration for children of, 78–80
Eve, 2
evidence-grounded approach, 189–90
exaggeration, 59, 61
excellence
  aretē as, 80, 198
  human ideal for, 10, 202–3
  moral, *See* virtue
existentialism, 24
external circumstances intent and, 51–52
outer mean of right action, 91, 92, 96, 98
eztli (blood), 219

face (*ixtli*)
  alignment of heart and, 59, 107
  character expressed as face and heart, 36, 59, 86, 112, 252
  development of, 37, 41, 112, 256
  philosopher's role to help others develop, 112, 256
  as seat of deliberation and judgment, 36, 37, 85
Face of Water (Axayacatl), 134–35
failure
  in life on slippery earth, 25, 26
  to live up to ethical assessment, 217
  reflecting on and adjusting after, 142, 155–56
  role of luck in, 52

self-conception after, 133
fairness, 147–49, 151
faith, 23–25
falsehood, 245
farting, 32, 106–7
fasting, 163–64, 176–78
Fasting Child, *See* Nezahualpilli
fate, 185–86
fears, facing, 101–3
feasting, 176, 178
Federal Bureau of Investigation (FBI), 45–46
fertility, 164
festivals, 167–68
Fides et Ratio (John Paul II), 24
filosofía nahuatl, La (León-Portilla), 230–31
filth *(tlazolli)*, 164
fiscal value, of future environmental harm, 123–24
Five Suns, legend of, 18, 22, 194–95
Flamingo Serpent (Quecholcohuatl), 134–36
Flayed Lord (Xipe Totec), 220
Flint (god), 222
Florentine Codex (Sahagún), 6
  on blood sacrifice, 219, 221
  on consistent habits, 142
  on daily rituals, 164, 165
  on ethical significance of trees, 64
  on fasting, 176
  on fragility of life, 15
  on habituation, 84, 85
  on happiness, 4
  on humility, 127–29

Florentine Codex (Sahagún) (*continued*)
  on the mean, 91–92, 96–97
  Nahuatl spelling in, 207
  on philosopher's role, 59, 110–13
  on prudence, 27–28, 44
  on right speech, 43
  on ritual structures for merchants, 114
  on sexual expression, 166
  on slippery earth, 27–28
  on temperance, 138–40
  translation of, 233–34
flow, 269
flower songs (*xochicuicatl*), 50
flowery war practice, 220
fluid synchrony, 79–80, 82
food preparation, 164–65
forethought, right action and, 96
Four Hundred Rabbits, 140, 263
Four Noble Truths, 18
fragility of life, 13–25
  Aztec philosophy on, 15–17
  and faith/reason, 23–25
  and living well/the good, 17–18
  and philosophical pessimism, 18–19
  on slippery earth, 29
  and structure of reality, 19–23
  for Emiliano Zapata, 13–15
Franklin, Benjamin, 77–78
Freud, Sigmund, 42
friendship, 203
  as "cardinal" virtue, 152–53
  for connectedness, 82
  mutual trust in, 160, 161
  relational agency in, 159–62
  shared agency in, 161–62
  vulnerability in, 161
fruitfulness, of approach, 190

Gage, Phineas, 261
Garibay K., Ángel María, 189
gender identity, 106–7, 174
general character justice, 148, 151, 262
General History of the Things of New Spain (Sahagún), 234
"Genie" (feral child), 117
Gilbert, Margaret, 249
Glaucon, 33
gluttony, 138, 262
goal-directed automaticity, 196
god as nature, 20–21, 23, 29, 81, 97, 189, 235
"golden fish," 27–28
the good, 197–98
  absolute, 197
  Aztec wisdom on, 16–18
  moral luck and, 242
  for Nietzsche and Machiavelli, 56
  qualli, yectli expression for correct and, 80
  qualli as, 200–201, 207
  relative, 197–98
  and right speech, 43
  rooted life for, 57, 58
  on slippery earth, 28
  standing upright for, 68
  virtues vs., 200–201
  virtuous action for, 76

gossip, 45, 46
great silk cotton tree (great ceiba), 64, 66, 66–67, 67
Greece, ancient; *See also* Stoicism; *specific philosophers*
  method of studying, 190–91
  organization of cosmos in, 53–54
  pessimism in tragedies of, 242
  unbalance in, 52–53
Greek Particles, The (Denniston), 34–35
grief, 162, 182–83
group action responsibility for, 73–74
group actions
  decision making, 109, 115–25
  ethical dimensions of, 72–76
Guadalupe, 227, 275

habits, 201
  consistent, 142–43
  of courage, 89
  cultivating, 82–86, 103–4
  defining, 82–83
  and right action, 96
  valuational agency and, 251
  and virtue, 82
habituation, 84–86, 92, 252
Haidt, Jonathan, 42
Handbook, The (Epictetus), 8–9
hand-holding rituals, 167
happiness, 1–11, 189
  Aztec philosophy on, 4–5, 8, 240
  and Aztec wisdom on living well, 16, 17

Index • 283

and inward vs. outward path to enlightenment, 8–11
metaphors for, 69
for parents, 2–4, 240
pursuing rooted life vs., 184
on slippery earth, 29
"Western" philosophy on, 1–4
and Western views of Aztec society, 6–7
Hart, Paul, 14
head, animating force centered in, 35, 41; *See also* face (*ixtli*)
heart (*yollotl*), 35
alignment of face and, 59, 107
animating force centered in, 31, 35
character expressed as face and heart, 36, 59, 86, 112, 252
habituation involving, 84
philosopher's role to satisfy one's, 112–13
as seat of desire, 36–37, 51
heart sacrifice, 219–26, 220, 273
heat (*tona*), 33
He By Whom We Live, 128
Hegel, G. F. W., 187, 265, 270
Heracles, 159
Heraclitus, 21–23, 192
Herrera, Antonio de, 174
History of the Conquest of Mexico (Prescott), 235
holding hands, 166–68
holistic coherence, 188–89
Holocaust, 225–26
Homer, 2

homosexuality, 135, 173–74, 273
hosshin stage, 9
House (TV series), 98
How to Be a Stoic (Pigliucci), 7
huehuetlatolli (discourses of the elders), 4, 36, 84; *See also Discourses of the Elders* (Olmos)
huellamati (happiness), 4, 5
Huexotzinco and Huexotzincas, 50, 68, 108
huey tlatoani (emperor), 249
Huitzilihuit (Hummingbird Feather), 179–80
Huitzilihuitzin, 49
Huitzilopochtli, 164
human sacrifice, 180, 216
humility, 203
as "cardinal" virtue, 152
and narcissism, 119
and parameters of right action, 98
and personal vulnerability, 132
in right speech, 45, 46
tololiztli as, 126, 260
and wisdom, 125–30
Hummingbird Feather (Huitzilihuit), 179–80
hunger, 177
Hungry Coyote, *See* Nezahualcoyotl
Hursthouse, Rosalind, 253

Iago, 161
ideal human beings, trees representing, 63–68
ideographic writing, 231
ihiyotl (animating force), 30, 32, 34, 41, 183, 262

imati (skill), 112
imprudent (*xolopitli*), 113
impulse control, 261
inamichuan (matching relations), 21–23, 35, 170, 178, 195
Indian philosophy, 54–55
Indigenous Mesoamerican heritage, collaboration for children of, 78–80; *See also specific groups*
individual agency, 70–72
individual deliberation, 116–17
individualist experiences of love, 173
inner mean of right action, 91–92, 98, 100
intelligence, 39–40
intensity, 154–56, 178
intention, 51–52, 90–92, 96
intimacy rituals, 169–73, 175
Introduction to Indian Philosophy (Chatterjee and Datta), 54
invulnerability, 11, 16, 17, 184
inward path to enlightenment, 8–11
isolation, 117–18
isopraxism, 45–46
ixiptla, 273
ixmimatiliztli (temperance), 137, 138
ixtlamatiliztli (practical wisdom), 110, 112, 129
ixtli, See face
ixtli, yollotl difrasismo (face and heart), 36, 86, 112
Ixtlilxochitl (historian), *See* Alva Ixtlilxochitl, Fernando de

Ixtlilxochitl (rival of Cacama), 72, 73

Jacobita, Martín, 234
Jade Doll (Moquihuix's wife), 172
Jade Doll (Nezahualpilli's love), 157–59, 186
jaguar, courage expressed as eagle and, 85, 100–101, 252, 274
Jefferson, Thomas, 1
Jesus Christ, loving actions of, 93–94
Jocasta, 53
John Paul II, 24
Johnson, Mark, 40, 69
Jones, Daniel, 268
Juana, Sor (Inés de Asbaje y Ramírez de Santillana), 93–95, 98, 102, 253
judgment, 37, 41, 51, 113, 132–33, 256
justice, 144–53, 203; *See also* character justice
as fairness, 147–49, 151
to follow the path, 149–51
heart sacrifice as form of, 224
for Doña Marina, 144–47
and other Aztec "cardinal" virtues, 152–53
political, 148
and temperance, 151–52

Kant, Immanuel, 199, 217, 247
karma, law of, 55
kind words, 45–46
king (*tlatoani*)
discipline for, 139, 140
Marina's role relative to, 147

obligations of, 75
social role of, 72, 97
trees and rulership, 66–67
Klein, Cecilia, 274
koan exercises, 9
Kohlberg, Lawrence, 148–49
Konrath, Sara, 258

Lakoff, George, 40, 69
Land of the Dead (Mictlan), 183–84, 220–21
language, thought and, 191
Lao Tzu, 192
Launey, Michel, 6, 189, 193
law of karma, 55
Legend of the Suns, 18, 22, 194–95
Lennon, John, 121
León-Portilla, Miguel, 189, 230, 235–36, 248, 256, 271
León y Gama, Antonio de, 228
Leopold, Aldo, 244–45
li (ritual), 200
Life Giver (Ayocuan), 68
Lincoln, Abraham, 181–82
liver, animating force centered in, 35, 41
living well, *See* the good
Lockhart, James, 191, 263
logical doubles, 21–23
López-Austin, Alfredo, 22, 34–36, 42
Lord and Lady of Duality, 33
love, 157–75
daily rituals to sustain, 162–66
and fragility of life, 16–17

intimacy rituals, 169–73
Sor Juana on, 93–94
for Nezahualpilli and Jade Doll, 157–59
and relational agency in friendships, 159–62
romance rituals, 166–69
sacrificing happiness for, 2
in same-sex relationships, 173–74
loyalty, 161, 162, 265–66

Machiavelli, Niccolò, 56, 57, 200
Madero, Francisco, 13, 14
Maffie, James, 192–93, 236, 243, 274
Magna Moralia, 191
magnanimity, 64, 66, 248
Mahayana Buddhism, 241
malinalli (movement), 222
Malintzin, *See* Marina, Doña (Daughter Child)
Mancera, Marquis de, 93
manliness, 80, 198
Marcus Aurelius, 154
Marina, Doña (Daughter Child, Malintzin), 87, 144–47, 153, 263
marriage, 159, 164, 166, 167, 170, 173
married man (*oquichtli*), 101
Martín, Don, 87–89, 99, 102, 104, 186
Mason, Alane, 243
matching relations *(inamichuan)*, 21–23
mati (perception), 112
Maya
Aztec merchants in territories of, 115
ceiba tree for, 64

Chontal, 145, 146
Chortí, 32
McCartney, Paul, 121
McGonigal, Kelly, 261
McKeever Furst, Jill Leslie, 32, 34
McRaven, William, 142
the mean, 89–95, 198, 213, 262
    central doctrine of, 253
    inner, 91–92, 98, 100
    outer, 91, 92, 96, 98
    parameters account of, 95–96
    practical wisdom and, 129–30
    temperance and, 138–39
meaningful life, 2–4
Mechoacan, 108
Medici, Lorenzo de', 56
Meier, Brian, 258
memento mori, 180–81
memories, *yolia* and, 31, 183
men
    courage for, 101–2
    daily rituals for, 162–63, 165
Mendieta, Gerónimo de, 164
mental health, solitary confinement and, 118
mental models, 249–50
merchants
    character justice for, 148–49
    rituals for, 115–16
Mesoamerican Humanism, 189–92, 271
metaphors, 40–41, 69
metaphysics
    Aztec, 18–21, 51, 189
    and Nahuatl language, 192–94
    and philosophical pessimism, 195
    unbalance and, 53

Metztitlan, 108
Mexican revolution, 228
Mexica people; *See also* Tenochtitlán
    conquest of Chalco by, 134
    conquest of Coatzacoalcos by, 144–45
    on *ihiyotl* and life force, 32
    Montezuma's surrender and, 146
    mythological history of, 269, 270
    Nezahualcoyotl's and nobility of, 57
michin, 6, 193
Mictlan (Land of the Dead), 183–84, 220–21
middle path, *See* the mean
Mignolo, Walter, 239
Milgram, Stanley, 124
Mill, John Stuart, 93
mind
    Aztec view of, 195–96
    embodied, 30, 35–40, 137, 138
    linking of soul, body, and, 34–36, 251
mindless routines, habits vs., 83, 84
mirroring, 45–46
Mischel, W., 136–37
mistakes
    making, 25, 28, 95–96
    reflecting on, 126, 142, 155–56
moderation, 90, 137, 203
modularity of mind, 196
Molina, Francisco de, 31–33
monogamy, 267
Montezuma (Motecuhzoma), 62
    coronation of, 71–73, 108–9, 255

headdress of, 70
    misconceptions about, 6–7
    surrender of, 146
Montezuma cypress, *See* ahuehuete tree
mood, group singing and dancing and, 168
Moore, G. E., 197
Moquihuix, 172
moral excellence, *See* virtue
moral luck, 28, 51–53, 242
moral peril, 242
Mosley, Michael, 176
Motecuhzoma, *See* Montezuma
mountain peak and the abyss, parable of, 91–92, 95–96, 138, 253
mourning rituals, 182–84
Museo Antropológico (Mexico City), 227, 228
mutual loyalty, 161, 162
mutual respect, 173
mutual support, 165–66
mutual trust, 160–62
mutual understanding, 120
Myer, D., 240

Nahuatl language
    and Aztec concept of habits, 82, 84
    Chimalpahin's histories in, 63
    grammar of, 193–94
    Latin translation of, 231–36
    López-Austin's analysis of, 34–35
    Marina as translator of, 146
    and metaphysics, 192–94

Nahuatl language
    (*continued*)
  nuclear clauses in,
    19–20
  orthography of, 240
  pronunciation guide,
    207–9
  stages of, 191
  structure of, 6, 193
Nahuatl society, *See* Aztec
    society
Nanahuatzin (Pimply
    Face), 222
narcissism, 118–19, 128,
    257–58
National Academy of
    Sciences, 121
National Congress of
    Venezuela, 241
natural environment, connection of body, psyche, soul, and, 251
natural virtues, 213–14
nature, god as, 20–21, 23,
    29, 39, 81, 97, 189,
    235
neltiliztli (truth), 69, 197
Neoptolemus, 160, 161
nepanotl (movement), 222
New England Courant,
    77–78
newlywed couples, seclusion for, 170–71
Nezahualcoyotl (Hungry
    Coyote), 48
  calmecac system of, 246
  on desire for connectedness, 81–82
  evidence supporting
    legend of, 192
  fate for, 186
  as king of Tezcoco,
    57–58, 72
  naming of successor
    by, 157
  Nezahualpilli and, 135,
    157

  as refugee, 49–51, 68,
    131, 133
  rooted life for, 8
  self-conception for,
    131, 133
  on transitory nature of
    life, 28–29
Nezahualpilli (Fasting
    Child), 135, 157–59,
    182, 186, 265
Nicomachean Ethics (Aristotle), 1, 191
Nietzsche, Friedrich
  character for, 201
  cosmic organization
    for, 55–57
  crises of faith inspired
    by, 24
  and moral peril, 242
  virtue ethics of, 200
Nine Inch Nails, 26
nobility (*pillotl*), 101, 102,
    254–55
nonbinary people, 174
Nordhaus, William, 123–
    24, 259
Norse culture, 18, 194, 242
"Northern" philosophy,
    239

Odysseus, 159–60, 185
Odyssey (Homer), 2
Oedipus, 53
Oedipus Rex (Sophocles),
    52–53
in ohtli, *See* outward path
olin; ollin (wave-like
    movement), 22, 31,
    222
Olmos, Andrés de, 232–
    33; *See also Discourses
    of the Elders*
ometeotl, 21, 22, 236
omnipredicative languages, 193
On Providence (Chrysippus), 54

ontology, 20, 194
"On What There Is"
    (Quine), 19, 194
oquichtli (brave man, married man), 101
Othello, 161, 162
Othello (Shakespeare),
    161–62
ousia, 189, 194
outer mean of right
    action, 91, 92, 96, 98
outward path (*in ohtli*)
  character justice to
    follow, 150–51
  connectedness and
    following, 82
  exposure to challenge
    on, 178
  fragility of life on,
    196–97
  good habits to stay on,
    151–52
  heeding council to stay
    on, 129
  progress along, 61
  reasons to follow, 200
  for rooted life, 10–11,
    201
  and wisdom of tradition, 264
Oviedo y Valdés, Gonzalo, 31

pantheism, 20
paqui (happiness), 4–5
parameters of right
    actions, 95–99
parents, happiness for,
    2–4, 240
Parmenides, 192
Passionate Lord, *See*
    Montezuma
    (Motecuhzoma)
passive dynamics, 38–39
patents, 121
path to enlightenment
    inward, 8–11

for Nietzsche and Machiavelli, 56
outward, *See* outward path *[in ohtli]*
patlache, 174
Paz, Octavio, 93, 242
pechteca (bow down), 260
Pelican Bay supermax penitentiaries, 117–18
Pennock, Dodds, 266
perception (*mati*), 112
performative actions, 200
permanence, true life for, 68
personality disorders, 118–19
personal vulnerability, 106, 131–33
pessimism, philosophical, 15, 18–19, 57, 194–97, 242
Phaedrus, 70–72
Phenomenology of Spirit (Hegel), 187
Philoctetes, 159–61, 265
Philoctetes (Sophocles), 159–61, 265
philosophers
 roles of, 59, 110–13
 tlamatinime as, 84, 110–12, 192
philosophy, distinguishing religion from, 275–76
phronēsis (practical wisdom), 212–14, 272
physical level of rootedness, 81, 82
Physics (Apollodorus), 54
Pigliucci, Massimo, 7
pillotl (nobility), 101, 102, 254–55
Pimply Face (Nanahuatzin), 222
pixcayotl, 251–52
pixtinemi (live with care), 252

piya (to guard), 84, 85, 209, 251
Plato, 255
 on afterlife, 185–86
 Alcibiades, 147–48
 Apology of Socrates, 255
 dialogues of, 240
 general character justice for, 151
 on justice, 147–48
 on parts of soul, 33–34
 on philosopher kings, 58
 on practical wisdom, 125
 Republic, 33–34, 58, 185–86
 Roman translations of, 198
pleasure-women (*ahuianime*), 174, 269
plural groups
 agency for, 162
 deliberation in, 72–76
 rituals in, 114–17
political justice, 148
political office, obligation of, 241
Potonchan, 145
Practical Intelligence and the Virtues (Russell), 7
practical reasoning, 89–90, 117–18, 122–24
practical wisdom, 109, 202, 211–15, 272
 and all other Aztec virtues, 129–30
 and courage, 100, 104
 difrasismo patterns for, 139, 262
 of Benjamin Franklin, 78
 humility and, 125–29
 ixtlamatiliztli as, 110, 112, 129
 phronēsis as, 212–14, 272

in plural group deliberation, 72–76
and shared agency, 113–14, 116, 129–30
temperance and, 139, 141
theoretical vs., 256
theoretical wisdom vs., 110–14, 122
praise, 165
Prescott, William H., 6, 235, 240–41
present value, 122–23
pride, 128
primary metaphors, 69
Primeros Memoriales (Sahagún), 149–50
Prince, The (Machiavelli), 56
Principles (Dalio), 125–26
pro drop fallacy, 19–20, 193
productive actions, 200
progressive exposure, 103
prosthetics, passive dynamics in, 38–39
prudence; *See also* practical wisdom
 as "cardinal" virtue, 152
 difrasismo for, 262
 Florentine Codex on, 27–28, 44
 of philosophers, 113
psyche, *See* soul
psychic level of rootedness, 81
psychopathy, 118–19
Puebla, Bishop of, 94
Purcell, Elyse, 264, 265
Pythagoras, 192

qualli (good), 200–201, 207
qualli, yectli difrasismo (good and correct), 80

quauhyot, oceloyotl difrasismo (eagle and jaguar), 85, 100–101, 252, 274
Quecholcohuatl (Flamingo Serpent), 134–36
Quetzalcoatl, 220–21, 274
Quinatzin, 163
Quine, W. V. O., 19, 187, 194

Ragnarök, 194
rank, in Aztec society, 115–16
reality, structure of, 19–23
real virtues, 213–14
reason, faith and, 23–25
reasoning
  ethical, 118–19, 122–25
  practical, 89–90, 117–18, 122–24
reciprocity of virtues, 94, 213–14
redemption, life without, 24–25, 184, 186
Reeve, C. D. C., 188–89
reflection
  and adjusting after failure, 142, 155–56
  building habits through, 103
  during fasting, 177
  on mistakes, 126
reflective deliberation, 39
relational agency, 159–62, 162
relationships, 11, 196–97; *See also* friendship; marriage
  Aztec views of healthy, 159
  enacting core virtues in, 153
  right speech in, 60–61
  virtues of, 264
relative good, 197–98

religion, distinguishing philosophy from, 275–76
religious rituals, 114
renewable energies, 274
Republic (Plato), 33–34, 58, 185–86
respect, mutual, 173
responsibility, for group action, 73–74
Restall, Matthew, 7
restaurants, secular rituals in, 114
Reznor, Trent, 26
right action, 86, 197–98; *See also* courage
  and enumeration problem, 152
  formula for, 103–4
  intention for, 90–92, 96
  mean of, *See* the mean
  parameters of, 95–99
  praise to encourage, 165
right speech, 43–46
  kind words, 45–46
  truthful words, 44, 46, 59–61
rituals, 200, 202
  for building habits, 142, 143
  daily, 162–66, 175
  exercising wisdom in, 114–17
  intimacy, 169–73, 175
  mourning, 182–84
  in response to tragedy, 181–84
  romance, 166–69, 175
  viewing love as a set of, 159
robotics, models of embodiment in, 37–38
Rogoff, Barbara, 78–79
romance rituals, 166–69, 175

Romances de los Señores de la Nueva España, 233
Rome, ancient; *See also* Stoicism; *specific philosophers*
  children's names in, 144
  method of studying, 190–91
  organization of cosmos in, 53–54
rooted life, 62–76, 184–85, 189, 197, 201
  in Aztec wisdom on living well, 17
  for Chimalpahin, 62–63
  collaboration for, 80
  fragility of, 16
  for living well, 57, 58
  metaphors and translation of, 69
  outward path for, 10–11
  and practical wisdom, 72–76
  pursuit of happiness vs., 8
  shared agency in, 70–76
  and trees representing ideal human beings, 63–68
  as "true" life, 68–69
  truthful speech for, 59
  virtuous action for, 81
rulership, trees and, 66–67
Russell, Daniel, 7, 264, 271
Russian language, 193

sacred vows, honoring, 163–64
sacrifice, 180, 270
  auto-, 274
  blood, 216–26
  heart, 219–26, 220, 273
  human, 180, 216

Sahagún, Bernardino de, 207, 233–34, 256, 264; *See also Florentine Codex General History of the Things of New Spain,* 234
Primeros Memoriales, 149–50
same-sex relationships, 135, 173–74, 273
San Antón Muñón Chimalpahin Cuauhtlehuantizin, Domingo de, *See* Chimalpahin
San Buenaventura, Pedro de, 234
Sandberg, Martin, 121
Santana, Alejandro, 236
Sapolsky, R. M., 261
Sartre, Jean-Paul, 242
satori (enlightenment), 9
Schopenhauer, Arthur, 242
scientific research, team-based, 121–22
Searle, John, 249
secular rituals, 114–17
Security Housing Unit syndrome, 118
self-conception, 131–33
self-esteem, 119, 168
self-estimation, accurate, 127, 128
self-worth, 128
service, to partner, 166
Set Theory and Its Logic (Quine), 187
sexual activity, 139, 167, 171, 174, 267
Shakespeare, William, 161–62
shame, 88, 123–33, 176, 180
shared agency
  in all Aztec virtues, 130, 152, 210–11
  in friendship, 160–62
  and practical wisdom, 113–14, 116, 129–30
  relational agency vs., 162
  in rooted life, 70–76
  as unique feature of Aztec virtues, 82, 152, 201–2
Shield Flower (Chimalxochitl), 179–80, 186, 216
Shoda, Y., 136–37
Silva Galeana, Librado, 189
Simeon, Remi, 248
singing, in groups, 167, 168, 267–68
Single Item Narcissism Scale (SINS), 258
skill (*imati*), 112
sleep management practices, 151, 154–55
slippery earth, 26–42, 197
  and animating forces of humans, 30–33
  Aztec philosophy on, 17, 26–30
  and embodied mind, 35–42
  fragility of life on, 15
  moral luck on, 51, 52
  and parts of the soul, 33–35
  Trent Reznor on failure, 26
  transitory nature of life on, 28–29
  true life on, 68, 69
social exercises, consistency in, 142
social expectations, violating, 106–7
social role(s)
  humility and performing, 127–28
  justice and fulfilling, 149–50
of kings, 72, 97
mourning ritual as reprieve from, 183
of nobles, 263–64
and parameters of right action, 96–97
in romantic relationships, 163
and temperance, 139–41, 152
social vulnerability, 105–7, 131
societal level of rootedness, 81
Socrates, 242
  and justice as fairness, 147–48
  knowledge above and below for, 255
  myth of Er told by, 185–86
  on parts of the soul, 33–34
  shared agency example, 70–72
  unity of virtues for, 211, 213
  wisdom of, 112
soft realism, 188, 191
solitary confinement, 117–18
songwriting, 121
Sophocles, 52–53, 159–61, 265
soul
  and Aztec's animating forces, 30–33
  linking of mind, body, and, 34–36, 251
  unbalance and, 53
  "Western" philosophy on parts of, 33–35
Soustelle, Jacques, 189
Spaniards
  blood sacrifice to justify colonization by, 216

Spaniards (*continued*)
  Marina/Malintzin's life with, 145–47
  torture of Martín Cortés by, 87–89
  view of Aztec culture by, 232–33, 275
Spanish-Aztec war, 6–7, 50, 234
Spanish language, 19–20, 193
spies, 115–16
Spinoza, Benedict de, 20–21, 23, 189, 235
spiritual exercises, 18
SSM Health, 43–44
standing upright (*tihcaz*), 67–68
Stanford marshmallow experiments, 136–37
Stern, Nicolas, 123–24, 259
Stockdale, James, 99–100, 103
Stockdale, Sybil, 100
Stoicism, 7
  Aztec philosophy and, 152, 254
  cardinal virtues in, 264
  on courage, 99–100
  on invulnerability, 16
  inward path of, 8–11
  on life without redemption, 24
  meditation on death in, 180–81
  organization of cosmos in, 53–54, 57
  temperance in, 137
  virtue and spiritual exercises in, 18
strength, 32, 184–86
suchioa, 174
suffering, 15
supermax penitentiaries, 117–18
support, mutual, 165–66

Sustenance, Lord of, 222
Swanton, Christine, 200
sweat baths, 217
sweeping practice, 142, 164
symbolism, 40–41
syncretic materials, 191

Tao Te Ching (Lao), 192
Taxodium mucronatum, *See* ahuehuete tree (Montezuma cypress)
telpochcalli (school for trade and war), 167
temperance, *See* willpower
Temple of Quetzalcoatl (Teotihuacán), 220
temptation, resisting, 136–37, 261
Tenochtitlán; *See also* Mexica people
  Ahuitzol's rule in, 182
  alcohol consumption in, 135, 140
  Chimalpahin's posting near, 62
  Doña Marina and fall of, 146, 147
  early colonial sexual expression in, 166
  heart sacrifice in, 220
  Huitzilopochtli as main god of, 164
  Jade Doll's execution and relations between Tezcoco and, 158–59
  for Nezahualcoyotl, 49, 57
  Nezahualpilli's allies in, 158–59
  social role of nobles in, 263–64
  in Spanish–Aztec war, 50
  Tlacaelel I and, 273
  Tlatelolco and, 172–73

teotl
  and Aztec metaphysics, 192–94
  as basic energy of universe, 20, 236, 243
  being vs., 19, 192–94
  and god as nature, 20–21, 23, 29, 81, 97, 189, 235
  inamic pair of *ometeotl* and, 22–23
  as Life Giver, 68
  as Lord and Lady of Duality, 33
  social obligations to, 97, 98
  societal rootedness and, 81
tequitlaqualiztli (gluttony), 262
textual evidence, of Aztec philosophy, 191
Tezcoco and Tezcocans
  Cacama's deliberations in, 72–75
  in histories of Alva Ixtlilxochitl, 265
  impact of Jade Doll's execution on relations with, 158–59
  for Nezahualcoyotl's family, 49
  Nezahualcoyotl's liberation and rule of, 8, 57–58, 157
  Nezahualpilli's rule in, 135, 158
Tezozomoc, 75
Thales, 192
theoretical wisdom, 109–14, 122, 256
"36 Questions That Lead to Love, The" (Jones), 268
thought, language and, 191
thoughtful speech, 44–46, 60–61

Index • 291

Thus Spoke Zarathustra (Nietzsche), 55, 56
tihcaz (standing upright), 67–68
time, metaphors for, 69
Tlacaelel I, 273
tlacoqualli, See outer mean of right action
tlalticpac, See slippery earth
tlamatiliztli (wisdom), 110, 112
tlamatinime, as philosophers, 84, 110–12, 192
tlanepantla, See inner mean of right action
tlanepantlacayotl, See the mean
Tlatelolco, 172
tlatoani, See king
tlatolli (bit of wisdom), 84, 129
Tlaxcala and Tlaxcalans, 50, 74–75, 108, 147, 220
tlazolli (filth), 164
Tlazolteotl, 164
"tl"endings, pronouncing, 209
"To Fall in Love With Anyone Do This" (Cantron), 169
tololiztli (humility), 126, 260
tona (heat), 33
tonalli (animating force), 30, 33, 41, 183
Townsend, Camilla, 7, 247, 261, 263
tragedy, 179–86
  defined, 270
  ethical, 265
  justification/redemption of, 225–26
  philosophy and strength to face, 184–86

rituals in response to, 181–84
Shield Flower's story of, 179–80
"Western" responses to, 180–81
trust, 160–62
truth
  courage to speak up for, 93–94
  neltiliztli as, 69, 197
  "true" life, 68–69
  truthful speech, 44, 46, 59–61
Turing, Alan, 273
Turquoise Lord, 222

unbalance, 49–58
  in Aztec wisdom on living well, 17, 18
  Greek vs. Aztec views of, 52–53
  moral luck as form of, 51–53
  for Nezahualcoyotl, 49–51
  and organization of the cosmos, 53–58
unconscious, origins of cognition in, 41–42
understanding, mutual, 120
unity of virtues, 211–15

Valeriano, Antonio, 234
valor, on the battlefield, 99–103
valuational agency, 251
value, expressions of, 83, 201
values, responsibility for group action and, 73–74
Vedānta, 54
Vegerano, Alonso, 234
Veracruz, 145–46
Vietnam War, 99–100

Vieyra, Antonio de, 93–94
Virgin Mary, 227, 275
virtue ethics
  Aristotelian, 130, 200, 202, 210–15
  Aztec, 130, 189, 198–99, 201–3, 210, 214–15
  Confucian, 130, 200, 201, 210, 215
  in "Western" philosophy, 198, 202
virtues
  Aztec vs. "Western" concept of, 80–82
  "cardinal," 152–53
  the good vs., 200–201
  as products vs. performances, 82
  real vs. natural, 213–14
  reciprocity of, 213–14
  of relationships, 264
  unity of, 211–15
virtuous action, 77–86
  in Aztec wisdom on living well, 17–18
  and cultivation of habits, 82–86
  and cultural differences in collaboration, 78–80
  by Benjamin Franklin, 77–78
  for good life, 76
  negation of, 151
  for rooted life, 81
virtus (manliness), 80, 198
von Humboldt, Alexander, 228, 235–36
von Humboldt, Wilhelm, 235
Voss, Chris, 45–46
vulnerability, 59
  in friendships, 161
  intimacy and, 170
  personal, 106, 131–33

vulnerability (*continued*)
and pursuit of invulnerability, 11, 16, 17, 184
social, 105–7, 131

Wall $treet Week (TV series), 125, 126
warmth, metaphors for, 69
Watts, Chris, 46
Werner, Heinz, 245
"Western" philosophy; *See also specific schools and individuals*
afterlife in, 30
cardinal virtues in, 152
concept of, 239
cosmological organization, 53–55
ego as seat of cognition in, 37
on happiness, 1–4
humility in, 126
justice in, 151
metaphysics, 20–21, 193
path to enlightenment, 10
on reality, 19
soul in, 31, 33–34
temperance for, 137
virtue ethics in, 198, 202
virtue in, 82
wisdom in, 109
"Western" societies; *See also* Spaniards
responses to tragedy, 180–81
view of Aztecs in, 6–7, 275
view of rituals in, 114
White, Ronald, 181–82
white lies, 60–61
Williams, Bernard, 242, 247
willpower (temperance), 134–41
Aztec philosophy on, 137–41
as "cardinal" virtue, 152
discipline, 103, 136–37, 139, 141, 152, 176–78, 261
drive, 136, 137, 154–56, 261
durability of, 136, 137, 142–43, 151, 261
in Flamingo Serpent story, 134–36
and justice, 151–52
practices to foster, 151, 155
wisdom, 108–30
exercising, in rituals, 114–17
from group decision making, 117–25
and humility, 125–30
and life on slippery earth, 27
of Montezuma, 108–9
practical, *See* practical wisdom

theoretical, 109, 109–14, 122, 256
tlatolli as bit of, 84, 129
women
courage for, 102
daily rituals of household for, 162–64, 174
mourning rituals for, 183

Xipe Totec (Flayed Lord), 220
Xochicoatl, 75
xochicuicatl (flower songs), 50
xolopitli (imprudent), 113

yectli (correct), 80, 200–201
Yoga, 54, 55
Yoki, Horoshi, 38–39
yolia (animating force), 30–32, 41, 183–84, 270
yollotl, *See* heart

Zapata, Emiliano, *12*
fate for, 186
fragility of life for, 13–15, 17, 29
the good and physical peril for, 242
rooted life for, 8
zazen practice, 9
Zen Buddhism, 8–11
Zorita, Alonso de, 232–33